1992

An Institutional Investor Publication

THE TRADING AND SECURITIZATION OF SENIOR BANK LOANS

John H. Carlson
Frank J. Fabozzi
Editors

PROBUS PUBLISHING COMPANY
Chicago, Illinois
Cambridge, England

This publication is designed to provide accurate and authoritative information in regard to the subject matter covered. It is sold with the understanding that neither the author nor the publisher are engaged in rendering legal, accounting or other professional service. If legal or other expert assistance is required, the services of a competent professional should be sought.

ISBN 1-55738-293-X

Printed in the United States of America

BB

1   2   3   4   5   6   7   8   9   0

Dedication

To our wives, Susanne Carlson and Dessa Fabozzi

and

Timothy and Billy Calder
Jack and Jill Carlson
Peter Bernard Carril
Julie and Claire Costello
Polly, Emily and Richie Howe
Eve Caldwell and Isabel Mary King
Eric Moses Gurevitch
Sean Michnowski
Brendon, Bridget, Christine, Daniel and Peter O'Brien
Lauren and Christopher Tortoriello

CONTENTS

v

CONTRIBUTORS

Jonathan D. Calder, Vice President, Citicorp Securities Markets, Inc.

John H. Carlson, C.F.A., Executive Vice President, Daiwa Securities America Inc.

Peter J. Carril, Jr., Senior Vice President, Daiwa Securities America Inc.

William M. Costello, Vice President, Security Pacific National Bank

Frank J. Fabozzi, Ph.D., C.F.A., Visiting Professor of Finance, Sloan School of Management, Massachusetts Institute of Technology

Jane Tripp Howe, C.F.A., Vice President, Pacific Investment Management Company

Brian J. LeWand, Assistant Vice President, Security Pacific National Bank

John E. McDermott III, Vice President, Daiwa Securities America Inc.

Steven C. Miller, Analyst, Loan Pricing Corporation

Meridee A. Moore, Farallon Capital Partners

Linda K. Moses, Structured Finance Group, Moody's Investors Service

Timothy M. O'Brien, Desk Manager, Garvin GuyButler Corporation

Christopher Regis Ryan, Vice President, Loan Product Manager, Lehman Brothers

Robert L. Tortoriello, J.D., Partner, Cleary, Gottlieb, Steen & Hamilton

Stewart L. Whitman II, Vice President, Long Term Credit Bank of Japan Ltd.

Preface

Historically, senior loans have been originated by commercial banks and syndicated to other banks and financial institutions. This market grew as a result of the large amount of bank loans issued in the 1980s. Institutional investors demonstrated a willingness to shift funds to this sector of the debt market because of their attractive yields and credit protection. Several dealer firms began committing capital and resources to facilitate the trading of bank loans and securities created from these loans.

Current and potential participants in the senior bank loan sector of the debt market must have the skills to identify and then capitalize on the opportunities available. The purpose of this book is to describe the institutional and investment characteristics of the senior bank loan market (both performing and distressed loans) and the market for securitized senior bank loans (both single loans and a pool of loans).

To be effective, a book of this nature should offer a broad perspective. The experiences of a wide range of experts are more informative than those of a single expert, particularly because of the diversity of opinion on some issues. We have chosen some of the best known practitioners who have been actively involved in the evolution of this market to contribute to this book.

ACKNOWLEDGEMENTS

We are grateful to the contributors and their organizations for allowing them to partake in this project. Daiwa Securities America provided support in various forms. In addition, we would like to express our appreciation to the following individuals who assisted us with this book or who have helped us along the way: Ichiro Abe (Daiwa), Bob Andres (Martindale, Andres and Godshalk), Joseph Bencivenga (Salomon Brothers), Stephen Bradley (Daiwa Securities), Bernie Feshbach (Feshbach & Sons), Frank Jones (Guardian Life Insurance of America), Chris Ray (consultant), and Martin Seneca.

A special thanks goes to Peter J. Carril, Jr. and Paula Marciante, both of Daiwa Securities, for their invaluable assistance at every stage of this project. Without their assistance this project could not have been completed on a timely basis.

Last, but certainly not least, we wish to thank our families for sacrificing lost weekends and evenings so that we could devote time to this project.

Chapter 1

Introduction

JOHN H. CARLSON, C.F.A.
EXECUTIVE VICE PRESIDENT
DAIWA SECURITIES AMERICA INC.

FRANK J. FABOZZI, PH.D., C.F.A.
VISITING PROFESSOR OF FINANCE
SLOAN SCHOOL OF MANAGEMENT
MASSACHUSETTS INSTITUTE OF TECHNOLOGY

Senior bank loans comprise the first priority debt obligations of a borrower. Bank debt is widely utilized as the senior financing for a leveraged buyout, acquisition or recapitalization. These are collectively referred to as "highly leveraged transactions" or "HLTs." The remaining financing required to complete an HLT transaction may be derived through publicly or privately issued bonds which are subordinated to the senior loan facility.

Historically, senior loans have been originated by commercial banks and syndicated to other banks and financial institutions. As this market has grown and liquidity in the high-yield bond market has declined, institutional investors have become increasingly active. The key features of senior loans that have made them attractive to institutional investors include:

Attractive yields. Senior loans are floating-rate instruments offering margins of 200 to 275 basis points over the London Interbank Offered Rate (LIBOR).

Senior, secured credits. Senior loans offer the investor excellent protection when compared with publicly-offered high-yield debt. Borrowers usually repay these loans as quickly as possible and ahead of other debt because of their senior position in the capital structure. High-yield bonds, which are most often subordinated obligations, tend to remain outstanding. Most senior loans are further secured by pledges of specific collateral, either in the form of assets and/or the equity of the borrower.

Strong covenant protection. Originating banks are able to negotiate covenants protecting the lender from a variety of adverse events or actions on the part of the borrower, and restricting uses of cash flow by the borrower in order to maximize the likelihood of timely payment of interest and principal.

In response to the large amount of bank loans issued in the 1980s and their strong credit protection, new participants have shown a willingness to commit capital and resources to facilitate trading as broker-dealers. The purpose of this book is to describe senior bank loans: their syndication, brokering, trading, valuation and securitization. Coverage includes not only performing loans but non-performing, distressed loans. In the case of the latter, the growth of trading in this market may be expected to parallel the trading of LDC loans which in 1989 had a trading volume of about $60 billion.

Securitization is an attractive technique to move loans off balance sheet. It can take various forms, often mimicing the origins and early direction of the mortgage-backed securities market.

Many institutional investors are interested in purchasing senior bank loans but are precluded from doing so because their investment charters prohibit this activity. Efforts are currently underway to place a *single* loan into a trust and distribute this product to interested investors. By placing the loan into a trust, the security can now be sold as a private placement (144A eligible) to a larger investor base. An extension of this is to direct the cash flow from one tranche to another so as to define and add an element of predictability to the maturity of the product. All rights and voting responsibilities remain with the holder of the trust certificate. Also, the trust structure reduces the amount of paperwork required when loans are transferred versus on an assignment/participation basis, in addition to reducing the minimum investment required by the prospective investor. This innovation recalls the early collateralized mortgage obligation (CMO) deals where cash flow was passed through and only slightly modified. Holders of large amounts of loans will favor this type of securitization for its ability to quickly and efficiently transfer loans off the balance sheet at *offer side, market* price. Investors favor this method due to reduced paperwork, increased liquidity, lower minimum of investment, and trust form purchase.

An extension of single loan securitization is the securitization of a pool of senior bank loans. Such structures are called *collateralized loan obligations* (CLOs). As with the securitization of a single loan, the cash flows can be tranched to produce a unique customized security to fit the particular needs of institutional investors. The first CLO was underwritten by Continental Bank in December 1988. This CLO, referred to as a floating-rate enhanced debt securities or FRENDS, was a $140 million transaction that was privately placed in Europe. The following summer, Continental Bank underwrote a $343 million FRENDS. Since then, approximately $1.5 billion of CLOs has been issued.

The remainder of this chapter provides an overview of the key characteristics of senior bank loans and what differentiates them from other fixed-income instruments. We then provide an overview of the book.

OVERVIEW OF SENIOR BANK LOANS

The yields on "HLT" senior loans compare well with yields on alternative investments when their credit characteristics are considered. Senior loans offer attractive returns while providing substantially more principal protection than high yield subordinated debt.

Senior loans have a priority position over subordinated lenders (bondholders) with respect to repayment of interest and principal. This arrangement is arrived at contractually among the borrower and its lenders, and also may be derived structurally. Contractual subordination results from the actual terms agreed to by the different classes of lenders under the various indentures. Typically, senior lenders require full repayment of principal before any principal payments may be remitted to subordinated lenders.

Senior debt has a shorter maturity date than subordinated debt, typically maturing in six to eight years. Senior lenders achieve this through scheduled principal amortization schedules, specified asset sale requirements and excess cash flow capture. Rigorous financial covenants required by the senior lender assist the borrower to maintain its stated business plan while restricting activities that may dilute its credit quality. Subordinated debt often does not mature for ten years, resulting in greater principal repayment risk compared to senior debt. This risk is even further intensified by the subordinated debt's lack of a scheduled amortization schedule.

Upon maturity of senior debt, by acceleration, or upon the distribution of assets as a result of bankruptcy, liquidation or reorganization, the senior loan will usually be entitled to receive payment in full before any payment is made to the subordinated lenders. Additionally, contractual subordination typically provides for a "blockage period" in favor of senior lenders. Should the senior loan go into default, senior lenders may block interest payments to the subordinated lenders for a specified period of time. This "blockage period" allows senior lenders more time, flexibility, and control in a default situation.

Structural subordination often occurs by placing the senior debt at the operating subsidiary and securing this debt with assets while structuring the subordinated debt as an obligation of the holding company. Also, if the senior loan is made at the holding company, the operating subsidiary may guarantee the loan and pledge its equity as security. This gives the senior lender additional control over the activities of the subsidiary, including liquidation if it becomes necessary.

Pricing Options

Senior loan pricing may allow the borrower to select a pricing option with respect to different indices. Typically, the borrower may select a pricing option based off the prime rate, LIBOR, or certificates of deposit (CDs), plus a credit spread. These options are established in the loan documentation and may be utilized at the *borrower's* discretion. The borrower may also select a new option on any "rollover date."

Prime Rate. Almost always, the agent bank's "base" rate is used in pricing an entire lending syndicates loans. The prime rate option may be the most expensive option for the borrower, but it provides the greatest cash management flexibility because there are not fixed periods nor prepayment penalties as there are with the LIBOR and CD options. Many HLT loans are priced at prime plus 150 basis points.

LIBOR. The borrower may select the LIBOR options of one, three, or six months. The loan will then reprice based upon current rates at the end of each rollover date. Many HLT loans are priced at LIBOR plus 200 to 250 basis points.

CD Rate. The CD rate is calculated on a manner similar to that of LIBOR except that U.S. domestic CDs are used instead of Eurodollars. Typical interest periods available are 30, 60, 90, or 180 days.

Reserve Adjustments

Many, *but not all* borrowing indices have a "reserve adjustment" mechanism. This feature compensates the lending institution for any increased borrowing costs associated with any reserve requirements which must be held against the loan.

Assignments Versus Participations

Senior loans are distributed by two methods—assignments and participations. Each has its advantages and relative disadvantages, with the transfer by method of assignment being the more desirable of the two. The practice of *novation*, which involves amending the original credit agreement, is rarely, if ever, used.

Assignments. When the holder of a loan is interested in selling his portion, he can do so by passing his interest in the loan by method of assignment. In this procedure, the seller transfers all his rights completely to the holder of the assignment, now called the assignee. The assignee is said to have privity of contract with the borrower. All fees and interest payments go directly to the assignee. Since the agent bank must change payment instructions and holder of record information on his books from the assignor to the assignee, there is also an agent fee which must be paid to the agent bank. In addition, the credit agreement will stipulate under what, if any, requirements are needed for the assignee to be an "eligible assignee." These often include net worth or net assets hurdles as well as a financial institutions test. Finally, assignments usually have minimum par amounts of $10 million or more. Because of the clear path between the borrower and assignee, the assignment is the more desirable choice of transfer and ownership.

Participations.   A participation involves a holder of a loan participating out a portion of his holding in that particular loan. The holder of the participation does not become a party to the credit agreement. His relationship is now not with the borrower but with the seller of the participation. Unlike an assignment, the holder of the participation does not have privity with the borrower. The holder of the participation can vote on certain legal matters concerning amendments to the credit agreement. These rights would include changes regarding maturity, interest rate, and matters concerning the loan collateral. There are no transfer restrictions regarding participations (if indeed they are allowed). The transfer represents "sale of assets" treatment with no recourse to the seller of the participation. A participation of a participation is called a *sub-participation*. The risks involved with a participation involve counterparty risk to the seller of the participation as well as non-inclusion of certain protective clauses.

OVERVIEW OF THE BOOK

The chapters that follow provide the information needed to capitalize on the opportunities available in the market for senior bank loans and to understand the future direction of this market. In the next chapter, the bank loan syndication process is described. There are four phases in that process: agent selection, underwriting group arrangement, primary syndication, and secondary syndication. The first three phases are explained in Chapter 2. The last phase involves the secondary trading of loans which is the subject of Chapter 3 and the brokering of loans which is the subject of Chapter 4. Chapter 5 addresses the legal concerns relating to the sale of loans and participations by banks.

Chapters 6, 7 and 8 cover the analysis of senior bank loans. Chapter 6 focuses on credit analysis. The syndicated loan market is placed in the context of the bond market in Chapter 7. In that chapter, some findings on default rates are also reported. An extensive framework for the valuation of HLT bank loans is set forth in Chapter 8. Four analytical tools are explained: intrinsic value, collateral value, expected recovery value and relative value compared with alternative investments.

The securitization of senior bank loans is the subject of Chapters 9 and 10. Chapter 9 describes the basic characteristics of CLOs: structure, investment considerations, credit support and cash flow mismatch. The rating process of CLOs is described in Chapter 10.

The last four chapters of the book focus on the distressed bank loan market. A description of the bankruptcy process is provided in Chapter 11. Chapter 12 provides an introduction to the emerging market for distressed bank loans and suggests two approaches as to how to think about these loans: interest rate play and asset play. Expanded coverage of the techniques for valuing distressed bank loans and the management of portfolios of these loans is described in Chapter 13. Opportunities in debtor-in-possession lending is discussed in Chapter 14.

PART I
Background

Chapter 2

Bank Loan Syndications

WILLIAM M. COSTELLO
VICE PRESIDENT
SECURITY PACIFIC NATIONAL BANK

Companies use bank loans to finance a variety of needs ranging from working capital to acquisition financing. To obtain these loans, a company will ask its relationship banks[1] for commitments within some broad structural parameters. The resultant proposals, while reflecting each bank's unique origination style, will likely include some basic similarities. For instance, the financing will be senior debt in the company's capital structure. The amount will probably be allocated among term and revolving facilities,[2] each maturing within eight years. Interest will be calculated on a floating base rate. The term loan will require annual amortization; yet, may be prepaid at any time without penalty. The win-

---

[1] The term "bank" will be used generically in this chapter to refer to any financial institution—bank or non-bank—providing bank loan financing.

[2] A term loan cannot be reborrowed once repaid. A revolver, on the other hand, is designed to be drawn (up to the commitment amount) and repaid any number of times. Interest is paid on the outstandings of both term and revolving facilities. Revolvers also earn commitment fees (on the unused/undrawn portions) and facility fees (on the amount available).

ning bid, therefore, usually depends less on the most creative structure and more on which bank commits the most money on the most favorable terms.

When its needs are such that they can be satisfied solely by its relationship banks, the company's main concerns will be the loan's price and covenants. When the financing requirements of a company grow beyond the capacity of these few banks, the best terms will include the deal's marketability. A bank loan syndication—the process by which a loan is marketed to a group of potential lenders—involves four major phases—agent selection, underwriting group arrangement, primary syndication and secondary syndication. This chapter will deal with the first three phases. Secondary syndication, also called trading or brokering, is covered in another chapter.

PHASE ONE: AGENT SELECTION

Once a company decides to access the bank debt market, it will ask its relationship banks to bid for the agency on a predetermined or to-be-negotiated structure. This serves the company in two ways. First, it is an effective way of ensuring that the total amount of required financing is committed. Becoming a company's agent bank is the goal of every relationship manager (RM).[3] Beside earning significant advisory and agency fees for the immediate loan request, agent banks often are given the right of first refusal on future banking needs. As RMs are measured (and compensated) on the amount and type of business done with their clients, the chance to bid for an agency is a very motivating event. Another reason companies put an agency to bid is so the agent can handle the tasks it is either unwilling or unable to perform: specifically, documentation, administration and syndication. Though usually performed by one bank, these responsibilities may be allocated among different banks within an underwriting group. As will be discussed below, while only one bank can be a documentation or administration agent, there can be several syndication agents.

---

[3] An RM is also called a lending officer or an account officer.

Documentation

This agent's major responsibility is to select the law firm that will represent the bank(s) in the legal negotiations with the borrower. Together, the agent and counsel will draft the commitment letter, summary of terms and conditions, and the credit agreement documenting the loan commitments. Since banks committing before the deal closes will want to review and possibly suggest changes to the drafts of the documents, the agent must also act as consensus builder and, when necessary, arbitrator.

Administration

This agent acts as a trustee for the parties to the loan, managing the flow of funds and information between the borrower and the banks. The administration agent collects from the borrower interest and fees which, along with required compliance documents, it distributes to the bank group.

Syndication

Ideally for the borrower, one bank commits to lend the entire amount of the facility on the borrower's terms and agrees to hold the whole loan in its portfolio. The borrower, then, would have to negotiate and deal with only one lender. For many borrowers this rarely happens for larger financing needs. The syndication agent is charged with marketing the loan to other banks when the size of the total facility is beyond the means of any one institution. This may be done by arranging an underwriting group or through a primary syndication. (In a secondary syndication, each bank in the deal is technically its own syndication agent). Although the major commercial banks have legal lending limits (i.e., the maximum amount that may be lent to any one borrower) of hundreds of millions of dollars, most manage their loan portfolios in such a way that their internally created comfort or hold level of exposure to any one borrower may actually be much less. Obviously, a bank's incentives to commit more than its hold level are the extra leverage and potential profit opportunity commensurate with a large commitment.

PHASE TWO: UNDERWRITING GROUP ARRANGEMENT

Assuming the deal is creditworthy, there are several possible outcomes to a borrower's bidding out a large agency. First, one or more banks each may commit to underwrite the entire amount. If the borrower accepts one bank's commitment, that bank must be prepared to lend the borrower the full dollar amount requested; that is, the bank incurs the syndication risk—the task of distributing the loan to other lenders until the bank reaches its hold level. That bank weighs the risks and rewards of potential syndication strategies. It may form an underwriting group and reduce risk by accepting large commitments from a few banks, but doing so will reduce its reward as several large commitments will cost more than many smaller commitments. On the other hand, going directly to a primary syndication while promising higher rewards involves the risk that many smaller commitments may not be readily obtainable. Second, several banks individually may commit less than the facility amount, but collectively commit enough to underwrite the deal. The company may ask these banks to combine their commitments and form an underwriting group (also called a *club*). In this case, several banks will be syndication agents; again they, not the company, will bear the syndication risk. Last, the deal is either so large or so risky that a few banks cannot or will not underwrite. Here, the company either invites more banks to try to create a club or selects a syndication agent(s) to attempt a best efforts syndication. In either event, no one bank's commitment is binding unless and until the entire deal is committed and underwritten. Hence, the company bears the syndication risk.

Whether one or several banks commit to underwrite depends on the availability of credit—both in the general market and for that borrower. In the current moderately tight environment, clubs are a popular strategy. For the borrower, the deal is underwritten and funds are provided relatively quickly. For the banks, all the club members enjoy the prestige of agency and syndication risk is spread over several institutions.

Once the club is formed, ground rules for the next phase of the syndication are established via a negotiated syndication agreement. Remember, bank loans are not securities and do not fall under the jurisdiction of the SEC.[4] A typical syndication agreement addresses two issues: how the market of potential loan buyers will be divided among the club and how commitments from the primary syndication will be allocated to reduce each bank's commitment. Generally, these decisions are based on the proportional commitment of each club member—when the financing is divided equally among the underwriting group, so are the market and any subsequent commitments. One club member with a larger commitment will usually be responsible for handling a disproportionately larger share of the market and will likewise garner an equally disproportionate share of subsequent commitments.

PHASE THREE: PRIMARY SYNDICATION

Now is when the deal is broadly distributed to the loan market by the syndication agent(s). Where there is more than one syndication agent, this phase is also called a pooled syndication, as both the market and any commitments are pooled and allocated according to the terms of the syndication agreement. For this section, "syndication" will apply to both primary and pooled syndications.

Syndication is chiefly a marketing effort. As in any other business, the underlying product being marketed, in this case a loan, must be solid in its own right for the distribution effort to succeed. The agent's deal team successfully marketed the deal within their own institution to get the loan approved. They know the strengths of the transaction and can reasonably explain any weaknesses. The art of syndication, then, is presenting the facts to a larger audience in a manner that convinces them to also commit to lend to the borrower.

The tasks required for a syndication, and their respective estimated times to completion, are delineated in Exhibit 1. Keep in mind that some of these steps, such as creating an Information Memorandum and staging a bank meeting, may be redundancies from phase two, especially for very large deals. The rest of this section will focus on detailing each step chronologically.

---

[4] Nevertheless, banks have taken the first steps toward self-regulation as evidenced by the loan sales committee created by the BCMA and later assumed by the ABA. Three sub-committees were established in mid-1990 to set Syndication Practices, Settlement Policies and Documentation Standards. Results from these committees should be announced late in 1991.

Exhibit 1
Bar Chart of Tasks in a Primary Syndication

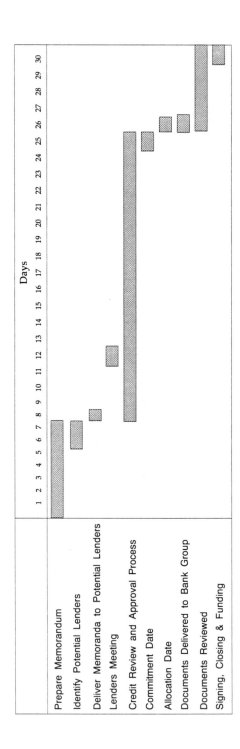

Prepare Memorandum

Public and non-public information is gleaned from various sources by all the participants: the borrower, the borrower's advisors (investment bankers, accountants, lawyers, consultants), and the banks (relationship manager, syndication specialist, staff research analysts). Although the banks may coordinate and arrange this data for the Memorandum, the borrower ultimately approves the version to be used in the marketing effort. Because of the sensitive nature of some of this information, borrowers may require that institutions receiving these packages be bound by a Confidentiality Agreement which restricts how the recipient uses and distributes non-public data. While there is no SEC regulated format, Information Memoranda generally follow the following outline:

Executive/transaction summary: This is a brief, one or two page synopsis of the events leading up to the transaction and the reasons for needing the financing. This section may also briefly outline the business of the borrower and provide summary financial historical and/or projected information.

Transaction highlights: These are bullet points of facts that should be considered when making the lending decision. Highlights may relate to any number of topics including the deal, the company, economic or competitive environments, or any other points that might explain the strengths or weaknesses of the loan.

Summary of terms and conditions: Also called a term sheet, this is an outline of the major deal points negotiated between the agent and the borrower from which the credit agreement will be drafted. Banks usually commit to the terms as outlined in the term sheet, though subject to satisfactory review of the final version of the credit agreement.

Business description: This provides a detailed review of the borrower's business. The goal here is to describe how the company did business in the past and how it plans to operate in the future. This section can include a review of historical financial results, a detailed description of the company's operations, an analysis of significant competitors, a discussion of current and future opportunities, and an analysis of the company's strengths and weaknesses. Confidential, non-public information is often presented for the banks, mainly to paint an accurate enough picture of the company's plans so that appropriate, not-too-restrictive covenants can be set.

Assumptions and projections: Here detailed written and numerical presentation of the borrower's plans is given. Projections of the borrower's financial statements are generally required for at least as many years as the bank loans are expected to remain outstanding. The assumptions are the underlying hypotheses on which the financial models are based.

Exhibits: This section will include any publicly available information which may be useful for a credit analysis; for instance, recent financial statements (Forms 10-Q or 10-K, quarterly or annual reports), news releases, press clippings, or research reports.

Identify Potential Lenders

The syndicators had a strong indication of the potential market for the loan when committing to lend. Now they formally identify and positively target the market. Broadly speaking, the market for bank loans can be divided into banks and non-banks. Beside the obvious regulatory differences between them, each group can be identified by its appetite for specific tranches of loans. Banks, having created revolvers to meet the seasonal and sporadic needs of their borrowers, are administratively equipped to handle the draw and repayment cycles inherent in these tranches. Regulatory accounting also encourages banks to dedicate part of their portfolios to revolvers because the commitment/facility fees paid on infrequently used commitments yield extraordinary returns on assets and capital. Hence, banks lend on a pro rata basis; that is, they commit to a proportionate share of all tranches in the facility. Non-banks, preferring the interest income on constant outstandings, are generally unwilling to purchase revolvers and will buy term loans on a non-pro rata basis. Banks and non-banks can be further described as follows:

US money center banks: This includes the largest commercial banks in the country. All have well established commercial/corporate lending departments. These banks are usually approached during the first two phases of the syndication process, as their stated preference is to be a lead bank in significant financings. The larger the financing, the more likely more than one money center bank will be involved.

US regional banks: These are loosely defined as every other substantial commercial bank in the country. The major difference from the money centers is that regionals tend to focus their attention on borrowers within their geographic area. This backyard borrower can be as narrowly defined as one having its headquarters in that region or as loosely defined as one having some sort of operations in the region. The largest of this group, called "superregionals," often do have a national corporate calling effort but are excluded from the money center category simply because of their size.

Foreign banks: This is a broadly defined group of institutions with offices across the U.S., but with headquarters outside this country. The major concentrations of foreign banks come from Europe, Japan and Canada. Many of these institutions are quite active in the first two phases of the syndication process. Generally, the larger foreign banks are much like the U.S. money centers and superregionals in that they have a national corporate calling presence and tend to be as much transaction driven as they are relationship driven.

Non-bank institutions: Included here are insurance companies, loan funds and leasing/finance companies (both domestic and foreign). Initially, non-banks bought loans to fill a floating rate need. Insurance companies used loans to match up with their own floating-rate liabilities (guaranteed investment contracts, for instance) whereas loan funds generally promise their investors a return at least equal to some floating base rate (usually the prime rate). Recent growth from this segment suggests both an appetite for the security of senior bank loans and an awareness of the favorable risk/reward ratio on loans.

Set Pricing

There are essentially two costs to a borrower for a bank loan that are relevant to a syndication: interest and upfront fees.[5] Interest rates are normally based on a floating-rate index plus some spread. Typical indices are the prime rate and London Interbank Offered Rate (LIBOR), each of which "floats" differently. Commercial banks set their prime rate according to their own corporate lending environment. While this rate may

---

[5] Commitment and/or facility fees payable on revolvers generally receive the same treatment as interest rates when that tranche is sold; that is, if interest rates are skimmed 1/8%, then commitment/facility fees are skimmed 1/8%.

theoretically change daily, it actually changes only a few times a year. LIBOR-based loans, on the other hand, are fixed for one, three, six, or twelve month periods and "float" at expiration when the principal amount is rolled into a new contract with a new rate. Spreads can range from a few basis points (for example, LIBOR plus 25 bp) for the strongest credits to hundreds of basis points on riskier loans. Loans are sold "with full rates" or are "skimmed." For instance, a loan contracted at LIBOR plus 25 bp sold at LIBOR plus 20 bp is said to have been sold with a 5 bp skim. So, for the remaining life of the loan, the borrower still pays interest at the original rate while the buyer receives LIBOR plus 20 bp and the seller earns his 5 bp skim. Syndicated loans rarely have interest rates skimmed; this practice is more popular in secondary syndications.

Upfront fees, paid as a percentage of the total facility, are the second major cost to a borrower and the most relevant pricing mechanism for a syndication, especially for the club and primary phases. An agent bank that charges a borrower 2% for a $100 million loan earns $2 million in upfront fees as compensation for providing financing quickly and for incurring the syndication risk inherent in a large commitment. To syndicate the deal, various levels of minimum commitments[6] will be offered, each with a unique fee level that increases with the size of the commitment.[7] Fees paid in a syndication are from the pool of fees paid to the agent by the borrower; any additional fee required to syndicate the loan would come from the agent's pocket.

Lenders' Meeting

Once pricing and commitment tiers are established, the packages are delivered to the targeted audience. Later, after having some time to review the information, interested parties may attend the lenders' meeting. Here the borrower's management has the chance to sell themselves and the deal to the potential lenders. Potential lenders also have a chance to meet and ask questions of the management team. The emphasis of this meeting is to let the key members of the management team describe their business so the audience can absorb the intangibles that didn't necessarily come through in the Information Memorandum. The underwriters

---

[6] Titles such as co-agent, lead manager, manager and co-manager are sometimes used to differentiate commitment levels.

[7] Lower fees paid on smaller commitments relate to the earlier discussion on the risk/reward decision of the syndication agent.

will occasionally arrange additional meetings where much more detailed questions regarding the projections and assumptions can be addressed.

Commitment Date

A few weeks after the lenders meeting, potential lenders will have completed their credit review and approval process. As extra encouragement, an early incentive fee is sometimes paid to banks responding by some date before the deadline. Banks responding by the commitment date, both verbally and by the form of commitment letter provided in the Memorandum, can usually be sure of getting allocated some part of the loan. If the syndication is over subscribed, however, they may not get as much as they committed.

Allocation Date

For a day or two after the commitment date, the underwriters will confer among themselves and with the borrower to determine how to allocate the loan among themselves and the newly created bank group. Any formula established in the syndication agreement will be used, but since this often applies only to reducing the commitments of the underwriting group, the allocations for the rest of the bank group must be handled individually. Custom dictates that the agents allocate themselves at the highest tier.

A syndication is said to be subscribed if the agents reach their hold level and the rest of the bank group is allocated their commitment amount. An over subscription implies the agents and/or the bank group were allocated less than their respective hold or commitment levels.

After allocations, documents are delivered to the bank group for review and execution. A funding date is set, on which day the administration agent will receive each lender's pro rata share of the principal amount for disbursal to the borrower. Only then will the agent release the fees to the lenders.

SUMMARY

This chapter described the business of bank loan syndication as a process with four distinct phases. The first two phases, Agent Selection and Underwriting Group Arrangement, are important, yet unpublicized steps leading to the much heralded Primary and Secondary Syndication phases.

Once selected to lead the financing, the agent will either syndicate the loan itself or arrange an underwriting group; the choice depending on the agent's risk/reward profile. The subsequent primary or pooled syndication, which lasts approximately one month, includes preparing an Information Memorandum, setting price, and marketing to banks and non-banks. Potential lenders successfully negotiating their internal credit approval process commit to lend, subject to satisfactory review of the credit agreement and related documents, by the commitment date. Having accumulated all commitments, the agent or underwriting group apply some formula to determine each lender's allocation. If the syndication is over subscribed, some lenders may be allocated an amount less than their commitment. As long as the total financing is subscribed (i.e., committed), documents evidencing the financing can be executed and the borrower can receive its funds.

Chapter 3

Secondary Loan Trading Market

JONATHAN D. CALDER
VICE PRESIDENT
CITICORP SECURITIES MARKETS, INC.

The commercial and industrial Loan ("C+I Loan") market is the sleeping giant of the financial industry. Equal in size to the single-family mortgage market, the C+I loan market is a complex, arcane, but quickly evolving sector in the financial markets. It was one of the principal engines of economic growth in the 1980s; a source of credit and financial innovation which contributed to the great stock bull market of the late 1980s. Some contend that the expansion in bank lending led to financial excesses whose consequences are now observed everywhere from the savings and loan crisis to the flood of Chapter 11 bankruptcy filings. More recently, the loan market has been reviled as the source of a "credit crunch" which caused an economic recession to begin in July 1990.

The development of a secondary market for bank loans is the direct result of the syndicated loan activities of the late 1980s. Large, widely distributed "deals" were catalysts for active trading. First, as a mechanism for distributing loans to asset-hungry foreign and U.S. regional banks, and later for transferring loans from those same banks (now asset-heavy), to non-bank loan buyers, the secondary loan market has developed to fulfill needs created by outside forces. The market will continue to be shaped by the forces impacting banks and the lending business. In the early 1990s the demand for greater public disclosure about the composition and quality of bank asset portfolios will drive the development of a loan market which is capable of handling large and complex asset portfolio restructuring and fine-tuning. Bank mergers, potential federal regulatory actions, and overall capital scarcity could be factors which cause an explosion in secondary loan trading volume in the near future.

Comparisons with some of the great growth markets of recent times provide clues to the future direction of the loan market. Parallels between loans and other instruments that rose to prominence in the 1980s are now evident. For example:

> **Swaps:** Interest rate swaps were cumbersome and illiquid until market participants formed the International Swap Dealers Association and agreed upon *standardized documentation and transfer procedures.* Now swaps are a highly liquid and actively traded instrument.

> **LDC:** Less developed country ("LDC") bank loans were very sparsely traded until 1986. Most banks were carrying the loans on their books at par, and almost no banks were willing to sell the loans at a loss. When federal regulators *mandated reserves* against Brazilian loans in 1986, trading volume doubled. When Citibank took its $3 billion reserve in 1987, volume doubled again. From $5 billion of annual turnover in 1986 (same as the secondary loan market in 1990), trading volume has continued to grow exponentially to today's $100 to $130 billion annual turnover figure.

> **Mortgages:** The majority of single-family home mortgages were originated and held by the thrift industry in the early 1980s. When the Volcker Federal Reserve tightened credit and sent short-term interest rates up to 20%, the thrifts, who had funded "short" against their long-term mortgage assets, began to hemorrhage money. Armed with *federal tax incentives* the thrifts *marked to market* pools of mortgages and sold them. Wall Street firms, banks, and the federal government *credit-enhanced and securitized the assets* which were then sold to institutional and individual investors. The mortgage market's explosive growth began with direct pass-through securities, and then redoubled in the mid to late

1980s with development of the *grantor trust* structure of the collateralized mortgage obligation ("CMO").

Any of the critical factors highlighted above could become the catalyst for growth in the secondary loan trading market. An effort to standardize documentation and settlement practices sponsored by the American Bankers Association ("ABA") is underway. Mandated reserves and "mark-to-market" are under consideration by federal regulators. Tax incentives are unlikely, but not inconceivable. And loan securitization efforts are widespread among banks, Wall Street firms, and numerous financial boutiques. Demand for loan portfolio management is growing. It is only a matter of time until the financial technology to satisfy this need is developed, and it is inevitable that an active secondary market will be a fundamental element of this progress.

This chapter is devoted to the secondary market for senior secured bank loans for highly leveraged transactions ("HLTs"), and is written from a general capital markets perspective. The term "price" is always used in the sense of "dollar price," meaning the percentage of par. Par is always one hundred percent of face value. The first section describes the size of the loan market, followed by an overview of trading practices. Secondary market pricing and loans as an investment vehicle are then discussed. The chapter concludes with a discussion of the future of the secondary loan market.

SIZING THE LOAN MARKET

The total size of the C+I loan market is approximately $1.6 trillion, about the same size as the single-family residential mortgage market. This is made up of about $800 billion of loans outstanding, and another $800 billion of unfunded commitments to lend (e.g. backstop lines, undrawn revolving credit facilities). Of the total outstandings, roughly $250 billion is classified as HLT. This compares to the LDC loan market of $400 billion and the high yield bond market of $200 billion. About 60% of the $250 billion is made up of deals with sufficient size to trade in the secondary market. About $60 billion is made up of "media" credits. It is estimated that $60 to $80 billion of HLT's are distressed (i.e., would trade at a price under 90 cents on the dollar) of which $35 to $45 billion are deals large enough to trade.

SECONDARY LOAN TRADING OVERVIEW

Development

Activity in the secondary loan market in 1988 through 1989 was primarily derived from the strength in the new issue, or "primary" loan syndication market. When a large new HLT borrower came to market the lead, or "agent" bank, usually put together a syndicate of underwriters sufficient to close the deal. Then the underwriters typically competed to "sell down" their primary positions to smaller banks and non-bank lending institutions with the largest and best-staffed banks having an enormous advantage in garnering sales. Secondary loan trading developed when aggressive banks would complete their sell-down, but continue to distribute loans (at risk) and cover positions by buying from other syndicate members.

With the slowdown in HLT loan origination in 1990, secondary trading shifted from trading new issues to brokering existing issues. The creation of loan mutual funds is the most important recent development in the loan market. At a time when most banks were under pressure to reduce assets, particularly in their HLT portfolios, the funds raised $6 billion to invest in HLT bank loans. Since the funds are diversified pools of loans, techniques emerged to swap loans, tie-in sales of certain loans with purchases or sales of certain others, and structure packaged deals. Non-bank brokers quickly entered the market when it was determined that capital was not required for this brokerage activity. Loan brokerage flourished while prices steadily declined throughout 1990. A fundamental unanswered question is whether the market will ultimately be a traded market with participants taking risk positions (advantage to banks and capital rich investment banks and funds) or a brokered market (advantage to the boutiques and other low cost producers).

Purpose and Function

The purpose of any market is to shift risk from those who do not want it to those who do. The loan market is no different, and as mentioned earlier, the roles it fills are determined by the external factors at any given time. In 1987 and 1988, the market provided investments for asset-hungry foreign and U.S. regional banks. In 1990 it provided an outlet for capital-hungry domestic and foreign banks to reduce assets and was the source of paper for the $6 billion of investable cash raised by the loan mutual funds. Going forward it will be the forum through which bank loan portfolio management is conducted.

"Par" vs. "Distressed"

As some HLT credits have soured while others have continued to perform well, the market has split into two discrete sectors. According to market convention, "par" loans are generally those that trade at a dollar price of 90 or better, while "distressed" loans are those bankruptcy and troubled credits that trade below 90 cents on the dollar. In general, bankruptcy credits tend to trade between 40 and 70 cents on the dollar dependent, obviously, on factors such as whether or not the borrower pays interest and how long bankruptcy is anticipated to last. There are three reasons for the 40–70 range. First, HLT loans are senior and secured and, even in bankruptcy, they tend to have real asset values they can attach, usually approaching 100 cents on the dollar. Second, most buyers of bankruptcy credits require approximately a 30% rate of return. Third, their average investment horizon (i.e., average time in bankruptcy) is about 2.5 to 3 years. Bond mathematics therefore determines that most senior secured bankruptcy loans will fall in this range.

Principal Players

During 1987–89, the market was composed of the large money-center banks as originators and traders, while the "retail" account base consisted of other banks, and some insurance companies. In 1989–90, some Wall Street investment banks became involved as brokers and traders as the loan funds and other expansion-minded insurance company portfolios became the dominant retail outlet for paper. In 1991, more Wall Street firms and boutiques entered the market. A great deal of interest stems from these firms' experience in distressed bonds, an area where the banks' market presence is non-existent. The distressed loan market is currently dominated by the bankruptcy boutiques who have access to investment capital for this purpose.

Standards and Practices

The loan market is undergoing its first concerted effort to standardize documentation and trading practices. Liquidity suffers greatly from lack of standardization as in the interest rate swaps market of the early 1980s.

The American Bankers Association (ABA) is the forum for discussions that are proceeding on three fronts: Settlement Practices, Documentation (i.e., Credit Agreements, transfer documents), and Syndicate Practices. The process was opened to all interested parties, and over 100 institutions are participating in some form. Market participants will benefit greatly from simple documentation standards and the adoption of a code of behavior. Below is a summary of current market practices, all of which are subjects of the ABA standardization efforts.

Currently, trades are agreed in writing (the "commitment letter") and are subject to satisfactory loan and transfer documentation. If a trade is arranged by a broker, the principals usually sign a commitment letter with each other, and a separate agreement with the broker detailing compensation and representing that the broker will be held harmless with respect to any problems that may result from the transaction. The two main modes of transfer are *assignments* and *participations*.

In an assignment, the buyer becomes a direct lender to the borrower under the credit agreement, and is entitled to all voting privileges afforded the banks under the agreement. Assignments are transferred directly between the two parties and recorded on the books of the agent. Usually the borrower's and/or agent's approval is required, but more recent credit agreements provide a definition of an "eligible assignee," with the more progressive agreements employing the SEC Regulation D definition.

In a participation, the buyer becomes a participant in a share of an assignee's loan. This form of transfer is transparent to the borrower, but is made without recourse to the assignee and is considered a full sale for accounting and regulatory purposes. Participations are administered by the assignee and therefore carry some additional credit risk. Most participation agreements do not transfer full voting rights. Most transfer only the right to vote on questions concerning "money terms" (maturity, amortization, coupon and fees, release of collateral, or forgiveness of debt). Participations are easier to create than assignments because they are usually not subject to the assignment definitions in the credit agreement requiring minimum amounts and standard pro rata shares in the various facilities. They tend not to be used for revolving credit facilities because the risk of the participant not funding is borne by the assignee. Participations are more difficult to transfer than assignments because the assignee may be unwilling to accommodate the trade, but must be imposed upon to prepare transfer documentation. Also, the section in a participation agreement which speaks to the right of transfer is never as specific as the same section in a credit agreement.

For either transfer method, settlement typically occurs within 30 days, with the majority of trades settling within 5 to 10 days. Credit risk currently transfers on the settlement date, as opposed to most bond markets where credit risk transfers on the trade date. For outstanding coupon interest periods, coupons are marked to market and the buyer receives the newly set rate (a process known somewhat inaccurately as "breakage"). Monies are transferred between buyer and seller either at settlement or on the coupon payment date(s) to ensure that each party receives the correct accrued interest. Traditionally, par loan trades have settled using at least three separate wire transfers: one from buyer to seller for the full par amount of the loan; one from seller to buyer for the full amount of the discount from par (known as "up front fees"); and at least one more wire to settle accrued interest. One goal of the ABA effort will be a mandate from a majority of players that all amounts should net and trades should settle with one wire transfer.

LOAN PRICING: SECONDARY MARKET PERSPECTIVE

Primary vs. Secondary Pricing

Primary pricing, or the pricing of new issue loan underwriting syndicates, is usually "tiered," with the larger underwriters receiving greater underwriting fees. Usually no member of the syndicate receives fees as large as the agent bank. Since banks do not make a secondary market to "protect" their new issues and insure an orderly secondary distribution, the primary fee tiers become very important.

Like in all syndicates, players must bet on the direction of the "break" at the end of the primary period. If the loans break up in price (down in fees) due to strong secondary demand, the market will normally stay quite orderly. If the loans break down in price (up in fees) on lower than expected retail demand, loans will usually trade to the highest fee tier level below the agent bank. Whereas new issue bond syndicates have an obligation to buy back bonds if the price drops, loan syndicate members will sell into the price drop down to the level of their cost price, then they will leave the market. These loans can become illiquid very quickly, with the underwriters stuck with large unsalable positions.

Cost Price vs. Sale Price: FASB 91

Under Generally Accepted Accounting Principles (GAAP) in the U.S. (specifically the Financial Accounting Standards Board ("FASB") rule 91), banks must account for loan holdings in three buckets: loans held for investment purposes, loans held for resale, and loans held for trading purposes. The first category, loans held for investment purposes, is not marked to market. Any upfront fees received are amortized (taken into income) over the life of the loan. FASB 91 allows underwriting banks in syndicated loans to take a portion of the underwriting fees into income at close, as long as a certain proportion of the loan is successfully distributed. In this case the remaining fees are amortized over the life of the loan. The second two categories are accounted for on a "lower of cost or market" (LOCOM) basis, and are used for syndication and trading inventories. Any fees received are booked into a reserve account and realized only when the asset is sold (or is repaid). The fees in the reserve account must be periodically compared to the market price, and if there is a shortfall, the account must be supplemented. The difference between book cost and sale price impacts the revenue account. Loans can be moved on a one-time basis from the loans held for investment purposes bucket to loans held for resale. Loans can be moved back to the investment account only if they become unsalable for credit reasons.

Loan Price Quotes

Few players in the loan market will sell a loan below cost price, and loans are not usually marked to market. Price quotes are either given as a percentage of par or as its complement, the "upfront fee." The coupon must also be stated because of the loan market technique called "skimming" where a bank sells a loan not only for lower fees than it received, but also for lower interest rates than it received.

Price History: Toward a Loan Price Index

These pricing practices have made relative value comparisons difficult. Now traders have begun to quote loans on a "percentage of par" basis (i.e., 100% less upfront fees paid to the buyer, or plus upfront fees paid to the seller). This seemingly minor development has paved the way for more sophisticated analysis of rates of return and pricing trends within the loan market. The yield and pricing behavior of loans can now be compared with similar measures of other investment vehicles.

Importantly, as in other markets, pricing histories of loans in the secondary market can be compiled into an index which numerically (or graphically) expresses market trends which previously have been "felt" by traders but not empirically confirmed. For example, during 1990 most loan market participants perceived that secondary market loan values (especially HLT loans) were declining in sympathy with values in the stock market and the high yield bond market. As can be seen in Exhibit 1, a price index of the twenty largest, most widely held and actively traded HLT loans clearly shows the downward trend in loan prices throughout 1990.

Comparative Yield Methodologies

Current yield. Most bond market investors are current yield buyers. Thus, the slope of the yield curve can be an important determinant of "non-traditional" buy interest in loans. That is, a "flat" or "inverted" yield curve is most advantageous for floating rate loan buyers who look at current yield. Current yield in the context of loans refers to actual LIBOR or prime, plus the appropriate interest margin stated in the credit agreement.

Discount margin. When the yield impact of the price discount from par is also considered, one arrives at the concept of discount margin. The discount from (premium to) par is spread ratably over the expected life of the loan, and increases (decreases) the effective interest rate margin earned by the holder of the loan. Discount margin is used by traders when determining current yield.

Yield to maturity. This fixed rate yield methodology has been borrowed by the floating-rate loan market as a way of comparing loan yields to their fixed rate counterparts. Floating and fixed rates are in general linked to each other via the interest rate swap market. This method, usually called "implied yield to maturity," makes the assumption that the floating-rate loan cash flows are swapped into fixed-rate cash flows using an interest rate swap. While interesting conceptually, loans are very difficult (or expensive) to swap due to the borrower's prepayment option.

Exhibit 1
C&I Loan Price Index—20 Large Capitalization (non-distressed) HLT Loans

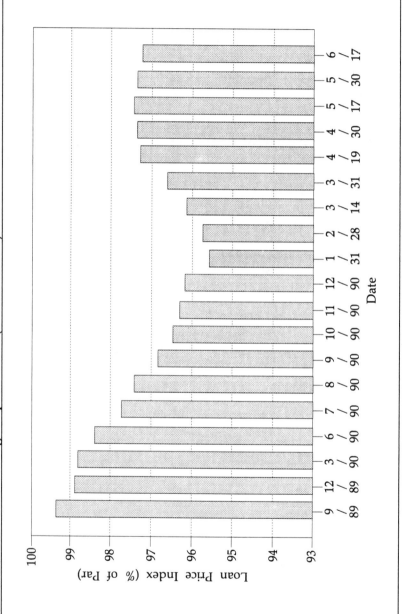

Interest Rate Swaps, the Yield Curve, and the Prepayment Option

In practice, an investor who swaps a loan from floating rate into fixed rate is increasing exposure to changing interest rates. Since a borrower can normally prepay a loan at any time, usually without penalty, the investor may be liable for compensation to the swap counterparty if rate movements have been unfavorable. When the yield curve between 3-month LIBOR and the 5- to 7-year sector is steep, the value of the prepayment option is at its greatest. In a steep yield curve environment, the potential current yield pickup from swapping a loan can be dramatic. The borrower pays a low floating-rate coupon, yet the investor receives a high fixed-rate coupon, with the interest rate swap market providing the difference. Since the prepayment option defines which loans can be swapped, the option takes on a significant value.

An interesting case in point was the RJR Holdings Capital Corp. 10.50% senior notes issue due in 1998. The notes were essentially equal in rank and just one year longer in maturity than the senior secured loans due in 1997. The loans had a coupon that floated 350 basis points over LIBOR. When the senior notes issue was brought to market, the loans paid a low floating-rate coupon of 9.56%, almost 100 basis points lower in current yield than the senior notes. However, swapped into a fixed-rate instrument, one would have been able to achieve a coupon of 12.20%, calculated as follows:

Interest rate swap margin:	T + 0.70%
7-year maturity T-note yield:	8.00%
Floating-rate loan margin:	LIBOR + 3.50%
Fixed-rate yield calculation:	
	0.70%
	8.00%
	3.50%
	————
Implied yield to maturity:	12.20%

In other words, the prepayment option is implicitly worth the difference between 12.20% and 9.56% to the company (or to an investor). An arbitrage opportunity exists because the market believes that a 10.50% fixed rate is more valuable than a floating-rate yield of LIBOR + 350 with an implicit, swapped yield to maturity of 12.20%, but a current coupon of only 9.56%. The role of the secondary market is to find a way to capture some of this arbitrage for investors.

LOANS AS AN INVESTMENT VEHICLE

In securities markets terms, loans are senior secured amortizing prepayable floating-rate instruments. They trade in book-entry form and clear through an agent bank. They carry extremely tight covenants, and the source document, the "credit agreement," is amended frequently. They trade by appointment in a thin secondary market that is unregulated, but is also free of any standard practices. So why would any investor want to buy a loan?

The main arguments for loans as an investment vehicle are: security translates into low loss experience (high recovery rate); floating-rate protects against principal loss in rising rate environments; attractive return vis-à-vis risk; and ability to invest in size. Other characteristics of loans as an investment vehicle are discussed below.

Dealing spreads/commissions. In general, the loan dealer community has not committed itself to guaranteeing the liquidity of the marketplace. While there have been isolated instances of dealers quoting two-way markets in certain issues (i.e., bid and offer prices as a "market maker" would in other markets), these cases have been rare. Nevertheless, an informal commission structure has developed along the lines of the corporate bond market. On average, dealers look to make a one-quarter point spread working orders, and a one-half point spread (or better) when taking a principal risk position.

Market movers. Like the junk bond market, loan market price movements tend to be very issue-specific. When prices move in general, they respond, like the high yield bond sector, to overall credit conditions in the economy. So, loan price movements are more likely to follow equity indices than Treasury bond prices. If there is one major difference between factors influencing high yield bond prices and HLT loan prices, it is the slope of the yield curve. Since investors are focussed on current yield, a steepening yield curve tends to hurt loan prices, while a flattening curve tends to help. As a rule-of thumb, loans generally follow the direction of the price movements in the high yield market, usually with a lag.

Loan price performance. The magnitude of price movements in the loan market is extremely small when compared to the bond market. There are two main reasons for this price performance. First, HLT loans are backed by collateral. Since they are usually the best-protected creditor in a company's capital structure, a severe deterioration in credit is usually required before the value of the senior secured loan becomes impaired. The second reason is the floating-rate argument again. In a rising interest rate environment, fixed-rate bond prices weaken, but a floating-rate instrument will continually reset its coupon to the market rate thereby muting any effect on price. When junk bond price indices traded down to 70 in late 1990, a similarly composed HLT loan index went only as low as 95 (refer again to Exhibit 1).

LOAN MARKET: WHAT'S IN STORE?

The secondary loan market will contine to be shaped by the forces impacting the banks and the lending business: pressure on bank earnings and capital; economic recession; consolidation (bank mergers); HLT and real estate loan exposure levels; S&L crisis; and federal regulatory environment.

These forces will continue to influence banks' risk appetite, and it is inevitable in this environment that bank loan portfolio management techniques will continue to be implemented. It is this very need for loan portfolio management that is likely to be the driving force behind further growth in the secondary loan trading market. First, portfolio analysis, then portfolio strategy, and then portfolio management/execution. An efficient secondary market will be one of the primary tools used in implementing portfolio management.

Will the market develop? A simple analysis of turnover (defined here as sell-side trading volume) of related products shows that there is an enormous capacity for growth in the secondary loan market:

Instrument	Market Size	Secondary Trading	Turnover
High yield bonds	$200 billion	$100 billion	50%
LDC loans	$400 billion	$100 billion	25%
HLT loans	$250 billion	$5 billion	2%

An increase in turnover to 10% would result in activity that is still extremely light when compared to the other two markets. But consider that an increase in turnover of only eight percentage points would cause a five-fold increase in annual trading activity to $25 billion. Given the abundance of factors that are crying out for a market to develop, it seems all that is required is for some "triggering mechanism" to start the explosion.

Certain mandatory "advances" are easy to identify. The current average ticket size of $10 million is too large. An average in the $1 to $5 million range would be more conducive to trading, and would also tend to increase the number of players prepared to commit capital to secondary market-making activities. And it goes without saying that standardized documentation and loan settlement procedures will be a boon to all participants. Slightly more esoteric, but equally important, will be the development of an efficient and reliable method for selling loans "short" and borrowing in loan "repo market."

The interest rate swaps, LDC debt, and home mortgage securities markets all went through similar growing pains in the recent past. While these other markets grew at different times, in different situations, they all shared the existence of powerful economic, regulatory, political, and cultural forces which defined and shaped their role and caused their explosive growth. The forces which caused those markets to take off in the 1980s were no more powerful than the ones observed now influencing the bank loan market.

Chapter 4

Brokering Senior Bank Debt

TIMOTHY M. O'BRIEN
DESK MANAGER
GARVIN GUYBUTLER CORPORATION

Every market has a broker; every market needs a broker. Intermediaries operate in markets as diverse as real estate, baseball cards, and third world debt. It should not be surprising to see brokers at work in the senior bank debt market. Naturally some markets, even within the financial world, are more easily brokered than others. However, the broker's constant role is providing a central location for pricing information and adding liquidity and efficiency to the market.

Characteristics common to every brokered market are presented in this chapter. We will analyze these characteristics and show how to apply them to the secondary market for senior bank debt. We will also see how brokers aided the development of this market, how it operates today, and where it might be tomorrow.

37

BROKER DEALERS VERSUS BROKER AGENTS

Before proceeding, it is important to distinguish between two types of brokers. The first is the broker dealer. Currently many investment firms and banks operate as broker/dealers. In most markets, broker dealers take positions and wait for a favorable price swing to make a profit. For example, broker dealers might position a transaction on which they received significant up-front fees either expecting increased demand or a complete restructuring of the deal. Dealers also may pass a position through their books without the price swing if both buyer and seller are matched. Typically, dealers make markets in types of transactions suitable for their books or portfolios. Therefore, the number of transactions in which they make markets may be limited.

Dealers in the senior bank debt market are further restrained due to credit policies and capital requirements. For example, many banks cannot position names which the bank does not already own. Or, if a bank's exposure in a particular credit is full, the trader cannot position any additional paper. Unlike other markets, there are no strategies to hedge their position.

This chapter is written from the perspective of a broker agent who operates much differently than the dealer. The major difference between dealers and agents is that dealers take positions. Conversely, agents never take a position in any transaction. In the exchange of senior bank debt, the broker agent never actually owns the participation or assignment and the buyer and seller are always introduced to each other. Whereas dealers may be limited in the names in which they make a market, agents will make a market in as many transactions as possible. Agents charge a fee for each transaction.

From an agent's standpoint, the perfect market would have an infinite number of possible buyers and sellers, all wishing to remain anonymous, and all with unlimited lines of credit. Trading would require little or no documentation. There would also be a constant stream of news causing price volatility.

However, this is not the case. Usually restrictions such as documentation or credit lines exist and these restrictions can vary widely from market to market. There are few documentation restrictions in the Eurodollar market, but in the lesser-developed country (LDC) debt market, the documentation can be prohibitively complicated. Whereas, the LDC broker works hard to complete a single transaction, the Eurodollar broker works equally hard to build and maintain market share. The volume of brokered transactions increases when there are fewer restrictions.

The three factors that determine the ease with which a particular product can be brokered are: (1) the nature of the product, (2) the types of players involved, and (3) the market itself. First, the product must be one that is widely accepted and understood. The product must be tradeable and involve relatively standard documentation. Second, the players should be plentiful and in a position to both buy and sell. All participants should be price sensitive, buying or selling depending upon price rather than relationship. Each player should also have a large available credit line for a variety of names. Finally, the market should be volatile, affected by events, rumors, and interest rate movements.

It was extremely difficult to first broker senior bank debt in the mid-1980s for many reasons. First, there were two distinct sets of sellers and buyers. Rarely did the two cross over. Banks were reluctant to disclose the names they were looking to buy or sell. Second, there were no available lines of credit. Rather, the broker had to wait for the credit process to be completed and for a line to be established, a process that generally took four weeks. Finally, once a bank bought into a transaction, it was not going to sell it. Who could blame banks? Why wait a month for an approval and then sell it? Banks were also hesitant sellers for fear of offending the borrower. Brokering opportunities were limited. However, this changed as the deals got larger and the number of banks in the primary syndicate increased. Although some improvements made brokering senior bank debt easier, two other problems exist that keep the volume of brokered transactions low as compared to most other brokered markets.

The first is the lack of price volatility associated with interest rate movement and speculative buying and selling. There is price volatility associated with credit changes. Activity in most financial markets increases when there is movement in interest rates. When the markets expect a discount rate cut or rising inflation, trading activity increases as traders adjust their positions. This doesn't happen in the senior bank debt market because most deals float according to LIBOR or PRIME. The holder of paper is not exposed to great interest rate risk.

The second obstacle is the buy and hold strategy of most market participants. This stems partially from the lack of price volatility and partially from the relationship aspect of banking. Once an institution approves the deal, it is not likely to be sold unless there is a serious deterioration in the borrower's credit standing. By this time, however, there are few buyers unless the seller offers it at a discount (which they are reluctant to do). Although opportunities are limited, broker agents provide advantages to buyers and sellers.

THE ROLE OF THE BROKER

The role of a broker in any market is to provide a central location for a market participant to price a transaction and to provide equal prices to all players regardless of their position (first tier, second tier, etc.) in the market. This role provides the market with efficiency, liquidity, and anonymity. The price is given in the form of a bid and offer. The bid is the buying price and the offer is the selling price. The closer the bid and offer are to each other, the more efficient the market. Brokers constantly canvass various institutions for prices and views of the market. Through this canvassing brokers know who can buy or sell, when, and at what price. This provides the market with additional liquidity which is vital for players who, for various internal and regulatory reasons, have to reduce exposure quickly. Brokers reflect the best unbiased prices in the market. Holders of paper naturally try to skew the price in their favor.

If a player wanted to price transactions, they could have called other players (Banks A, B, C) as shown in Exhibit 1. A problem arises if only Bank A was called. The customer receives the best price on transaction W (with 50 basis points upfront) but not on transaction X. Bank B is offering 37.5 basis points while Bank A is only offering 25 basis points. Bank C, on the other hand, only has a bid on transactions W and X. Thus, to receive the best pricing, the customer should call all possible buyers and sellers. This is difficult, however, when there are many possible holders of the paper. Alternatively, the customer could have all the transactions priced with a broker.

ADVANTAGE TO THE SELLER

In recent years brokers expanded the number of potential buyers for institutions that did not have a large sales force. Many banks had relationship buyers and did not find it necessary to expand. However, as the size of the transaction and syndicate groups grew, there was a need for banks to look beyond their traditional buyers. It is easier and more economical

Exhibit 1
Variation of Upfront Fees

		Bank A	Bank B	Bank C	Brokers
		Bid/Offer*	Bid/Offer*	Bid/Offer	Bid/Offer*
Transaction	W	/50	/12.5	60/	60/50
	X	/25	/37.5	30/	30/25
	Y	75/	50 /	/45	50/45
	Z	50/	/25	35/	35/25

*Indicates upfront fees expressed as basis points. Bank A is offering 50 basis points to buyers of transaction W.

for an institution to utilize a broker's existing distribution network than to develop its own. As the market developed, the lines between the buyers and sellers have blurred.

Brokers quickened the selling pace. This was important for bankers who applied for larger lines to obtain higher upfront fees, but had to sell some to reduce their exposure. Speed was also important for large transactions in a publicity-adverse market.

Brokers distributed many leftover or seasoned deals. In many cases, banks sold most of a transaction, but had a small piece remaining. Brokers developed a niche selling these seasoned transactions. The market was previously educated on the transaction and there was usually a buyer with a late approval.

ADVANTAGES TO THE BUYER

For the buyers, brokers expanded the range and number of transactions available. Although buyers dealt with banks who were involved in many transactions, there were always more available. Thus, brokers presented new transactions which were attractive to buyer's portfolios.

Many deals were so large that several banks were involved in the primary syndicate group. Many of the larger transactions had 40 or more syndicate members. Unless a buyer received a price from every bank in the syndicate, there was a good chance they were not obtaining the best price. This is where the broker market receives its impetus. The prices offered by various sellers differed by as much as 50 basis points.

Brokers provided an additional supply of paper to buyers. Many times a bank got a name approved only to find the original seller sold out. They could source this paper through the broker. New buyers are often looking from some seasoned or odd lot paper which brokers can often find. In summary, brokers provided distinct benefits for both buyer and seller. The main benefit was providing a central location to obtain an unbiased price on any transaction.

The above benefits established a broker's place in the secondary market. Originally, the primary benefit was finding a new buyer or seller. As the number and size of deals grew, trading activity increased, and a broker's purpose was to provide updated pricing and speed of execution. Now as the market has slowed, brokers are assisting buyers and sellers in shaping their portfolios.

DISADVANTAGES OF USING A BROKER

Many buyers and sellers felt that dealing through a broker reduced their chances of developing a direct relationship with the counterparty, or may damage an existing one. Buyers assumed that if they didn't buy directly, they would be left out of the next deal. For this reason, a buyer felt obliged to buy from the bank who showed the transaction originally, or who assisted with the analysis. This was often true even when the offering price was more attractive through a broker. On the other hand, some selling banks would not sell a transaction away from a relationship buyer, for fear the buyer would not buy the next deal from them. Sellers felt obliged to sell to one of their relationship banks even if a better bid was available elsewhere. This practice became less prevalent as more transaction-oriented players entered the market.

Broker agents might not be as familiar with the intricacies of the deal as the buyer or seller. As stated earlier, institutions spend a good deal of time analyzing the transaction and many other factors that might influence the transaction in the future. The account officer or transaction leader can therefore highlight the strengths and explain any other aspects of the loan.

IMPORTANT MARKET DEVELOPMENTS

Some development that increased the broker's activity in the secondary market for senior bank debt include:

- The vast number of takeover and leveraged buyouts in the 1980s and the increased size of syndicate groups.

- The upfront fee structure for buying a deal: In many deals, the upfront fees were positively correlated with the size of the deal bought. The larger the piece bought, the more the upfront fee. For example, a $25 million purchase received an upfront fee of 50 basis points. However, a $50 million purchase received 75 basis points. Thus, many banks bought larger chunks, with the intention of selling some in the secondary market just to receive the higher fee.

- There were changes that made it easier to buy assignments rather than participations. This reduced the risk of losing a deal due to counterparty risk, which is a bigger problem for brokers than for buyers and sellers. If a buyer or seller has a problem with another player, they do not call that player. Brokers, on the other hand, cannot be aware of a particular bank's guidelines. Although the reality of the problem is actually small, the thought is always gnawing on the broker's mind when closing a transaction. Another similar change permitted assignments in a particular facility such as a term loan, rather than a pro-rata assignment which might include a revolver and letter of credit.

- The increase in the number of non-bank buyers and sellers who tend to be more trade- and transaction-oriented than banks.

- Banks' changing views on portfolio management. This development will become more important in the coming years as new capital adequacy requirements and other regulatory guidelines force institutions to review their portfolios and to actively manage them. Institutions are currently achieving this goal through outright purchases and sales or asset swaps. Asset swaps, popular in the third world debt market, are simply institutions selling a transaction where they might be overexposed, and simultaneously buying into another transaction where their exposure is less. Recently, asset swaps include HLT for HLT, term loan for revolving credit, and corporate for sovereign.

THE MECHANICS OF A TRADE

While canvassing the market, the broker presents available bids and offers on various transactions. If a party expresses an interest in buying a particular deal, has an approval in place, and would like to purchase it, brokers relay this to the selling bank. The reverse is true if a party has something to sell.

Once both parties agree on the terms, (i.e., the particular facilities to be purchased and applicable interest rates and fees), brokers send a confirmation fax to the buyer and seller. Although the parties are still unknown to each other, neither side should have a problem signing the confirmation because it clearly states that the completion is subject to satisfactory documentation. In practice, a responsible broker should not match buyer or seller if the broker thinks one party would be unacceptable to the other. To do so would be a waste of time for the three parties involved and would eventually reduce the broker's credibility in the market.

Once the broker receives the signed confirmation, the parties are introduced to each other. When introduced, the counterparties complete the documentation which is executed directly between the seller and buyer. Although a broker facilitates the process, the broker's name never appears on the document thereby keeping documentation and legal liability limited. The flow of principal and interest is directly between the buyer and seller, so there is no third party settlement risk. However, the upfront fees may flow through the broker depending on the wishes of the other parties.

Once the particular deal is complete, all correspondence regarding the particular deal is between the buyer and seller.

One variation of this process occurs when the potential buyer does not have an approval for the transaction. In this instance, a broker will supply as much of the credit information as possible. When the buyer completes an initial credit review and is still interested, a broker will introduce such a buyer to the potential seller for all credit questions. A reputable broker never makes any representations about the borrowing company or transaction. All investors are required to perform their own credit analysis.

CONCLUSION

The market will develop in numerous ways. Many players will shed or pare down their portfolios. As many credits mature or amortize, the portfolios of most institutions will naturally decrease in size. Once the portfolio reaches a certain level, the institution may choose to sell the remainder rather than pay the administrative cost associated with its maintenance. Regulatory requirements will force other institutions to sell. Still other players realize that it may be a while before the flurry of deals completed during the 1980s are seen again, and they may decide to exit the business totally in order to concentrate on other activities.

The market will continue to provide golden opportunities for institutions that are able to participate. Most large banks and investment houses currently have personnel trading senior bank debt, both at par and distressed levels. Their activity and the number of nontraditional players will continue to increase as the players become more familiar with the market and the opportunities available. More crossover between buyers of high yield bonds and high yield bank debt can be expected, as junk bond investors view senior bank debt as an alternative investment.

Chapter 5

Bank Loan Sales Activities: Selected Banking and Securities Law Considerations

ROBERT L. TORTORIELLO, J.D.
PARTNER
CLEARY, GOTTLIEB, STEEN & HAMILTON

Recent developments in the loan sales market, coupled with evolving judicial guidance as to when a "note" constitutes a "security" for federal securities law purposes, have brought to the forefront issues with respect to how banks and other financial institutions can or should structure their loan sale/participation activities to accommodate market realities and to assure compliance with federal securities laws and the Glass-Steagall Act. This chapter addresses the very significant developments which have occurred with respect to loan and loan participation sales in

The author wishes to express his appreciation to Steven Lofchie for his assistance in the preparation of this chapter.

recent years and discusses the banking and securities law issues which these developments implicate.[1]

BACKGROUND TO THE LOAN SALES MARKET

The intermediation function that commercial banks provide in financial markets generally is nowhere more evident than in the loan sales market. The nature of that market—its size and scope, the identity of its principal participants and the regulatory and documentary framework surrounding its operation—are critically important to understanding the impact of banking and securities law considerations on its evolution.

Market Participants

Commercial banks sell loans and loan participations to diversify risk, improve liquidity or comply with capital requirements and lending limits.[2] In addition, as the financial markets become more integrated and the nature and scope of commercial banking continue to develop, the business of commercial banks has evolved to make the origination of loans for sale an important profit-generating activity.

> The rapid expansion of sales of loan participations by some money center and large regional banks reflects a fundamental change in the way many of these banks view this traditional activity. Whereas the sale of participations previously had been viewed primarily as a correspondent banking product, it is now viewed primarily as an increasingly important technique for meeting the credit demand of the most creditworthy wholesale borrowers. Many of

---

[1] This chapter is current as of January 1, 1992.

[2] A study by the Federal Reserve Bank of Chicago found that loan sales have little effect on bank risk, despite their goal of asset diversification (which could be expected to reduce bank risk), and despite the fear that banks are likely to sell their best loans (which could be expected to increase bank risk). This study, which analyzed three key reasons for loan sales—funding, diversification and capital requirements—found little support for the argument that banks sell appreciated loans to realize the gain for regulatory capital purposes. Pavel, "Loan Sales Have Little Effect on Bank Risk," *Economic Perspectives* (Federal Reserve Bank of Chicago), March/April 1988.

these banks now originate loans to such borrowers primarily for distribution to others through the sale of participations rather than for their own portfolios. In certain
respects, this form of intermediation more closely resembles the distribution of commercial paper by investment
banks than traditional lending by commercial banks.[3]

Sales of loans and loan participations have been particularly important in major bank commercial lending transactions, including—in the
past decade, at least—financing of merger and acquisition ("*M&A*") and
leveraged buyout ("*LBO*") transactions as well as other highly leveraged
transactions ("*HLTs*"). In fact, it was the ability of lead banks to sell and
participate away most or all of the exposure that they initially acquired
in a large HLT that allowed banks to increase the scope of their participation in such transactions in the first place.[4]

The major *purchasers* of loans and loan participations include the U.S.
and foreign branches and agencies of foreign banks, as well as insurance
companies, thrift institutions, pension funds, corporations, money market
and other mutual funds and institutional investors.[5] The most important
sellers in the market are large commercial banks, many of which are striv-
ing to reach more, and more diverse, purchasers, and which, at least
until recently, have been increasing their sales forces. While medium-
sized regional banks, non-bank affiliates of commercial banks, foreign
banks and investment banks (as syndicators and as sellers of loans to
institutional clients) and institutions such as General Electric Capital Cor-

---

[3] Board of Governors of the Federal Reserve System ("*Board*") Senior Loan Officer Opinion Survey, April 11, 1986, pp. 8-9.

[4] See the discussion of HLTs later in this chapter.

[5] See Board August 1988 Senior Loan Officer Opinion Survey (September 28, 1988)
("*1988 Board Survey*"); *see also Asset Sales Report,* March 4, 1991; *American Banker,* November 28, February 9, 1990, November 22, 1989; *Investment Dealers Digest,* July 9,
1990; *Bank Letter,* May 21, 1990; Gorton and Haubrich, The Loan Sales Market (Research paper; September 1988) (describing, analyzing and quantifying the evolution of
the loan sales market).

poration also participate in the market, large banks have established an increasingly dominant position.[6]

Sales Procedures

Guidelines of the Comptroller of the Currency (the "*Comptroller*") require national bank purchasers and sellers of loan participations to follow prudent business practices, and identify information and documentation that must be provided in connection with the purchase and sale of loan participations.[7] These guidelines require:

1. Written policies and procedures for loan participation.

2. Disclosure by the selling bank of complete and regularly updated credit information on the obligor during the term of the loan and on the loan's accrual status and related matters.[8]

3. An independent analysis of credit quality by the purchasing bank.

4. Written documentation of all parties' rights and obligations in any arrangement to buy back loans or participations.

Two trade groups, the American Bankers Association and Robert Morris Associates, have also developed loan sale guidelines for originat-

---

[6] During the fourth quarter of 1986, for example, the top 10 banks in loan sales had less than 60% of the market and the next 40 banks had 18%, while the remaining 4,700 smaller banks that participated in the market had 22%; during the third quarter of 1990, the market share of the top 10 banks in loan sales was approximately 86%, the market share of the next 40 banks was 8%, while the share of the smaller banks declined to 6% of the market. See, for example, *Asset Sales Report*, June 17, 1991, May 15, 1989; *American Banker*, February 25, 1991, September 4, May 19, 1990; *1988 Board Survey*, footnote 5.

[7] Comptroller Release NR 83-87 (1983), *revised*, Comptroller Banking Circular No. 181, August 2, 1984, CCH Fed. Banking L. Rep. ¶ 60,799 (the "*Comptroller Loan Participation Guidelines*").

[8] Complete information is required, regardless of whether the borrower is a public company that files with the Securities and Exchange Commission (the "*SEC*"). *See* Letter, dated December 18, 1985, from William Glidden, Assistant Director, Legal Advisory Services Division, Comptroller.

ing banks, participants and participation agreements.[9] These guidelines include the following:

1. Originating banks should (i) provide participants with complete and current credit information; and (ii) keep bank examiners' loan classifications secret unless the relevant regulator provides written approval. However, the facts underlying an examiner's loan criticisms and the originating bank's internal classifications may be furnished.

2. Participants should (i) exercise due diligence regarding the originating bank as well as the borrower; (ii) perform their own credit analysis and not rely on the originating bank's; (iii) maintain current and complete credit information on the borrower, as though they had originated the loan; (iv) when using a participation agreement, have counsel review all relevant documents; (v) consider the reputation of the originating bank and its expertise in the given type of transaction and industry; and (vi) ensure that the obligation of the originating bank to provide current credit information throughout the life of the loan is included in the participation agreement.

3. Participation agreements should (i) be structured as a non-recourse sale of a share in the underlying loan; (ii) limit the power of the originating bank to modify material provisions without the consent of all parties; (iii) provide that, on the insolvency of the originating bank, its agency terminates and all loan documents are assigned to the participants; (iv) address the consequences of a participant's default; and (v) require the approval of the originating bank and all participants for any sub-participation.

Product Developments

The development of loan note and participation sale efforts is changing not only the market for loans, but also the nature of the product itself, as commercial and investment banks strive to create, package or trade instruments more likely to obtain a ready market acceptance. Efforts in this area have gone in a number of complimentary directions. Loan originators have been trying to create loans that are more standardized in both

---

[9] *Loan Participation Agreements: ABA/RMA Industry Guidelines; American Banker,* November 4, 1987.

form and content. For example, some banks omit promissory notes from some loan agreements, which may make the secondary market for these loans more liquid. Efforts by banks to quote to loan sale customers rates at which they would be prepared to repurchase participations sold, and to develop "transferable loan certificates" have also been noted, as has the possible use of such "standardizing" elements as Standard & Poors ratings on commercial loan products.[10] In addition, a number of banks are working actively to formalize sales operations in the area of distressed domestic and foreign bank debt, and banks with large distribution networks that want to fill demand for secondary paper have bought and sold options on loans and participations in the secondary market for large commercial credits. Moreover, in structuring transactions with particular borrowers, banks are trying to maximize the amount of term loans and to minimize the revolver loan portion of credits so as to appeal more directly to non-bank buyers of loans which may not have the back office capacity to track a revolving credit, the amount of which may vary widely over time.[11] Recent investment and commercial bank efforts to

---

[10] The implications of such a rating program under the federal securities laws and under the Glass-Steagall Act, if coupled with aggressive loan note or participation sales to non-traditional purchasers, could be important. The Securities Industry Association ("SIA") has expressed "obvious concerns" respecting such a program. See Mortgage-Backed Securities Letter, February 6, 1989; Asset Sales Report, May 2, January, 25, 1988.

[11] See, for example, Int'l Financing Rev., December 21, 1991 (reporting Board concern as to the surge in the volume of trading in the debt of less-developed countries and the ability of banks and other market participants to handle that volume without abuses), July 7, 1984; Asset Sales Report, June 24, 10, 1991; The Wall Street Journal, June 11, 1991; Mortgage-Backed Securities Letter, June 10, 1991; American Banker, May 15, 1991, April 25, February 22, 1989; Bank Letter, March 25, 1991, September 12, 1988, March 16, January 19, 1987; Financial Times, July 9, 1984.

In the area of international syndication efforts, devices worthy of note include note issuance facilities ("NIFs") and revolving underwriting facilities ("RUFs"). In a NIF, the borrower and its investment bank formalize a procedure for the issue by the borrower of notes during the facility's duration. Frequently, banks participate in NIFs as members of so-called "tender panels," which may bid for notes when an issuer proposes to borrow. In a RUF, which is essentially a NIF with a firm commitment backup, banks agree to provide the borrower with revolving credit for funds which the investment bank is unable to raise through securities sales. A RUF thus combines a revolving credit facility, a backup-up line of credit behind a borrower's sale of notes and a credit syndication in which participating banks may "participate out" their committed shares. A twist to the development of NIFs and RUFs is the so-called "stand-by floater," a transferable (but only within a "closed universe" of preapproved lending banks) lending commitment.
continued

create special purpose vehicles to issue commercial paper backed by short-term loans to companies which would have difficulty selling their own commercial paper directly, provide yet another example of the interplay of securities and loan sale markets, coupled with asset pooling efforts.

Efforts to broaden the potential market for loan notes and participations also include "loan swaps"—in which lenders agree to exchange secondary bank loan paper as well as so-called "controlled sell-downs," whereby members of a primary bank syndicate pool the unwanted amounts of their loan holdings, which are then sold to buyers in the secondary market through agent banks, with sales reducing the shares of all pool members *pro rata*. The aim of the process is to avert a price war in the secondary market, as well as to allow smaller banks in the primary syndicate to benefit from the distribution capabilities of larger banks.[12]

Commercial and investment banks also continue to expend significant efforts on loan pooling and other arrangements for the aggregation and securitization of commercial loans. Although, in general, banks have had only limited success to date in such arrangements, it is very likely an area of important future developments as risk-diversification and liquidity become ever more important aspects of bank balance sheet management.[13] In part, securitization difficulties arise from the fact that

---

continued

The Board's Regulation K, 12 C.F.R. Part 211, permits foreign affiliates (but not foreign branches) of U.S. banks to engage in a full range of underwriting and dealing activities respecting debt securities outside of the United States; however, U.S. banks may not themselves underwrite or deal in corporate securities, whether as part of a NIF or RUF or otherwise.

[12] *See*, for example, *Bank Letter*, February 25, 1991; *American Banker*, August 21, 1990.

[13] *See*, for example, *The Wall Street Journal*, January 4, 1991, September 26, 1990; *Asset Sales Report*, November 26, 1990; December 26, 1989; *American Banker*, September 29, 11, 1989; *N.Y. Times*, September 12, 1989.

A development related to the pooling of HLT bank loans is the securitization of pools of high yield securities or junk bonds in so-called "collateralized bond obligations" or "CBOs." In 1989, CBOs represented less than 1% of the $200 billion junk bond market, and a number of CBO transactions that were reportedly long in the works never made it to the market. *See*, for example, Letter, dated May 14, 1990, from SEC Chairman Richard Breeden to Representative John Dingell (reviewing the development of the CBO market); *Mergers & Acquisitions Report*, March 26, 1990; *Bond Buyer*, February 22, 1990; *American Banker*, September 29, 1989.

commercial loans usually have complex covenant provisions and irregular payment structures and are heterogeneous. Thus, it is expensive for third parties (especially non-banks) to evaluate pools of these loans. Moreover, the manner in which banks comply with regulations like those set forth in the Comptroller Loan Participation Guidelines in participating in such pools, as well as issues under the Glass-Steagall Act for banks prohibited from acquiring corporate stock or less-than-investment grade (or illiquid) "securities," must still be addressed. On the other hand, bank loans, by way of favorable comparison with junk bonds, often are secured and occupy the most senior position in the borrower's capital structure. Nonetheless, it would appear that the greatest likelihood of successful pooling would exist with respect to commercial loans with standard contractual provisions and collateral, such as leases and trade receivables.[14] Securities law-related issues, particularly under the Securities Act of 1933 (the "1933 Act") and the Investment Company Act of 1940 (the "1940 Act"), must also be addressed.

Highly Leveraged Transactions

The growth of the loan sales market in the 1980's was closely bound to the willingness and ability of banks to provide lending in support of HLTs. As the market exploded, however, banking regulators and others began to sound increasingly cautious notes concerning the scope of bank participation in LBO financings, particularly as the level of criticized HLTs increased relative to total outstanding HLTs; as HLT credit terms and structures deteriorated due to increased competition; and as agent banks experienced greater difficulties in selling some transactions, increasing large bank aggregate risk exposure. Moreover, there has been a growing reluctance on the part of many banks to participate in HLT financing because of concerns as to recourse, disclosure and information issues, all of which has lead to a decline in HLT exposure over the past

---

[14] *See,* for example, *Asset Sales Report,* March 12, 1990; *Institutional Investor,* July 1989; *Mortgage-Backed Securities Letter,* May 8, 1989.

few years.[15] Nonetheless, HLTs still account for a significant portion of outstanding bank commercial credits and, thus, remain an important component both of commercial bank loan portfolios and of the loan sales market.[16]

Just what constitutes an HLT has been the subject of significant discussion by banking and securities regulators and by market participants. Until recently, no standard definition of an HLT existed and the scope of disclosure concerning HLTs had been inconsistent.[17] In October 1989, the three federal banking regulators jointly adopted a definition of an "HLT" (subsequently clarified in February 1990). The definition includes a financing transaction (i) the purpose of which is a buyout, acquisition or recapitalization, and (ii) which (a) doubles the subject company's liabilities and results in a leverage ratio higher than 50%, or (b) results in a leverage ratio higher than 75%, or (c) is designated an HLT by a syndica-

---

[15] *See*, for example, *Investment Dealers Digest*, February 4, 1991; Remarks before Robert Morris Associates, Robert Clarke, Comptroller (November 14, 1989); *see also American Banker*, November 15, 1989.

The 25 banks with the largest HLT portfolios were reported as of year-end 1990 to have outstanding over $60 billion in HLT loans (with Citicorp having the largest HLT portfolio, one containing $7.2 billion in HLT loans). (This reflects a decline from nearly $70 billion at the end of the first quarter of 1990.) HLT portfolios accounted on average for more than 4% of the total assets of the most active market participants, with Bank of Boston Corporation reporting the largest percentage, at 9.65%. *American Banker*, April 5, 1991.

[16] *See*, for example, *Recent Developments in the High Yield Market* (March 1990), SEC Staff Report prepared by Divisions of Corporation Finance, Investment Management and Market Regulation and the Office of Economic Analysis; *Federal Reserve Bank of San Francisco Weekly Letter*, December 8, 1989; *Corporate Financing Letter*, May 29, 1989; *cf. High Yield Bond Market* (Congressional Research Service, July 5, 1990); *see also* Comptroller Interpretive Letter No. 517 (August 16, 1990), CCH Fed. Banking L. Rep. ¶ 83,228 (approving an arrangement in which Citibank would act as investment advisor to, and a Citibank subsidiary would, in conjunction with an investment bank, become a general partner in, a limited partnership making bridge loans to finance LBOs and recapitalizations in transactions in which the limited partnership ordinarily would receive, in addition to interest income, warrants, stock appreciation rights and/or profit participation rights); Comptroller Interpretive Letter No. 411 (January 20, 1988), CCH Fed. Banking L. Rep. ¶ 85,635 (to similar effect).

[17] *See*, for example, "An Open Letter to LBO Lenders," *Keefe Bank Review* (September 1, 1988). By the time of the preparation and dissemination of 1990 Annual Reports, however, it was apparent that, in general, banks were adhering closely to the "standard" HLT definition. *See Bank Letter*, March 25, 1991.

tion agent. In February 1991, the three federal banking regulators further clarified the HLT definition (i) to exempt court-approved debtor (or trustee)-in-possession financing for a business in Chapter 11 bankruptcy reorganization from HLT designation, and (ii) to provide for deducting credits from HLT status if they meet certain specific performance criteria, even if the borrower's leverage ratio continues to exceed 75%. In addition, the regulators indicated that loans to subsidiaries of highly leveraged companies must be treated as HLTs, even if the subsidiaries themselves do not meet the "highly leveraged" definition.[18] It is expected that, at some point in 1992, the federal banking agencies will discontinue mandated HLT reporting in recognition of lower HLT volumes as well as more sophisticated and complete examination standards.

The federal banking regulators have each issued guidelines to be followed by examiners in reviewing bank financing of HLTs which are intended, among other things, to enable examiners to determine if banks have adopted appropriate policies, procedures and controls with respect to HLTs. The Comptroller's guidelines, for example, mandate (i) an appropriate policy statement which defines the bank's philosophy and objectives in financing HLTs, (ii) HLT lending policies (including provisions for a separate HLT loan review and approval process), (iii)

---

[18] *See* Board/Comptroller/Federal Deposit Insurance Corporation (*"FDIC"*) Release (February 15, 1991), CCH Fed. Banking L. Rep. ¶ 49,274; Board/Comptroller/FDIC Release (February 6, 1990), CCH Fed. Banking L. Rep. ¶ 49,273; Board Release SR-89-23 (October 25, 1989), CCH Fed. Banking L. Rep. ¶ 87,859; Comptroller Banking Circular No. 242 (October 30, 1989), CCH Fed Banking L. Rep. ¶ 49,272; FDIC Release FIL-18-89 (November 20, 1989), CCH Fed. Banking L. Rep. ¶ 87,859.

In July 1991, the Board/Comptroller/FDIC issued a request for public comment on the supervisory definition of an HLT, including in particular (i) on the use of a standardized cash flow criterion in conjunction with designating and delisting HLTs, (ii) the pertinent time frame, economic and financial data relevant to delisting HLTs, (iii) the appropriateness of designating organizations with investment-grade debt as HLTs, (iv) the application of the definition to subsidiaries and their parent organizations, and (v) the degree of flexibility and judgment that may be exercised by bank management in designating credits as HLTs. *See* Board/Comptroller/FDIC Release, 56 Fed. Reg. 31464 (July 10, 1991)

Banks have taken steps to protect themselves against the risk that loans made as non-HLTs will later be classified as HLTs by the regulators (for example, by including provisions that, should a loan be classified as an HLT, the borrower must negotiate in good faith on the extent to which there should be an increase in fees, interest rates and/or margins to reflect the then current market requirements for HLTs). *See,* for example, *American Banker,* July 30, June 13, 1990.

HLT portfolio analysis, management information and bank reporting systems, (iv) policies and procedures on sales, purchases and distribution of participations in HLT financing, (v) policies for internal HLT review and controls designed to supplement the normal management loan review process, (vi) policies respecting the level of equity participation and mezzanine and bridge financing in an HLT, (vii) policies addressing whether separate HLT valuation reserves are needed, and (viii) policies respecting review of the legal and regulatory issues posed by HLTs, including potential conflicts of interest and securities law compliance.[19]

---

[19] Comptroller News Release, May 8, 1989. *See also* Letter, dated December 15, 1988, from Comptroller to Chief Executive Officers of all National Banks; Comptroller Examining Circular EC-245 (December 14, 1988), CCH Fed. Banking L. Rep. ¶ 87,529; Memorandum to Each Officer in Charge of Supervision at each Federal Reserve Bank, from William Taylor, Staff Director, Board Division of Banking Supervision and Regulation, SR 89-5 (February 16, 1989), CCH Fed. Banking L. Rep. ¶ 35,325; Memorandum to Chief Executive Officers of FDIC-Supervised Banks, BL-21-89 (May 10, 1989), CCH Fed. Banking L. Rep. ¶ 49,271.

In a 1989 Study, *Leveraged Financing and National Banks,* the Comptroller discussed the full range of leveraged financing activities by banks and bank holding companies, including senior debt, bridge loans, revolving credit, mezzanine financing and equity investments, and reviewed how banks in the survey established and implemented policies on HLTs, how they analyzed and reached decisions on funding LBOs and other HLTs, how they analyzed risk and monitored performance of their leveraged portfolios and how they sold participations in individual transactions. The extent to which bank holding companies have begun to take equity positions in LBOs that their banks have arranged was also noted. In a letter accompanying the Study, the Comptroller stated that his inquiries did not lead him to conclude that national bank participation in leveraged financing posed undue safety and soundness concerns. *Cf. also Leveraged Buyouts* (General Accounting Office 1991) (case studies of the impact of selected LBOs on the companies themselves and their communities).

One area of increasing concern with respect to the trading of HLT loans is the extent to which fraudulent conveyance law can have an impact on the ranking of these loans in a bankruptcy situation. Essentially, such laws—at both the state and federal level—can provide creditors of corporations acquired in an HLT a basis on which to challenge the validity of the financing arrangements incident to the HLT. Often, this challenge is designed to eliminate the collateral security granted to certain of the lenders that provide HLT financing, or to change the ranking of such lenders with respect to preexisting creditors. In general, these laws may be triggered if a borrower fails to receive a fair consideration or reasonably equivalent value for incurring the debt represented by a loan and if, after giving effect to such loan, the borrower is insolvent, has unreasonably small capital or has incurred or expects to incur debts beyond its ability to repay. Under these circumstances, a court could decide—for example, in the *continued*

The size of banks' HLT exposure, and the importance to banks of the performance of their HLT-related loans, has also attracted the attention of the SEC, which has issued an interpretive release regarding the disclosure required of bank holding companies in, among other documents, their annual reports concerning participation in high yield, highly leveraged and non-investment grade loans and investments. The required disclosure includes: (i) relevant lending and investment policies, (ii) the amount of holdings (stated separately by type), (iii) the level of activity (*e.g.*, originations and retentions), (iv) the amount of holdings (if any) giving rise to significantly greater risks than are present in other similar transactions or instruments (*e.g.*, where the issuer is bankrupt or has issued securities on which interest payments are in default, or where there are significant concentrations in an individual borrower, industry or geographic area, particularly where those concentrations are in securities with relatively low trading market liquidity), and (v) the actual and reasonably likely material effects of the above matters on income and operations.[20]

---

continued

context where a loan is made to an acquisition vehicle secured by an upstream guarantee or pledge of assets by the newly acquired operating subsidiaries—to invalidate the loan (and any related security interest) as a fraudulent conveyance or subordinate the loan to existing or future creditors of the borrower/guarantor and direct a return of all or a portion of interest or principal payments previously made. For a number of recent cases which discuss fraudulent conveyance issues in the HLT context (which issues are beyond the scope of this chapter), see, for example, *Mellon Bank, N.A. v. Metro Communications, Inc.*, 945 F. 2d 635 (3d Cir. 1991); *Crowthers McCall Pattern Inc. v. Lewis*, 129 B.R. 992 (S.D.N.Y. 1991); *Moody v. Security Pacific Business Credit, Inc.*, 127 B.R. 958 (W.D. Pa. 1991); *In Re O'Day Corp.*, 126 B.R. 370 (Bankr. D. Mass. 1991). *See also* Investment Dealers' Digest, November 5, 1990.

[20] SEC Release No. 33-6835 (1989). *Cf. also* letter from Gene A. Gohlke, Acting Director, SEC Division of Investment Management (October 16, 1990) ("thorough explanation" needed of high yields in junk bond mutual funds); letters from Carolyn Lewis, Assistant Director, SEC Division of Investment Management (February 27, 1990, October 3, 1989) (staff suggestion that investment companies adopt standard disclosure language regarding junk bond holdings).

The rating agencies have also expressed concern about the exposure of banks to both junk bonds and LBO loans in a weak market. *See*, for example, *American Banker*, February 15, 1991, March 30, 1990.

SECURITIES LAW STATUS OF LOAN NOTES AND LOAN PARTICIPATIONS

As the loan sales market evolves, it is not entirely clear whether loan notes or loan participations constitute "securities" under federal or state securities laws. However, without slighting the importance of that question, it is important not to overemphasize the implications of a negative answer. Particularly in an uncertain economy, with financial institutions under credit and earnings pressure, there is a greater restiveness on the part of loan purchasers whose acquired loans do not perform as well as expected, and a greater willingness to sue selling banks for violating purported standards of disclosure or fiduciary responsibility, whether those standards are mandated by securities laws or by principles of state common law. Thus, in the context of any particular sale of a loan note or participation, the determination that the instrument in question is not a security does *not* lead to the conclusion that the selling bank is free from risk that a purchaser may not make a claim of a "securities law nature." Courts may well conclude that the obligation of a loan seller to a loan purchaser—in terms of disclosure of non-public information, fiduciary responsibilities and the like—is essentially the same regardless of the applicability of federal or state securities laws.

Statutory Definitions and Consequences

The Supreme Court has determined that the definitions of "security" in the 1933 Act and in the Securities Exchange Act of 1934 (the *"1934 Act;* together with the 1933 Act, the *"Securities Acts"*)[21] are functionally equivalent and are to be interpreted similarly. Both definitions expressly state that, "unless the context otherwise requires," a note is a "security," and that a participation in a security is itself a "security." The 1934 Act definition of "security" excludes "any note . . . which has a maturity at the time of issuance of less than nine months."[22]

If a loan note or participation *is* deemed a "security" under the 1933 Act, its sale would invoke the full registration and prospectus delivery

---

[21] 15 U.S.C. § § 77c(2), 78c(10). *See,* for example, *Landreth Timber Co. v. Landreth,* 471 U.S. 681 (1985); *Tcherepnin v. Knight,* 389 U.S. 332 (1967).

[22] It should also be noted that state law offering circular, anitfraud and similar provisions could all be relevant if a loan note or participation is characterized as a state-law "security" whether or not it would also be deemed to be a "security" under the Securities Act.

requirements of the Act,[23] unless an exemption is applicable. Exemptions exist under the Act which can relate either to the *transaction* or to the *security* in question. The "private placement" exemption of Section 4(2) of the 1933 Act (which applies to "transactions by an issuer not involving any public offering") and the so-called "Section 4 (1-1/2)" exemption derived from market practice and SEC interpretation[24] (which applies essentially to institutional transactions in privately placed securities in the secondary market) would likely apply to most sales of loan notes and participations, given the level of sophistication (and limited number) of purchasers, and the size of the instruments ordinarily employed.[25] The SEC appears to regard Section 4(2) as the traditional exemption from registration for sales of bank loans.[26] The implication of this position, how-

---

[23] *See* 15 U.S.C. § § 77e-77l.

In short, the essence of the 1933 Act is that a "public offering" of "securities" in the United States must be "registered" under the 1933 Act by filing a comprehensive "registration statement" disclosure document with the SEC; no sales of "securities" can be made until the "effective date" of the relevant registration statement.

[24] *See* SEC Release No. 33-6862 (1990) (adopting Rule 144A under the 1933 Act, 17 C.F.R. § 230.144A, which provides a non-exclusive "safe harbor" from the registration requirements of the 1933 Act for certain resales of eligible securities to qualifying buyers).

[25] With respect to NIF and RUF obligations, if such instruments are "securities," international placements and resales could rely not only on Section 4 (2)/4(1–1/2) of the 1933 Act, but also on a "foreign offering" exemption. *See* SEC Release No. 33-6863 (1990) (adoption of SEC Regulation S, 17 C.F.R. § § 230.901 *et seq.*, clarifying the extraterritorial application of the registration requirement of the 1933 Act).

[26] *See* SEC Release No. 33-4552 (1982).

Pursuant to a complex body of law that has developed with regard to the definition of a "private placement," a number of conditions must be satisfied to qualify an offering as such. For example, debt securities must be offered to a limited number of prospective purchasers who are sophisticated investors, able to bear the economic risk of investment, have a certain amount of information concerning the borrower and do not themselves intend to distribute the securities to the public. In addition, securities sold in a private placement usually bear a restrictive legend to the effect that they have not been registered under the 1933 Act and may not be sold unless they are so registered or unless they are sold in another transaction that is itself exempt from the registration requirements of the 1933 Act. Moreover, even though privately placed securities are exempt from registration under the 1933 Act, they are still subject to the "antifraud" provisions of both the 1933 and 1934 Acts, which impose civil and criminal penalties on a borrower as well as its agents if securities are sold pursuant to a disclosure document containing false or misleading statements.

ever, is that bank loans could qualify as "securities" the sale of which without registration requires an exemption.[27]

If a loan note or participation is deemed to be a "security" under the 1934 Act, the Act's antifraud provisions, most notably Section 10(b) and SEC Rule 10b-5 thereunder, would apply.[28] Section 10(b) forbids the use of any "manipulative" or "deceptive" device in connection with the purchase or sale of any "security." Rule 10b-5 prohibits the use of any device, scheme or artifice to defraud; the making of any untrue statement of a material fact or the omission of a material fact necessary to make the statements made not misleading; or, broadly, the engaging in "any act, practice or course of business" which would operate to deceive any person in connection with the purchase or sale of any security.[29]

Another aspect of Rule 10b-5 that could be of importance to loan note or participation sellers is that the rule is the source of the prohibition of "insider" trading: engaging in a securities transaction while in possession

---

[27] *See Equibank Corp.* (avail. July 9, 1983) (sales of loan participations to depository institutions and other accredited investors are not subject to the registration requirement of the 1933 Act); *cf. Security Federal Savings and Loan Assn.* (avail. August 17, 1990) (SEC staff refusal to concur that participations in interests in short-term construction loan notes do not constitute 1933 Act "securities"); *Bankers Mortgage Funding Corporation* (avail. May 8, 1990) (sales by non-bank financial institution of secured real estate loans to institutions and individual investors may require registration of loans under the 1933 Act and registration of seller of loans as a broker-dealer under the 1934 Act, notwithstanding the fact that the loan seller provides the buyer with sufficient information to perform an independent credit evaluation).

An argument could also be made that, since the "issuer" of a loan participation is a bank, not the original borrower, if a loan participation is a "security," the "security" is an "exempt security" under Section 3(a) (2) of the 1933 Act, which exempts from registration, among other things, "securities issued or guaranteed by any bank." It is not clear, however, that the SEC would concur with that conclusion. *See* Letter, dated July 2, 1987, from then-Chairman John Shad to Representative John Dingell; *Buffalo Savings Bank* (avail. October 25, 1982); *Bank of America* (avail. May 19, 1977); *First State Bank of Dodge City* (avail. November 21, 1975).

[28] 15 U.S.C. § 78j(b); 17 C.F.R. § 240.10b-5.

[29] Although Section 10(b) does not by its terms create a private claim for aggrieved parties to recover damages, the courts have long held that Congress intended that such suits be authorized under this section and the SEC rule implementing it. A civil claimant under Rule 10b-5 must allege and prove that the person engaging in the prohibited behavior acted with "scienter"; that is, wrongful intent. *See*, for example, *Ernst & Ernst v. Hochfelder*, 425 U.S. 185 (1976). Although the courts have developed various interpretations of the scienter requirement, a plaintiff must ordinarily prove, at a minimum, that the defendant acted recklessly.

of material non-public information. Lenders, for example, with knowledge of undisclosed material information about a corporation are prohibited from selling a corporation's securities until such time as the material information has been disclosed, or is otherwise available, to the purchaser. While a key prerequisite to insider trading liability under Rule 10b-5 is that the trader has breached an obligation to keep undisclosed information confidential and not to use such non-public information for its private purposes, this obligation can arise from a variety of sources, including, potentially, by reason of a confidential borrower-lender relationship.[30]

Pre-1990 Case Law

Courts have been nearly unanimous in holding that a loan or loan participation sold by one bank or financial institution to another is *not* a "security" for purposes of the Securities Acts (or under applicable state laws). However, the legal analyses on which they based their respective decisions were not consistent. The major variations in legal analyses that courts have employed include:

1. *The "Literal" or "Family Resemblance" Approach.* In *Exchange National Bank of Chicago v. Touche Ross & Co.,*[31] Judge Henry Friendly stated a presumption that all notes are "securities" unless they bear a "strong family resemblance" to certain consumer loans (including mortgage loans), secured commercial loans and loans by commercial banks for current operations. Applying the *Exchange National* test, the court in *Equitable Life Assurance Society v. Arthur Anderson & Co.,*[32] for example, found certain promissory notes not to be "securities," as they

---

[30] Although usually thought to be principally a problem respecting corporate stock transactions, "insider trading" issues can arise in the context of debt securities as well. The SEC, for example, is reported to be investigating whether certain Harcourt Brace Jovanovich and Fort Howard high yield bond investors have been trading on inside information. *Business Week,* April 22, 1991. *Cf. SEC, Report of the Division Market Regulation on Transparency in the Market for High-Yield Debt Securities* (September 6, 1991) (concluding that substantially more information should be publicly available on the high-yield debt market).

[31] 544 F.2d 1126 (2d Cir. 1976) ("*Exchange National*"), *modified, Chemical Bank v. Arthur Anderson & Co.,* 726 F.2d 930 (2d Cir.), *cert. denied,* 469 U.S. 884 (1984).

[32] 655 F. Supp. 1225 (S.D.N.Y. 1987); *see also,* for example, *Commercial Discount Corp. v. Lincoln First Commercial Corp.,* 445 F. Supp. 1263 (S.D.N.Y. 1978) ("*Commercial Discount Corp.*").

bore "a strong family resemblance" to short-term commercial loans, based on the agreement governing the loan transaction and the high degree of control that was granted over the borrower's operations.

2. *The "Investment/Commercial" Approach.* Some courts focused on the prefatory language "unless the context otherwise requires" in the 1933 and 1934 Act definitions of "security" as the basis for an interpretation which would exclude loan notes or participations from necessary inclusion within that term. These courts attempted to distinguish "commercial" from "investment" transactions, based on such factors as whether note sales were to a large class of investors, the characterization of the instruments in the business community and by the parties, the use of proceeds, the extent of reliance on efforts of others, collateral, the number of notes issued, the dollar amount of the transaction in question and the length of the instrument's term. These courts concluded that "commercial" loan notes or participations are not "securities."[33]

3. *The Howey or "Risk Capital" Approach.* Certain courts, relying principally on *United Housing Foundation, Inc. v. Forman*[34] and *SEC v. W.J. Howey Co.*,[35] attempted (i) to draw a line between conventional loans and those representing "risk capital" by looking at such factors as the duration of the transaction, collateralization, the relation between the amount borrowed and the size of the borrower's enterprise, the terms of the transaction, the form of the obligation, the contemplated use of proceeds, the bargaining position of the parties, the intent of the parties and the contractual nature of the arrangements; and/or (ii) to determine whether the transaction constituted an investment in a

---

[33] *See,* for example, *Futura Development Corp. v. Centex Corp.,* 761 F.2d 33 (lst Cir.), *cert. denied,* 474 U.S. 850 (1985) (*"Futura"*); *American Fletcher Mortgage Co. v. U.S. Steel Credit Corp.,* 635 F.2d 1247 (7th Cir. 1980), *cert. denied,* 451 U.S. 911 (1981); *Bellah v. First National Bank of Hereford,* 495 F.2d 1109 (5th Cir. 1974) (focusing on the manner in which the notes were offered, the lender's purpose for taking the notes and the use to which the borrower put the money); *Lino v. City Investing Co.,* 487 F.2d 689 (3rd Cir. 1973); *but see Zabriskie v. Lewis,* 507 F.2d 546 (10th Cir. 1974) (notes at issue found to be "securities" since they were issued in isolated transactions outside of normal commercial circles to a person not in the business of making loans for the purpose of obtaining funds to promote a corporation).

[34] 421 U.S. 837 (1975).

[35] 328 U.S. 293 (1946) (*"Howey"*).

common venture with a reasonable expectation of profits to be derived from the entrepreneurial or managerial efforts of others.[36]

The Reves Decision

In *Reves v. Ernst & Young*,[37] the Supreme Court held that publicly distributed, unsecured, demand notes, not guaranteed by any government entity, are "securities" for purposes of the Securities Acts and that demand notes do not fall within the 1934 Act exception for "any note . . . which has a maturity at the time of issuance of less than nine months." In reaching its conclusion, the Supreme Court adopted the analysis set out in *Exchange National* for the purpose of determining whether any particular note is a "security." *Reves* also approved of the "investment/commercial" test, describing that test as another method of "formulating the same general approach." However, *Reves* specifically rejected the method of analysis used in those circuits that had relied upon *Howey*, stating that the *Howey* analysis was applicable to a determination of whether an *investment contract* is a "security," but is *not* applicable to a determination of whether a *note* is a "security."

In analyzing whether any particular note is a "security" (the portion of the decision most relevant to the sale of loan notes and participations), *Reves* stated that (i) the starting point for analysis is the "presumption that every note is a security"; (ii) exceptions to this presumption are certain types of notes "for which the context otherwise requires," such as notes delivered in consumer financing, home mortgage notes, short-term notes secured by a lien on a small business or some of its assets, bank loans to individuals, short-term notes secured by an assignment of accounts, notes formalizing open-account debt incurred in the ordinary course of business, and notes evidencing loans by commercial banks for current operations; and (iii) another exception is any note bearing a "family resemblance" to the foregoing exceptions. *Reves* developed the "family resemblance" analysis by setting out a list of four crucial factors a court should examine in determining whether a particular note is a "security":

---

[36] *See*, for example, *McVay v. Western Plains Service Corp.*, 823 F.2d 1395 (10th Cir. 1987); *Union National Bank of Little Rock v. Farmers Bank*, 786 F.2d 881 (8th Cir. 1986); *American Bank and Trust Co. v. Wallace*, 702 F.2d 93 (6th Cir. 1983); *Amfac Mortgage Corp. v. Arizona Mall of Tempe*, 583 F.2d 426 (9th Cir. 1978).

[37] 494 U.S. 56 (1990) ("*Reves*").

1. *Motivation for the Transaction.* If the seller of a note does so to finance the purchase of a minor asset or consumer good, to correct a cash-flow difficulty, or "to advance some other commercial or consumer purpose," the note is less likely to be considered a "security" than if the seller's purpose is to raise money for the general use of a business enterprise or to finance substantial investment and the buyer is interested primarily "in the profit the note is expected to generate." "Profit," in the view of the *Reves* Court, includes "a valuable return on an investment" and is specifically said to "include interest."[38]

2. *Plan of Distribution.* A note in which there is "common trading for speculation or investment," or that is sold to a "broad segment of the public" is more likely to be considered a "security" than a note that is not.

3. *Expectations of Purchasers.* If the "investing public" has "reasonable expectations" that the note in question is a security, a court could consider that instrument to be a "security" on the basis of such "public expectations."

4. *Alternative Regulation or Government Guarantee.* If there is a governmental scheme that significantly "reduces the risk of the instrument" such that the Securities Acts are not necessary, the note is less likely to be considered a "security."[39]

Application of Reves Factors to Loan Notes and Loan Participations

Commercial loan notes and participations would appear to bear a "family resemblance" to at least one type of instrument cited in *Reves* as excepted from the presumption that "notes" are "securities": notes

---

[38] 494 U.S. at 68 n.4.

[39] *See,* for example, *Marine Bank v. Weaver,* 455 U.S. 551 (1982) (partially FDIC-insured certificate of deposit sold by a bank is not a "security" as the regulatory scheme applicable to bank deposits sufficiently protects the purchaser's interest so as to render the protections of the Securities Acts superfluous).

evidencing loans by commercial banks for current operations.[40] Even assuming that they would not be excluded from the definition of "security" on that ground alone, however, the application of the *Reves* factors in this context may be analyzed as follows:

1. *Motivation for the Transaction.* Under the first factor of the *Reves* analysis, courts will likely look to the motivation of both the *underlying borrower* which is the original issuer of the note and of the *bank* that sells the instrument. While a *borrower* may have borrowed money for its general use or for a substantial investment—motivations arguably consistent with finding the borrower's note to be a "security"—it is strongly arguable that *any* borrowing from a commercial bank is for a "commercial purpose" (and, thus, that the related note would not be a "security"), and that any participation in such a borrowing is in furtherance of that purpose.[41] Moreover, while loan note/participation buyers are presumably motivated by their evaluation of the income to be derived from the note/participation purchased, it is hard to characterize that interest as different from the motivation that would exist if the buyer had made a loan *directly* to the borrower, rather than *indirectly* through the medium of a purchase (instead of through an origination) of the note or participation in question. With

---

[40] Building on that analysis, for example, Judge Milton Pollack recently concluded in *Banco Espanol de Credito v. Security Pacific National Bank,* 763 F. Supp. 36, (S.D.N.Y. 1991) ("*Banco Espanol*"), *appeal docketed,* No. 91-7563 (2d Cir. June 7, 1991), that participations in short-term (less than six months) working capital loans to a regular customer sold by a U.S. bank to domestic and foreign commercial banks, pension funds and corporations pursuant to master participation agreements were not "securities" or "investment contracts" under the Securities Acts. These master agreements provided that the participations were "loans" and were not readily transferable and that the participation purchaser was to make its own credit analysis of the issuer of the note underlying the participation. While dealing with only a subset of the type of loans, nature of seller and form of participation agreement employed in the loan sales market, *Banco Espanol* provides an important precedent for the analysis of the implications of *Reves* for the loan sale market in general.

[41] *Cf. Banco Espanol,* 763 F. Supp. at 42, ("because the plaintiffs here did not receive an undivided interest in a pool of loans, but rather purchased participation in a specific, identifiable short-term . . . loan, the loan participation did not have an identity separate from the underlying loan"); *Mishkin v. Peat, Marwick, Mitchell & Co.,* 744 F. Supp. 531 (S.D.N.Y. 1990) (a participation in a banker's acceptance does not have an identity that is separate from the banker's acceptance itself). *But cf. Commercial Discount Corp.,* footnote 32 (concluding that a participation in a loan may be a security, even though the underlying loan is not).

respect to the motivation of the bank which sells a loan note or participation (of which the bank is the technical issuer), it is clear that loans or participations are sold for a number of reasons[42] and it is not entirely clear which reasons a court would regard as consistent with the determination that a particular instrument is a "security" or a "loan."[43] Moreover, with respect to secondary market transactions, it is important to note that one court has concluded that there is "nothing anomalous" in finding in the appropriate circumstances that a particular note is not a "security" when originally sold, but may become a "security" if sold in a later transaction.[44] On the other hand, to the extent that the "business of banking" includes financial intermediation as a principal element, it is hard to see how institutional loan transactions, absent egregious drafting or characterization problems, should be viewed as involving "securities."

2. *Plan of Distribution.* The second factor of the *Reves* analysis is also somewhat ambiguous in the loan note/participation context. For example, it is arguable that a broad-based institutional sale of HLT-generated loan instruments or of distressed credits could result in "common trading for speculation or investment," especially if it is the intention of a lead bank to make the instruments attractive to purchasers by standardizing the instrument or by providing assurances as to the creation of a secondary market. Further, if a loan note has a Standard & Poors rating attached and the selling bank hires an investment bank to locate potential purchasers or plans to solicit purchases by publicly traded mutual funds, it could be argued that the

---

[42] *See* the discussion in the previous section.

[43] *In Banco Espanol*, 763 F. Supp. at 42-43, Judge Pollack found the motivation of the selling bank—to enable it to increase its lines of credit to the borrower and to diversify its risk—consistent with *commercial*, rather than investment, characterization.

[44] *Mercer v. Jaffe, Snider, Raitt and Heuer*, 736 F. Supp. 764, 769 (W.D. Mich. 1990) ("*Mercer*") ("first mortgage notes" qualify as "securities" insofar as they were sold by a broker-dealer to individual investors on a mass market basis), *aff'd sub. nom. Schreimer v. Greenburg*, 931 F. 2d 893 (6th Cir. 1991).

plan of distribution for the loan is much like the plan of distribution for a "security."[45]

On the other hand, *Reves* states that the plan of distribution for a note most resembles that for a "security" when the note is offered to a "broad segment of the public," a factor which the Court characterized as *"necessary* to establish the requisite 'common trading' in an instrument."[46] This would seem to indicate that courts should look to the type and sophistication of loan purchasers, rather than to some arbitrary number of purchasers, in evaluating this factor. Moreover, assuming that a public sale of the notes or participations in question is not effected, it is not clear that the selling bank's technique of institutional distribution would necessarily be a determinative factor.

Focusing on the *type of purchaser* is consistent with the purposes of the Securities Acts, which are intended to protect passive investors, not commercial lenders.[47] Nonetheless, there is language in lower court opinions that can not be considered directly overruled by *Reves* which indicates that both the *number* of purchasers *and* the method of distribution could be considered factors in a court's determination of whether a particular note is a "security."[48]

3. *Expectations of Purchasers.* The third factor of the *Reves* analysis is largely a restatement of the "investment/commercial test" that *Reves* cited approvingly, and one that has resulted generally in the charac-

---

[45] In *Banco Espanol,* 763 F. Supp. at 40, 43, Judge Pollack took comfort in determining that the participation in question was not a "security" in the facts that the selling bank had not included individuals in its participation program (but rather limited the program to "sophisticated or commercial institutions and not to the general public") and that the participations were not freely negotiable. In that context, the fact that the selling bank provided the purchasers with the Standard & Poors rating of the borrower's commercial paper was not viewed as particularly relevant.

[46] 494 U.S. at 68 (emphasis added).

[47] *See,* for example, *Hunssinger v. Rockford Business Credits, Inc.,* 745 F.2d 484 (7th Cir. 1984) (*"Hunssinger"*).

[48] *See,* for example, *Developer's Mortgage Co. v. TransOhio Savings Bank,* 706 F. Supp. 570 (S.D. Ohio 1989) (loan participation sold to only one purchaser not a "security"); *Crocker National Bank v. Rockwell International Corp.,* 555 F. Supp. 47 (N.D. Cal. 1982) (use of investment bank to approach a large number of financial institutions through marketing channels designed for sale of securities is indicative that note is a "security").

terization of commercial loan notes/participations as "non-securities." Each case that *Reves* approved for following the investment/commercial approach focused in part at least on the character of the underlying transactions to determine whether the instruments involved in those transactions were "securities."[49] In approving the investment/commercial test, *Reves* described the test as one made "on the basis of *all the circumstances surrounding the transactions.*"[50] Further, *Reves* did not recommend consideration of such inherent characteristics of a note as its duration or whether it is collateralized in determining whether it is a "security." Thus, the Court may have implicitly rejected cases that analyzed notes in terms of such inherent characteristics.[51]

It is thus difficult to see how the sale—to a sophisticated institution capable of evaluating and understanding the implication of the characterization—of an instrument *called* a *"loan note"* or *"loan participation"* and treated and characterized as a "loan" by both buyer and seller would ever fail the third prong of the *Reves* test; that is, if an institutional purchaser of a note represents to the seller that it regards its purchase as "the making of a loan," it would appear that a court would be quite unlikely to consider the note a "security."[52] One fac-

---

[49] *See Futura,* footnote 33 (the investment/commercial approach directly focuses on an investor's dependency on efforts and expertise of others and on his need for financial disclosure provided by others; seller of property held to have received note from purchaser in "commercial" rather than "investment" context); *McClure v. First National Bank of Lubbock, Texas,* 497 F.2d 490 (5th Cir. 1974), *cert. denied,* 420 U.S. 930 (1975) (notes that evidenced bank loan which were neither offered to a class of investors nor acquired for speculation are not "securities"); *Hunssinger,* footnote 47 (Securities Acts are intended to protect investors and to exclude from the Acts' protection borrowers and lenders in commercial settings); *Holloway v. Peat, Marwick, Mitchell & Co.,* 879 F.2d 772 (10th Cir. 1989), *cert. granted and remanded,* 494 U.S. 1014, 110 S. Ct. 1314, *aff'd,* 900 F.2d 1485 (10th Cir.), *cert. denied,* ___ U.S. ___ , 111 S. Ct. 386 (1990) ("*Holloway*") (factor of foremost importance in determination that note is a "security" is that issuer of note solicited the general public; issuance of notes to a broad class of investors usually indicates a "security"); *see also Noyd v. Claxton, Morgan, Flockhart & Vanliere,* 463 N.W. 2d 268 (Mich. App. 1990) (in determining whether an instrument is a "security" under Michigan law proper focus is on the "nature of the transaction").

[50] 494 U.S. at 63 (emphasis added).

[51] *See,* for example, *Great Western Bank & Trust v. Kotz,* 532 F.2d 1252 (9th Cir. 1976).

[52] *See Banco Espanol,* footnote 40; *cf. Mercer,* footnote 44 (when offering circular for mortgage notes stated that the sale of the notes was subject to federal securities law, it was reasonable for purchaser to believe notes were "securities").

tor that may be considered of importance in determining the expectations of a loan purchaser in this regard is whether the purchaser relied on the seller either to evaluate the quality of notes or to add
value to them by, for example, promising to buy them back or make
a market in them.[53] This analysis obviously puts a premium on great
care in drafting documentation.

4. *Alternative Regulation or Government Guarantee.* The final factor of the
Reves analysis, viewed in the commercial loan context, could be considered consistent with a finding that a bank loan is a "security" in
the usual case when the loan is not government guaranteed. However, it is more reasonable to conclude that *Reves* suggested the
fourth prong of its test so as to focus on any special "risk-reducing
factor" that would suggest an instrument that otherwise would appear to be a "security" on the basis of an evaluation of the first three
factors should be found *not* to be a "security."[54] Accordingly, the

---

[53] *Compare,* for example, *First Citizens Federal Sav. and Loan v. Worthen Bank,* 919 F.2d 510
(9th Cir. 1990) (bank participant in secured loan that did not rely on managerial or
entrepreneurial skills of principal bank lender did not have rights based on Arizona
securities laws against principal bank lender), *and First Financial Federal Sav. & Loan v.
E.F. Hutton Mortgage,* 834 F.2d 685 (8th Cir. 1987) (purchaser of mortgage loans in "as
is" condition that acknowledged it was a sophisticated institution with knowledge and
experience in evaluating mortgage loans, that had been granted access to all information concerning the loans and that acknowledged that no person employed by the
seller had been authorized to give any information concerning the loans could not
claim protection of Securities Acts), *and Union Planters National Bank v. Commercial
Credit Business Loans,* 651 F.2d 1174 (6th Cir.), *cert. denied,* 454 U.S. 1124 (1981) (when
bank perceived loan participation as a routine commercial loan and its officers who
purchased the participation were the same officers who normally passed on direct
loans, the bank cannot claim protection of Securities Acts), *and United American Bank of
Nashville v. Gunter,* 620 F.2d 1108 (5th cir. 1980) (bank that acknowledged it evaluated
purchase of loan participation in same manner as it evaluated direct loan application
and that treated loan participation as a loan on its books for regulatory purposes may
not sue selling bank on basis of Securities Acts), *with Gary Plastic Packaging Corp. v.
Merrill Lynch, Pierce, Fenner & Smith,* 756 F.2d 230 (2d Cir. 1985) (although FDIC-insured certificates of deposit sold by bank were not "securities," they became "securities" when distributed by investment bank under circumstances where the investor
relied on the investment bank to maintain a liquid market in the certificates, to find
bank-issuers offering the best price and to monitor the solvency of bank-issuers).

[54] *See,* for example, *Holloway,* footnote 49.

fourth factor would *not* appear to be relevant to an analysis of commercial loan notes/participations.[55]

On the other hand, since banks are heavily regulated in terms of the manner in which they evaluate and acquire loans,[56] it is arguable that the fourth *Reves* factor would treat the loans as non-securities under the Securities Acts.[57] Nonetheless, this approach does require reading broadly that portion of *Reves* which requires that the relevant government regulation "reduce [ ] the risk of the *instrument*."[58]

Implications of Reves and Post-Reves Case Law

Prior to *Reves*, the general trend of the courts was clearly in the direction of holding that notes evidencing loans by banks, or participations in such loans, are not "securities" for purposes of the Securities Acts. This trend did not embody any consistent mode of analysis, nor did the cases involve public sales of loan notes or participations. Following *Reves*, it appears that courts will focus more explicitly on the context of a transaction than on the instrument that is the subject of the transaction. That is, it would appear that, under *Reves*, determination of whether a loan note or participation is a "security" is likely to depend less upon *what* is distributed (in terms of the purpose of the underlying credit extension) than *to whom and how* it is distributed.

Following *Reves*—as before it—a public distribution of loan notes or participations is very likely to be found to be subject to the Securities Acts. However, it does not appear likely that direct placement of loan notes or participations with sophisticated institutional investors— whether banks, thrift institutions, insurance companies or other likely

---

[55] *See generally*, for example, *State of Washington v. Saas*, 792 P.2d 554 (Wash. App. 1990) (absence of government regulation is irrelevant in determination that notes negotiated in private loan transactions were not "securities" under Washington law).

[56] *See*, for example, Comptroller Loan Participation Guidelines.

[57] Such an approach to government regulation would appear to be consistent with at least two judicial decisions following *Reves*, *Banco Espanol*, footnote 40 (focusing on Comptroller Loan Participation Guidelines), and *Singer v. Livoti, O'Grady & O'Hare*, 741 F. Supp. 1040 (S.D.N.Y. 1990) (concluding that a state regulatory scheme surrounding the recordation of mortgages was relevant under the fourth factor in the *Reves* analysis).

[58] 494 U.S. at 67 (emphasis added).

loan purchasers—would be characterized as an offering of "securities" if the purchasers of the loans are engaged in the business of making commercial loans or acquiring similar instruments and have the credit expertise to evaluate the notes or participations placed, and if the purchasers are aware of and acknowledge that the instruments sold were originated and are being sold as "loans" and not as "securities." On the other hand, the SEC is expected to file a brief in support of the complaining purchasers in the appeal of *Banco Espanol,* and to argue that only the most "traditional" loan notes or participations fall outside the definition of "security."

Reves does not provide explicit guidance either as to the relative weights to be accorded to the four factors in its analysis, nor as to whether satisfaction of the "security" definition under any one (or more) factors would be sufficient for characterization of a particular instrument as a "security." Thus, great sensitivity to securities law issues is needed with respect to any loan note or participation sale program. Banks should be quite careful in the manner in which they structure sales to institutions (such as mutual funds) that are not involved generally in direct credit extension (especially when the bank retains no part of the loan in question). They should make a case-by-case determination that the purchaser has sufficient financial sophistication to evaluate the underlying borrower's creditworthiness and has no expectation that it will benefit from the Securities Acts. It would also be prudent if the manner of, and restrictions in respect of, loan note or participation sales are such as to prevent a broad-based distribution of the instruments outside of a universe of sophisticated institutional investors of a type that makes commercial loans or acquires loans or similar interests.

The selling bank should also take care to provide sufficient credit information for the purchaser to evaluate the loan and should not allow the purchaser to rely on the seller's expertise.[59] It may also be useful for the seller to obtain certification from the purchaser that the purchaser has not relied on the seller's credit evaluation, and that (if the purchaser is a bank) it has evaluated the instrument in accordance with sound banking practice and will treat the instrument on its books for regulatory and all other purposes as a "loan."

As discussed in the previous section of this chapter, a number of developments in capital markets generally are putting increasing pressure

---

[59] These guidelines would be consistent with the Comptroller Loan Participation Guidelines and similar regulatory pronouncements.

on the distinction between "loans" and "securities." First, large lending transactions can be expected to create a great incentive for bank loan sellers to find new types of purchasers and to satisfy those purchasers' need for liquidity in the loan notes or participations acquired. Care will also be needed to minimize the risk that loan purchasers would rely not only on the credit of the underlying borrower, but also on the ability and willingness of the selling bank to repurchase or to make a market in the loans sold. Otherwise, the seller may be found not only to have added value to the loan, but also to have changed the nature of the instrument sold so that it more closely resembles a "security" in the context of the sale.

Second, some loan notes and participations "look" more like "securities" in form and structure. This is consistent with what appears to be an increasing trend for investment banks to move into the loan syndication area, once thought well beyond their "traditional" field of activity, as well as with expanded institutional trading of privately placed securities, some of which may appear to be very similar to loan notes. Indeed, as discussed in the next section of this chapter, banks may justify their acquisition of privately placed securities under certain circumstances by classifying them as "loans" for banking law purposes.

Third, as Standard & Poors and other statistical rating services begin to assign ratings to commercial loans, although neither *Reves* nor *Exchange National* placed particular reliance upon the form of the instrument in making the determination as to whether any particular note is a "security," and although *Banco Espanol* did not seem to view this factor as particularly important, this development could be significant from a securities law perspective as it could imply either that the purchaser of the loan is not relying on its own credit analysis or that the purchaser expects that the rating will make the loan easier to resell.

Fourth, as loan pooling advances in the commercial loan area, the distinction between "loans" and "securities" can be expected to compress even further.

In summary, a variety of factors could be significant to any securities law analysis (although none should necessarily be viewed as determinative)—such as (i) the nature of the purchasers of the loan notes or participations—that is, commercial banks or "institutional purchasers" generally and, if "institutional purchasers", whether they are in the business of originating or purchasing loan notes or participations or similar instruments, (ii) the "name" put on the transaction—that is, that the purchaser of the loan note/participation acknowledge that the economic substance of the transaction is a "loan" made by the purchaser to the original borrower, (iii) the nature of the seller of the instrument (with sales by the originating bank more easily characterizable in general as nonsecurities), (iv) the amount of information provided to the purchaser, the ability of the purchaser to seek more information from the borrower, and the capacity of the purchaser to evaluate the information, (v) the minimum size of the loans or participations sold, (vi) whether the seller makes any agreements or arrangements with respect to a secondary market in which the notes or participations may be sold, (vii) whether the loans sold or participated are loans of a type which the seller would keep on its own books, (viii) the number of purchasers, (ix) whether the purchaser is involved, or is capable of being involved, in administration of the loan, (x) whether the seller retains for its own account a portion of the loan sold or participated out, and (xi) whether "form" loan sale or participation agreements are put into place prior to disbursement of the loan.

LOAN NOTE AND LOAN PARTICIPATION SALES UNDER THE GLASS-STEAGALL ACT

Origins and Purpose of the Glass-Steagall Act.

The Glass-Steagall Act—officially, the Banking Act of 1933—was adopted as omnibus legislation in the wake of the stock market collapse and the banking crisis of the preceding several years. It was intended to separate the activities of investment and commercial banking and thereby to protect the safety and soundness (both real and perceived) of commercial banks. The Glass-Steagall Act has been interpreted by the Supreme Court to reflect two general concerns: (i) a concern about the inherent risks of the securities business and a consequent intention to separate commercial bank operations from investment banking activities, and (ii) a concern about the "more subtle hazards" that arise when investment banking activities conflict in fundamental ways with the institutional role of commercial banks.[60] It has been asserted that the principal cost of Glass-Steagall has been the absence from the marketplace of the effective competition to investment banks that commercial banks and their affiliates could provide.

---

[60] *See*, for example, *Board v. Investment Company Institute*, 450 U.S. 46 (1981).

While the Glass-Steagall Act is the most significant law governing the securities-related activities of banking organizations, a complex series of additional federal legislation also implements Glass-Steagall's policies and purposes. In particular, the Bank Holding Company Act of 1956 (the "*BHCA*")[61] was intended, in the Supreme Court's words, "to maintain and even to strengthen Glass-Steagall's restrictions on the relationship between commercial and investment banking."[62]

Statutory Provisions of the Glass-Steagall Act

The Glass-Steagall Act has four key provisions: two are aimed at preventing direct combinations of commercial and investment banking and two are aimed at preventing indirect combinations (that is, combinations by corporate affiliation and by personnel overlap):

Section 16. National banks and state Federal Reserve System member banks are barred by Section 16 of the Glass-Steagall Act[63] from "dealing in, underwriting and purchasing" securities *except*:

i. A bank may purchase and sell securities "without recourse," solely upon the order and for the account of customers (but in no case may a bank "underwrite any issue of securities or stock");

ii. A bank may underwrite, deal in, purchase and sell certain federal government securities without limitation (referred to as "Type I" securities in regulations of the Comptroller);

iii. A bank may underwrite, deal in, purchase and sell securities of certain federal agencies and certain state and municipal securities ("Type II" securities), within certain limitations; and

iv. A bank may purchase and sell (but not underwrite or deal in) certain readily marketable "investment securities" ("Type III" securities, comprising essentially "non-speculative" marketable

---

[61] 12 U.S.C. §§ 1841 *et seq.*

[62] *Board v. Investment Company Institute,* 450 U.S. 46, 69 (1981).

[63] 12 U.S.C. § 24 (Seventh).

debt, including corporate debt) as prescribed by the Comptroller, within certain limitations.[64]

Section 21. Section 21 of the Glass-Steagall Act[65] provides that no person or organization engaged in the business of "issuing, underwriting, selling, or distributing" securities (except to the extent permitted under Section 16) may engage "at the same time to any extent whatever" in deposit-taking. Section 21 reaches all banks (state or federal, Federal Reserve System-member or not) and probably all other deposit-taking entities as well. It is designed to approach the separation of commercial and investment banking from the investment banking side, and draws the same line as Section 16.

Section 20. Section 20 of the Glass-Steagall Act[66] bars Federal Reserve System-member banks[67] (including national banks) from being "affiliated"[68] with an organization "engaged principally" in the "issue, flotation, underwriting, public sale or distribution" of any "stocks, bonds, debentures, notes, or other securities."

Section 32. Lastly, Section 32 of the Glass-Steagall Act[69] bars personnel interlocks between Federal Reserve System-member banks and entities "primarily engaged" in the issuance, underwriting, public sale or distribution of securities, except such limited classes of relationships as may be permitted under general regulations of the Board.[70]

---

[64] 12 C.F.R. Part 1.

[65] 12 U.S.C. § 378.

[66] 12 U.S.C § 377.

[67] In applying the BHCA, the Board applies the restrictions of Section 20 to bank holding company subsidiaries irrespective of whether any of the holding company's bank subsidiaries are Federal Reserve System-member banks. *See,* for example, 12 C.F.R. § 225.125(b); *Banco di Roma,* 58 Fed. Res. Bull. 940 (1972).

[68] "Affiliates" are defined in 12 U.S.C. § 221a(b) to include subsidiaries, parent companies, sister companies and companies having interlocking directorates (in each case involving a majority of stock or directors).

[69] 12 U.S.C. § 78.

[70] 12 C.F.R. Part 218.

Application of the Glass-Steagall Act to Loan Note and Loan Participation Sales

What little authority there is seems to indicate, in general, that loan notes and participations should *not* be characterized as Glass-Steagall "securities" and, accordingly, that the sale of loan notes and participations to financial and institutional purchasers should *not* be found to violate the Glass-Steagall Act. However, the factors that enter into a determination as to whether particular notes are 1933 or 1934 Act "securities" (as discussed in the previous section) could also be relevant (although not necessarily dispositive) for Glass-Steagall purposes.

Section 16 of the Glass-Steagall Act specifically authorizes national and state member banks to "discount . . . and negotiat[e] promissory notes," and banks have traditionally bought and sold loan notes and participations subject to lending limit and other credit evaluation standards applicable to loan origination. However, a broad-based or "retail" sale of loan notes or participations is arguably similar to a corporate debt underwriting and could be seen as posing some of the financial risks and conflicts of interest at which Glass-Steagall is directed.

In *SIA v. Board*,[71] the Supreme Court held that commercial paper is a "security" for purposes of Glass-Steagall. Given the Supreme Court's broad interpretation of "notes" and "securities" for Glass-Steagall purposes in that case and the Court's focus on both the nature of the financial instrument involved and the role of the bank in the transactions at issue, the possibility of Glass-Steagall coverage of transactions in loan notes and participations under certain circumstances cannot be ignored.[72] This possibility becomes more important as banks broaden the universe of institutions to which they ordinarily sell loan notes and participations, appear to fill the role more of "seller" than "lender," move to standardized documentation, begin on a more widespread basis to quote rates to loan sale customers at which they would be prepared to repurchase notes or participations sold, and develop "transferable" or "book entry" loan certificates.

The Board's Legal Division has stated, however, that "the business of commercial banking" includes "sales of loan participations . . . to other

---

[71] 468 U.S. 137 (1984).

[72] Moreover, the SEC staff has expressed its view that "absent greater elaboration, sales of loan participations may raise questions under Glass-Steagall." Letter, dated June 26, 1979, from SEC General Counsel to Board General Counsel.

commercial banks and *other institutional purchasers.*"[73] Moreover, in its order approving limited securities corporate underwriting and dealing activities for bank holding company subsidiaries under the BHCA and Section 20 of the Glass-Steagall Act, the Board continued to endorse the characterization of bank loan sale activities as part of the business of banking by stating that "banks have sought to continue to service their traditional customer base, within the boundaries of current statutory restrictions, by providing certain types of investment banking or functionally similar services such as . . . syndicating and selling bank loans."[74]

---

[73] *Commercial Paper Activities of Commercial Banks: A Legal Analysis* 8 (June 28, 1979) (emphasis added).

[74] *J.P. Morgan & Co., Inc.,* 75 Fed Res. Bull. 192, 197 (1989). The Board apparently also views purchasers and sales (as principal or broker) of commercial loans, mortgage loans, loan participations and other extensions of credit, as well as loan marketing and advisory services, as incidental to the activities of a commercial finance company (an activity permitted to bank holding companies under 12 C.F.R. § 225.25(b) (1) (iv) and (4) of the Board's Regulation Y). *See,* for example, *Great Lakes Financial Resources, Inc.,* 56 Fed. Reg. 4065 (February 1, 1991) (Board solicitation of public comments) (approved February 27, 1991); *Toronto-Dominion Bank,* 76 Fed. Res. Bull. 573 (1990); *Manufacturers Hanover Corp.,* 55 Fed. Reg. 31441 (August 2, 1990) (Board solicitation of public comments) (approved August 17, 1990); *Dai-Ichi Kangyo Bank, Ltd.,* 55 Fed. Reg. 22099 (May 31, 1990) (Board solicitation of public comments) (approved August 10, 1990); *F.N.B. Corp.,* 54 Fed. Reg. 47407 (November 14, 1989) (Board solicitation of public comments) (approved November 29, 1989) (approval granted in reliance on commitment not to purchase, underwrite, guarantee or take any position in connection with loans marketed); *Fuji Bank,* 54 Fed. Reg. 43487 (October 25, 1989) (Board solicitation of public comments) (approved November 14, 1989); *Bank of Tokyo, Ltd.,* 54 Fed. Reg. 32394 (August 7, 1989) (Board solicitation of public comments) (approved August 3, 1989) (trading loans, loan participations and others interests in loans and extensions of credit to public and private sector borrowers in less developed countries, including consulting and support services to other market participants with respect to purchases, sales and debt-equity conversion programs); *Union Planters Corp.,* 54 Fed. Reg. 1993 (January 18, 1989) (Board solicitation of public comments) (approved February 4, 1989); *Bryn Mawr Bank Corp.* 74 Fed. Res. Bull. 329 (1988); *United Jersey Banks,* 53 Fed. Reg. 23311 (June 21, 1988) (Board solicitation of public comments) (approved July 7, 1988); *Sovran Financial Corp.,* 73 Fed. Res. Bull. 939 (1987); *National Westminster Bank PLC,* 52 Fed. Reg. 7487 (March 11, 1987) (Board solicitation of public comments) (approved June 12, 1987); *Texas Commerce Bancshares,* 51 Fed. Reg. 5803 (February 18, 1986) (Board solicitation of public comments) (approved 72 Fed. Res. Bull. 803 (1986)); *Bankers Trust New York Corporation,* 49 Fed. Reg. 12748 (March 30, 1984) (Board solicitation of public comments) (approved August 29, 1984); *Post-och Kreditbanken, PKbanken,* 68 Fed. Res. Bull. 787 (1982); *Société Générale,* 67 Fed. Res. Bull. 453 (1981).

continued

The Comptroller has stated that "banks . . . engage every day in the sale of . . . loan participations, . . . which can be considered securities in certain contexts" but which were not so considered for purposes of the Glass-Steagall Act.[75] In addition, the Comptroller has reaffirmed his conclusion that instruments representing bank mortgage loans are not Glass-Steagall "securities" in the context of even the public sale of those instruments.[76] While this conclusion was upheld in *SIA v. Comptroller and*

---

continued

The Board has also approved applications by bank holding companies under Regulation Y to engage in asset management services for failing financial institutions, which services would include the management and disposition of loans and collateral acquired through foreclosure on loans. *See*, for example, *Michigan National Corp.*, 78 Fed. Res. Bull. 65 (1992); *First Interstate Bancorp.*, 77 Fed. Res. Bull. 334 (1991); *Banc One Corp.*, 77 Fed. Res. Bull. 331 (1991); *NCNB Corp.*, 77 Fed. Res. Bull. 124 (1991); *First Florida Banks Inc.*, 74 Fed. Res. Bull. 771 (1988).

In addition, the Board has approved applications by bank holding companies under Regulation Y to engage in "mezzanine" financing in connection with acquisitions and to take equity positions in companies being acquired to the extent permitted by the BHCA § 4(c)(6). *See*, for example, Board approval letters in connection with *National Westminster Bank PLC*, 54 Fed. Reg. 5677 (February 6, 1989) (Board solicitation of public comments) (approved March 24, 1989); *Banc One Corp.*, 54 Fed. Reg. 8597 (March 1, 1989) (Board solicitation of public comments) (approved March 6, 1989); *Matewan BancShares, Inc.*, 54 Fed. Reg. 66 (January 3, 1989) (Board solicitation of public comments) (approved January 14, 1989); *Signet Banking Corp.*, 53 Fed. Reg. 15733 (May 3, 1988) (Board solicitation of public comments) (approved June 22, 1988); *Fleet/Norstar Financial Group, Inc.*, 53 Fed. Reg. 3456 (February 5, 1988) (Board solicitation of public comments) (approved Feb. 18, 1988); *First National Boston Corp.*, 47 Fed. Reg. 40236 (September 13, 1982) (Board solicitation of public comments) (approved October 7, 1982).

[75] Letter, dated March 30, 1977, CCH Fed. Banking L. Rep. ¶ 97,093 (concerning sale of pass-through mortgage-backed securities).

[76] Comptroller Interpretive Letter No. 388 (June 16, 1987), CCH Fed. Banking L. Rep. ¶ 85,612. *See also*, for example, Comptroller Interpretive Letter No. 539 (January 15, 1991), CCH Fed. Banking L. Rep. ¶ 83,251 (providing that, pursuant to its authority to engage in correspondent banking, a national bank may provide asset management services (including services relating to the disposition of assets, which would include the sale of loans) for the FDIC and the RTC as conservator or receiver of failed financial institutions and, in certain instances, for third parties who purchase assets from either such entity); Comptroller Interpretive Letter No. 387 (June 22, 1987) ("*Letter No. 387*"), CCH Fed. Banking L. Rep. ¶ 85,611 (national bank brokerage of mortgage loans). *Cf. also* Comptroller Banking Circular No. 254 (June 14, 1991) (setting forth guidelines for national banks and their operating subsidiaries which provide asset management services).

Security Pacific National Bank,[77] the Second Circuit did so on other grounds, and did not resolve the question of whether loans on the books of, and sold by, a bank are ever Glass-Steagall "securities."

It is not always easy to determine for regulatory purposes whether a particular instrument is a "loan" or an "investment security" (or can be characterized as either, at the election of the interested bank).[78] It would appear, however, that at least under circumstances where a bank characterizes such instruments as loans for all purposes (including internal classification and monitoring, credit review, reporting, lending policy compliance, allowance and provision for loan losses, lending limits, etc.) and performs a credit review of (and maintains a credit file on) the issuer comparable to that for a loan, such a bank would have the authority to purchase and sell (but not necessarily underwrite or deal in) privately placed instruments which are clearly "securities" for purposes of the Securities Acts in reliance on its power to make, buy, and sell loans and other extensions of credit.

If loan notes, participations or other instruments are Glass-Steagall "securities," then, depending on the circumstances, the sale of such notes or participations could constitute prohibited "underwriting," "dealing" or "selling." Nonetheless, the better argument appears to be that, at least where (i) a full credit review is made with respect to the loan or participation to be sold, (ii) the instrument is of the type that the bank would, in general, be prepared to keep on its books, (iii) the purchasers are all sophisticated financial institutions, and (iv) the bank does not use a broker-dealer to effect widespread sales to entities which do not ordinarily purchase loan notes or participations, the risks of a significant loan/loan participation sale program being viewed as violative of the Glass-Steagall Act are relatively small. In this context, it appears that bank regulators are not likely to clamp down on the loan/loan participation market, and that most regulatory staff would conclude that the line between a per-

---

[77] 885 F.2d. 1034 (2d. Cir. 1989), *rev'g* 703 F. Supp. 256 (S.D.N.Y. 1988), *cert. denied,* 493 U.S. 1070 (1990).

[78] At one time, the Comptroller's staff was preparing guidelines to identify regulatory issues arising from the identification of whether an instrument is a "loan" or an "investment" and to list characteristics that should be reviewed when making the distinction. *See* "Differentiating Loans From Investments," dated September 23, 1988 (draft). *Cf.* Comptroller Interpretive Letter No. 506 (October 31, 1989), CCH Fed. Banking L. Rep. ¶ 83,204 (national banks may treat bonds issued by Mexico in connection with its 1989–92 Financing Package either as loans or as investment securities, at their one-time election).

missible "loan sale" and an impermissible "securities operation" has not been passed in the existing market, nor should it be if proper precautions are taken.[79]

CONCLUSION

The loan note and participation market is a large, vibrant and innovative arena of commercial bank funds intermediation. Liquidity and flexibility have become increasingly important components of that market, and efforts to promote the ready transferability of loan instruments, and to package loan components in unique and risk-spreading ways, continue to compress the distinctions between "loans" and "securities" under federal banking and securities laws. Care in the structure, documentation and sale of loan notes and participations is thus critical in order to minimize the prospect of bank liability under these laws, while creativity— from both a business and a legal perspective—remains essential to reconcile applicable legal considerations with the banking industry's needs to assure the existence of the most responsive and liquid market possible.

---

[79] With respect to NIF and RUF obligations, a number of steps (not all of which would appear to be necessary to assure compliance with the Glass-Steagall Act) can be taken which would strengthen the argument that NIF/RUF resales do not involve Glass-Steagall "securities." Participating banks could resell NIF or RUF obligations only to institutions which normally purchase loan participations. The NIF or RUF certificates could also bear a legend restricting subsequent resale or transfer to such institutions and bank-owned NIF or RUF certificates could be physically distinguishable from notes sold by an investment bank. It may be helpful if the NIF/RUF agreement provides that, in lieu of purchasing notes, a bank can make an advance (that is, a "loan") equal to the principal amount of the notes that it was otherwise obligated to purchase. Transfers of bank NIF or RUF certificates should be accompanied by such documentation and credit information as is typically provided in loan participation sales. Documentation should also establish the transferee's performance of its own credit analysis and its lack of reliance on the transferring bank with respect to such matters as the borrower's creditworthiness or the collectibility or enforceability of the obligation.

PART II
Credit Analysis and Valuation

Chapter 6

Credit Analysis for Senior Bank Debt

JOHN E. MCDERMOTT III
VICE PRESIDENT
DAIWA SECURITIES AMERICA INC.

BRIAN J. LEWAND
ASSISTANT VICE PRESIDENT
SECURITY PACIFIC NATIONAL BANK

STEWART L. WHITMAN II
VICE PRESIDENT
LONG TERM CREDIT BANK OF JAPAN LTD.

The emergence and development of a secondary market for senior bank debt creates new opportunities for corporate investment. Senior bank debt provides investors with the unique opportunity to realize attractive returns while participating as the senior (secured) creditor of a corporate borrower. The potential for attractive returns is primarily predicated on the continued ability of the corporate borrower to produce the necessary cash flows to maintain its debt service obligations. Alternatively, and if necessary, the potential for refinancing and/or the sale of operating or other assets must be reviewed as a secondary source of repayment. Credit analysis involves the measurement and assessment of a company's debt service capability. Accordingly, credit analysis is prudent to the investment decision in senior bank debt. Also embedded within the due diligence of credit analysis is the analysis of the existing creditor rights prescribed and preserved in the senior bank debt credit agreement. These senior creditor rights hold certain advantages relative to alternative corporate debt investments. Specifically, senior bank debt, through the use of security or partial security interests, strict financial and legal covenants, scheduled amortization requirements and monetary penalties for noncompliance, provide the senior creditor with certain control and protection advantages not afforded debt investors of other creditor classes.

The chapter will provide a general overview of the credit analysis approach toward better assessing the investment risk in senior bank debt. The focus will be on analyzing the credit quality of the borrower coupled with a review of potential control and protection advantages of participating as a senior creditor in a bank debt facility.

REASON FOR A BORROWER'S INDEBTEDNESS

In order to assess the credit quality of the borrower and its ability to service its debt obligation, it is first important to understand the reason for a borrower's indebtedness. A significant portion of the investment activity in the secondary senior bank debt market relates to corporate borrowers that were classified as Highly Leveraged Transactions (HLTs) by the Federal bank regulators. (The reporting requirement by banks for this classification of loans was pending rescindment in early 1992.) Accordingly, a large portion of the senior bank debt that is available for investment was incurred as an obligation of such a corporate borrower through a leveraged transaction. This means that the bank debt borrowings incurred by the corporation were the result of a particular transaction that resulted in the leveraging of that corporation's balance sheet. These leveraged transactions primarily include the following specific types:

Leveraged Buyout:

A leveraged buyout involves the acquisition of a company that is financed primarily through the use of debt. Such a transaction is typically undertaken by management (Management Buyout), employees (ESOP Buyout), and/or outside financial investors. The transaction results in balance sheet leverage through the use of senior and subordinated borrowings.

Leveraged Acquisition:

This is the acquisition of one company by another company that is financed primarily through debt. These transactions, usually undertaken by strategic corporate buyers, typically result in increased leverage for the merged companies.

Recapitalization:

A recapitalization involves the utilization of debt to finance the repurchase of a substantial portion of a company's stock. Such a transaction may occur as a defense against a potential takeover. A recapitalization results in additional leverage for the company and a reduction in its net worth.

In order to gain an understanding of the corporate borrower, it is necessary to identify the type of transaction that resulted in that borrower's indebtedness. Although not all secondary senior bank debt investment opportunities include leveraged borrowers, it is always important for potential investors to understand the reason for the existence of a corporation's borrowings. Other senior bank debt investments would include obligations of middle market and emerging growth companies that are precluded from accessing public debt markets.

PRIMARY SOURCE OF REPAYMENT

This section will focus on the senior creditors' primary source of repayment: the corporate borrower's ability to produce sufficient levels of cash flow from its business operations to service its debt requirements. There is no magic formula that accurately determines whether or not a corporate borrower will or will not default on its borrowing obligations. Therefore, potential investors must assess the default risk of a corporate borrower through a fundamental and diligent credit analysis process. This process should begin with an understanding of the company's industry, the company itself, its anticipated ability to provide continued cash flows for its debt requirements, and a review of any potential contingent risks.

Industry

An overall analysis of the industry or industries for the company's businesses is an integral part of the credit analysis process. It is important to understand the characteristics of the particular industry(ies) in which the company is operating. Industry risk is a factor that impacts the debt servicing capability of a company. While industry analysis itself is complicated and intensive, extensive industry analysis and statistics by research experts are available for most industries. Fundamental credit analysis requires that the industry be researched and understood. Specific industry factors which impact the company need to be carefully analyzed. While there are many factors that need to be reviewed, the following summarizes some of the broad industry factors that should be assessed:

- vulnerability to cyclical downturns

- degree of recessionary impact

- effect of changing commodity prices

- industry/market size

- industry stage—mature vs. growth

- industry composition/competition

- traditional industry customer base

In particular, it is important to review the potential negative impact of certain industry characteristics to ascertain to what extent, if any, they could lead to future lower cash flows for the company. Such a review should be followed by a determination of the sensitivity of the company's cash flows to such events, an exercise that will be reviewed later in this chapter.

Fundamental credit analysis includes determining whether an industry is stable or subject to downward cycles, and if so, to what extent. This analysis should continue to analyze what degree of impact a recession might have on an industry. For example, certain industries, such as construction or those that are construction-related, are more prone to downward business cycles than other industries. Severe downward business cycles may negatively impact future cash flows of a company and thus impair its debt service capability. Other industries such as food retailers (grocery stores) have a much more stable business demand and thus are less susceptible to downward cycles.

A recession may have a much more significant negative impact on certain industries such as general merchandise retailing and textiles than it does on those that are health care or utility related. The degree of recessionary impact varies with different industries and should be understood before investing in a particular industry.

Changing commodity prices are also a major factor that affect the cash flows of companies in many industries. In particular, industries that include commodity producers such as non-ferrous metals or oil and gas are vulnerable to lower commodity prices. On the other hand, rising commodity prices tend to squeeze cash flows of companies in industries that must purchase these commodities for production of their own products such as chemical or airline-related businesses.

The size and state of the industry, as well as the composition of its participants, are also significant aspects to the fundamental credit analysis. Large, mature industries might offer more predictability for future revenues and costs, and thus more stable cash flows, than some new or growing industries such as technology and entertainment-related industries where there is less historical information. Industries whose products rely on technology and discretionary consumer demand may change quickly and thus result in altering cash flow patterns for some companies.

The composition of industry participants is extremely important to the credit analysis. The analysis should encompass the number of competitors, relative market share of these competitors, the barriers to entry and the capital structures of a particular peer group. If, as in the food retail business, many companies are leveraged, cost structures of the competing companies will be similar. The result is that one's competitors will have a more difficult time increasing their market share through price cuts in periods of lower demand. If, however, competitors are not leveraged, they may be able to achieve gains in market share through price and cost cutting during periods of lower demand. Additionally, the same disadvantage occurs if industry-wide costs increase. A leveraged company may have a more difficult time passing the costs on to customers through price increases if its competitors abstain from such practices.

The customer base of an industry is also important to understand. Industries that rely on few corporate customers or the public sector may be more susceptible to lower cash flows due to lack of renewal business than industries such as retail and consumer-oriented businesses across which demand is more randomly distributed.

This industry overview does not purport to state which industries might present more risk relative to other industries, but attempts to highlight certain industry characteristics that should be identified and analyzed as part of the overall credit review process. Of course, the existence of certain characteristics offers a higher degree of risk than others. Such degrees of risk must be taken in context with the overall credit analysis to uncover the full extent of credit risk while determining which mitigating factors exist.

Company Analysis

Fundamental credit analysis relies on a diligent and extensive review of the businesses operated by the company. While there are many points and issues that need to be analyzed, the following is a general outline of factors relevant to a company's credit analysis.

- market position/proven product

- proprietary products or services/franchise value

- expected growth prospects

- predictability of cash flows

- cash flow analysis

- management

- capital expenditure/working capital requirements

- contingent risks

It is necessary to determine if the company is producing a proven product, the continued production and sale of which will result in sufficient cash flow levels needed to service its debt. The analysis of the potential for and expectation of cash flows are the essential elements required in measuring debt service capability. Such analysis requires a review of market components to determine if the company indeed has a proven product while also assessing growth prospects for the product. This analysis combined with a careful interpretation of management's capability and future capital requirements are helpful in ascertaining the company's ability to sustain the product and its associated cash flow levels. These factors contribute largely to the resulting cash flow analysis that will be discussed later in the chapter.

Market position is an important element in determining if the company is producing a proven product. A proven product is identified by its leadership in the marketplace supported by a relatively large market share, depending on the size of the market. Proven products with an entrenched market share usually provide more stable and predictable cash flows as they are less sensitive to competitive factors and cyclical downturns, factors which negatively effect cash flows.

Proven products are further identified as proprietary products. Proprietary products help to provide protection from generic substitutes produced by the competitor(s) that may result in loss of market share. While market share protection is important, long-term stability is created by proprietary products with low obsolescence risk.

The future value of a company's product and its market share are further stabilized through a strong franchise value. Strong franchise value provides for stable and channeled distribution. This has enormous value in a company's ability to retain and even increase its share.

A company's future growth prospects can be determined, in part, by analyzing historical performance coupled with the assessment of its ability to retain and gain market share while maintaining costs. Increased revenues due to industry growth and/or market share gains, while maintaining costs and/or margins, will result in higher future cash flows for the company. This expected growth scenario should be compared to the cash flow requirements necessary to service the senior bank debt amortization. A flat or no growth performance should also be considered as to its effect on cash flows that are needed to meet the scheduled debt payments.

The management of a company is critical to its success and, therefore, important to, if not the most important element of, the credit analysis of a debt investment in that company. While an on-site meeting with management is important for purposes of secondary market investment, that may be difficult to undertake. However, a review of management's performance and background is imperative. Management's capabilities are a major determinant in future success and resultant cash flow levels realized by the company.

Future capital requirements, both short and long term, play an important role in determining future cash flow levels that are available for debt service. Capital-intensive companies, such as those that are manufacture-related, require substantial capital outlays for maintenance and improvements in order to maintain production levels. Some producers require higher levels of research and development spending than others to maintain their market share. Such companies must devote a portion of annual cash flows to capital requirements in order to maintain proven product status. Significant debt requirements may pressure or restrict potential capital spending.

Lower levels of cash flows might reduce capital spending and thus may further negatively impact future cash flows. Initially, cash flows for capital spending in excess of maintenance may be earmarked for debt service. However, this practice may have a negative effect as reduced capital spending levels deteriorate the proven product status. The most desired scenario is one where the company's expected cash flows adequately service debt while allowing a cushion for planned capital spending.

Working capital availability or liquidity is essential to the production and distribution process, and requires cash to be available for its use. Seasonal business operations or slowing business activity may result in draining cash flow. Companies should have the available liquidity and support from a working capital facility to meet seasonal business demand and inventory buildup without having to make a substantial drain on internally generated cash flows.

One of the most important tools employed during the credit analysis process is cash flow analysis. The statement of cash flow, now presented along with the balance sheet, income statement, and statement of retained earnings in any package of audited financial statements, assists a creditor in appraising the ability of a borrower to repay its debts as well as provides insight into the firms financing methods, investment strategy, and dividend policy.

The statement of cash flows can be presented in many different forms, though the underlying purpose quite simply is to provide a "cash" basis picture of a company. This is especially helpful because revenues and expenses as reported in the income statement for a period differ in amount from cash receipts and disbursements for the period. The differences arise for two principal reasons:

1. The accrual basis of accounting is used in measuring net income. Thus, the recognition of revenues does not necessarily coincide with receipts of cash from customers. Likewise, the recognition of expenses does not necessarily coincide with disbursements of cash to suppliers, employees, and other creditors.

2. The firm receives cash from sources that are not related directly to operations, such as issuing capital stock or debt. Similarly, the firm makes cash disbursements for such things as dividends and acquisition of fixed assets.

The cash flow statement is broken down into three distinct categories: operating activities, investing activities, and financing activities.

1. Operating activities yield cash flow from the selling of goods and services. Cash is produced principally through the collection of receivables from customers and is used for the payment of obligations to suppliers and employees. All non-cash items that were charged through the income statement, such as depreciation, amortization, non-cash interest, and deferred taxes, are recaptured in this section of the cash flow statement.

2. Investing activities generally account for an outflow of cash associated with the purchase of plant, property, and equipment. This outflow is net of any proceeds received from the sale of such non-current assets.

3. Financing activities relate to the cash effects of debt and equity transactions, most notably the issuance/redemption of long-term debt and capital stock, as well as the payment of cash dividends.

The following illustration will assist in understanding the application of cash flow analysis in the credit process.

Throughout the early and mid 1980s XYZ Manufacturing, Inc., established in 1977, produced record profits and strong cash flows. In the early months of 1987, however, a foreign competitor with a newly developed product line invaded XYZ's marketplace and suddenly financial performance began to suffer. Though XYZ had spent adequately on R&D and capital expansion programs, the Company suffered from management neglect resulting in lagging the market in the development of new product lines and marketing strategies. Sales, which traditionally enjoyed double-digit growth, suddenly flattened, and though the Company was able to rebound somewhat after the initial shock, profit margins never regained their historical levels (Exhibit 1).

In the latter half of 1989, XYZ's parent company, ABC, Inc., decided to sell XYZ. Though ABC knew that XYZ had a proven product and strong market franchise, the subsidiary required increasingly more attention over the previous few years. This, coupled with the fact that XYZ was always viewed as a non-strategic business unit, motivated ABC to seek a buyer for the Company.

A well-known leveraged buyout fund, Stellar Capital, purchased the Company on 12/31/89. Security Atlantic Bank agented the senior bank financing with a major insurance company providing the mezzanine debt. The sources and uses of funds at 12/31/89 were as follows ($s millions):

Sources			Uses	
Bank Revolver	$0.0	0.0%	Common Stock Purchase	$420.0
Bank Term Loan	231.0	55.0%		
PIK Sub Debt	63.0	15.0%		
Equity	126.0	30.0%		
	$420.0	100.0%		$420.0

It is now 1991 and there exists investment opportunities in XYZ's senior bank debt. The Company has been right on target with management's original projections, and the senior bank debt is currently being offered at par value.

An investor may be provided by the Agent bank with the original financial package, including historical data from 1986 through 1989 and projections through 1995 (herein "Management Case"). As mentioned earlier, XYZ came in right on target for fiscal year 1990. The credit analysis undertaken to assess the potential risk of this senior bank debt investment now concentrates on the cash flow analysis.

First, some key definitions and ratios:

EBITDA

Earnings before interest, taxes, depreciation, and amortization. EBITDA is a commonly used measurement of pre-tax operating cash flow, or, more specifically, cash earnings (taken right from the income statement), though it does not take into consideration changes in working capital.

EBIT

Earnings before interest and taxes. This is used as a measurement of profitability.

EBITDA/Total Interest

This ratio is a good measurement of how well a company can service its interest obligations, and measures how many times interest charges have been earned by the corporation on a pre-tax basis.

EBITDA/Cash Interest

This ratio is an important indicator of interest coverage when a capital structure includes a tranche of debt bearing non-cash interest expense such as PIK (payment-in-kind; holder of the paper receives additional paper in lieu of cash) interest.

EBITDA-CAPEX/Cash Interest

Since capital expenditures (CAPEX) are arguably the most important cash outflow for a company (and often higher in priority to management than debt service), this ratio gives a more realistic indication of cash interest coverage.

Senior Debt/EBITDA

Useful in measuring both leverage and purchase price multiples, this ratio shows what the company must be resold for in order to make the senior lenders whole. The inverse of this cash flow multiple will generate a breakeven interest rate (i.e., if the multiple is 6.5:1, than senior debt interest coverage is 1:1 at a rate of $1/6.5$, or 15.4%).

Fixed Charge Coverage

This is widely used as a measurement of how well a company can cover its capital expenditures and interest and principal payments from pre-tax cash flow (EBITDA). "Fixed" denotes mandatory obligations of the company, thus the ratio must at all times remain above 1:1.

During the period 1987 through 1989, the Company experienced what some might view as a lackluster period (Exhibit 1). Though XYZ did show admirable operational results and strong cash flows following the troubled 1987 period, Stellar Capital viewed the buyout as a good investment opportunity. The Company was a market leader with a proven product base, and there existed considerable potential. Sales growth and margins had fallen from historical averages, and the Company needed what amounted to a renewed focus, drive, and direction.

Various factors, including manufacturing inefficiencies and loose cost controls, had led to a reduction in profitability and mismanagement of working capital. Though the Company's financial performance trended upward in recent years, relative to historical averages EBITDA margin had fallen by over 1.5%, from 16.2% to 14.7%, and inventory turns had slowed noticeably.

Considering that prior to 12/31/89 XYZ had no debt on its books, from a credit standpoint historical cash flows were more than adequate. The Company had been able to sufficiently cover the working capital uses of cash as well as continue a minor capital expansion program (CAPEX greater than depreciation).

The 12/31/89 LBO involved XYZ borrowing a $231 million term loan at LIBOR plus 225 basis points (swapped into an 11% fixed rate) and having it amortize over a six year period according to the following schedule:

Year	Principal Payment	% Repaid
1990	$20.0 million	8.7%
1991	25.0	19.5%
1992	35.0	34.6%
1993	45.0	54.1%
1994	50.0	75.8%
1995	<u>56.0</u>	100.0%
	$231.0 million	

Exhibit 1
XYZ Manufacturing Inc. Management Case—Worksheet Assumptions and Results

FYE 12/31/xx
Millions $

WORKSHEET ASSUMPTIONS & RESULTS

	Historical				Management Projected					
	1986	1987	1988	1989	1990	1991	1992	1993	1994	1995
OPERATING ASSUMPTIONS										
Sales Growth	10.0%	2.0%	6.0%	6.0%	8.0%	3.0%	10.0%	6.0%	6.0%	6.0%
Cost of Goods Sold	65.8%	68.0%	67.0%	67.0%	67.0%	67.0%	66.0%	66.0%	66.0%	66.0%
Operating Expenses	18.0%	18.5%	18.5%	18.3%	18.0%	18.0%	17.0%	17.0%	17.0%	17.0%
Margins:										
EBITDA	16.2%	13.5%	14.5%	14.7%	15.0%	15.0%	17.0%	17.0%	17.0%	17.0%
EBIT	13.2%	10.4%	11.4%	11.6%	11.4%	11.3%	13.4%	13.3%	13.3%	13.2%
Net Profit	7.9%	6.2%	6.8%	6.9%	3.5%	3.7%	5.5%	5.9%	6.3%	6.7%
Interest - Bank Debt	n/a	n/a	n/a	n/a	11.0%	11.0%	11.0%	11.0%	11.0%	11.0%
Interest - Sub Debt	n/a	n/a	n/a	n/a	14.0%	14.0%	14.0%	14.0%	14.0%	14.0%
Tax Rate	40.0%	40.0%	40.0%	40.0%	40.0%	40.0%	40.0%	40.0%	40.0%	40.0%
WORKING CAPITAL										
Receivables/Sales	18.5%	18.0%	18.5%	18.7%	18.0%	18.0%	18.0%	18.0%	18.0%	18.0%
Inventory/COGS	18.0%	22.0%	21.0%	20.0%	19.0%	18.0%	17.0%	17.0%	17.0%	17.0%
Accounts Payable/COGS	17.0%	18.0%	17.0%	17.0%	18.0%	18.0%	18.0%	18.0%	18.0%	18.0%
Accrued Expenses/Sales	4.0%	4.0%	4.0%	4.0%	4.0%	4.0%	4.0%	4.0%	4.0%	4.0%
Receivable Days	67	65	67	67	65	65	65	65	65	65
Inventory Days	65	79	76	72	68	65	61	61	61	61
Payable Days	61	65	61	61	65	65	65	65	65	65
KEY RATIOS										
EBIT / Total Interest	n/a	n/a	n/a	n/a	2.16	2.38	3.40	4.11	5.21	7.11
EBITDA / Total Interest	n/a	n/a	n/a	n/a	2.85	3.16	4.32	5.25	6.68	9.13
EBITDA-CAPEX/ Tot. Int.	n/a	n/a	n/a	n/a	2.24	2.43	3.45	4.17	5.28	7.20
EBITDA/Cash Interest	n/a	n/a	n/a	n/a	3.92	2.73	7.40	11.50	25.75	n/a
EBITDA-CAPEX/Cash Interest	n/a	n/a	n/a	n/a	3.07	3.64	5.91	9.11	20.54	n/a
Fixed Charge Cov. Ratio	n/a	n/a	n/a	n/a	1.46	1.42	1.59	1.54	1.61	1.68
Total Funded Debt/EBITDA	n/a	n/a	n/a	n/a	3.05	2.80	2.05	1.68	1.32	0.97
Senior Debt/EBITDA	n/a	n/a	n/a	n/a	2.27	1.95	1.27	0.84	0.42	0.00

Also extended by the Agent bank was a $60 million revolving line of credit to cover seasonal working capital and letter of credit needs.

At the time of the LBO, Stellar Capital compiled a detailed set of projections that were predicated upon months of research and forecasting as well as the abilities of a new management team with years of experience and a proven track record. Management indicated at the recent bank meeting that their new five year budget was unchanged from the original projections.

The cash flow analysis portrayed in Exhibits 1 through 4 attempts to review the Management Projections and then is adjusted to create a reasonable worst case scenario which is reflected in Exhibits 5 through 8. The sensitization of the Management Case to this "worst case" is an important aid in determining whether or not this is an attractive investment.

For a LBO, the financing structure appears acceptable, with senior bank debt accounting for 55% of total capitalization at closing. The purchase price of $420 million represented a multiple of 5X 1989 EBITDA, which when compared in a peer group analysis, is in line with other acquisitions. Following the $20 million amortization of term debt during 1990, senior bank financing at 12/31/90 represented a conservative 2.27X 1990 EBITDA. The subordinated debt has a 10-year bullet maturity and pays PIK interest for the first 7 years.

1990 was a good year for the Company, as the new management team was able to accomplish its goals during the first projected period following the buyout. XYZ met its forecasted level of 8% sales growth and a mild improvement in EBITDA margin to 15%, and working capital returned to more normalized levels (Exhibit 1). Resulting cash flow from operating activities of $59.6 million (Exhibit 3) easily funded CAPEX and fulfilled the $20 million amortization requirement; EBITDA-CAPEX/Cash Interest and Fixed Charge Coverage were very favorable at 3.07X and 1.46X, respectively (Exhibit 1).

The Management Case (Exhibit 1) projects a recessionary economic environment in 1991 with a rebound in 1992 and level, above-inflation (assume inflation of 4%) growth thereafter. Cost of Goods Sold (COGS), as a percentage of sales, decreases to 66% by 1992 as management believes that they can improve margins through new technologies and enhanced manufacturing efficiencies. SG&A expenses decrease to 17% of sales in 1992 and thereafter due to continued streamlining of personnel and an overall cost reduction program being established to cut out well documented waste. On the working capital side, a complete overhaul of

Exhibit 2
XYZ Manufacturing Inc. Management Case

FYE 12/31/xx
Millions $

INCOME STATEMENT	<---- Historical ---->				Management Projected <------------------->					
	1986	1987	1988	1989	1990	1991	1992	1993	1994	1995
Sales	500.0	510.0	540.6	573.0	618.9	637.4	701.2	743.3	787.9	835.1
Cost of Goods Sold	329.0	346.8	362.2	383.9	414.6	427.1	462.8	490.6	520.0	551.2
Gross Profit	171.0	163.2	178.4	189.1	204.2	210.4	238.4	252.7	267.9	283.9
(%)	34.2%	32.0%	33.0%	33.0%	33.0%	33.0%	34.0%	34.0%	34.0%	34.0%
Operating Expenses	90.0	94.4	100.0	104.9	111.4	114.7	119.2	126.4	133.9	142.0
EBITDA	81.0	68.9	78.4	84.2	92.8	95.6	119.2	126.4	133.9	142.0
(%)	16.2%	13.5%	14.5%	14.7%	15.0%	15.0%	17.0%	17.0%	17.0%	17.0%
Depreciation	15.0	16.0	17.0	18.0	19.0	20.0	22.0	24.0	26.0	28.0
Amortization	0.0	0.0	0.0	0.0	3.4	3.4	3.4	3.4	3.4	3.4
EBIT	66.0	52.8	61.4	66.2	70.5	72.2	93.8	99.0	104.6	110.6
(%)	13.2%	10.4%	11.4%	11.6%	11.4%	11.3%	13.4%	13.3%	13.3%	13.2%
Interest Expense	0.0	0.0	0.0	0.0	32.5	30.3	27.6	24.1	20.1	15.5
EBT	66.0	52.8	61.4	66.2	37.9	41.9	66.2	74.9	84.5	95.0
Provision for Inc. Taxes	26.4	21.1	24.6	26.5	16.5	18.1	27.8	31.3	35.2	39.4
Net Income	39.6	31.7	36.8	39.7	21.4	23.8	38.4	43.6	49.3	55.7
(%)	7.9%	6.2%	6.8%	6.9%	3.5%	3.7%	5.5%	5.9%	6.3%	6.7%

Exhibit 3
XYZ Manufacturing Inc. Management Case

FYE 12/31/xx
Millions $

	Historical				Management Projected					
CASH FLOW STATEMENT (1)	1986	1987	1988	1989	1990	1991	1992	1993	1994	1995
Net Income	39.6	31.7	36.8	39.7	21.4	23.8	38.4	43.6	49.3	55.7
Adjustments to Reconcile Net Income to Cash:										
Depreciation	15.0	16.0	17.0	18.0	19.0	20.0	22.0	24.0	26.0	28.0
Amortization	0.0	0.0	0.0	0.0	3.4	3.4	3.4	3.4	3.4	3.4
Deferred Taxes	2.0	2.0	2.0	2.0	2.0	2.0	2.0	2.0	2.0	2.0
Non-Cash Interest	0.0	0.0	0.0	0.0	8.8	10.1	11.5	13.1	14.9	17.0
(Increase) Decrease in Working Capital	1.5	(9.5)	(7.6)	(2.9)	5.0	1.5	(4.3)	(5.6)	(5.9)	(6.3)
Cash Flow from Operating Activites	58.1	40.2	48.2	56.9	59.6	60.8	72.9	80.4	89.7	99.7
Cash Flow from Investing Activities:										
Capital Expenditures	(22.0)	(22.0)	(22.0)	(22.0)	(20.0)	(22.0)	(24.0)	(26.0)	(28.0)	(30.0)
	(22.0)	(22.0)	(22.0)	(22.0)	(20.0)	(22.0)	(24.0)	(26.0)	(28.0)	(30.0)
Cash Flow from Financing Activities:										
Bank Term Loan Amortization	0.0	0.0	0.0	0.0	(20.0)	(25.0)	(35.0)	(45.0)	(50.0)	(56.0)
Bank R/C Draw / (Paydown)	0.0	0.0	0.0	0.0	0.0	0.0	0.0	0.0	0.0	0.0
Common Dividends	(36.1)	(18.2)	(26.2)	(34.9)	0.0	0.0	0.0	0.0	0.0	0.0
	(36.1)	(18.2)	(26.2)	(34.9)	(20.0)	(25.0)	(35.0)	(45.0)	(50.0)	(56.0)
Excess Cash	0.0	0.0	0.0	0.0	19.6	13.8	13.9	9.4	11.7	13.7
Beginning Cash Balance	10.0	10.0	10.0	10.0	10.0	29.6	43.3	57.3	66.7	78.4
Plus Excess Cash Generated	0.0	0.0	0.0	0.0	19.6	13.8	13.9	9.4	11.7	13.7
Ending Balance Sheet Cash	10.0	10.0	10.0	10.0	29.6	43.3	57.3	66.7	78.4	92.1

(1) For presentation purposes, the 1989 cash flow does not reflect the sources and uses of the proposed transaction.

Exhibit 4
XYZ Manufacturing Inc. Management Case

FYE 12/31/xx Millions $	<---- Historical ---->				Closing Adjustments	Post-Closing 1989	<---- Management Projected ---->					
	1986	1987	1988	Pre-Closing 1989			1990	1991	1992	1993	1994	1995
BALANCE SHEET												
Cash & Mkt. Securities	10.0	10.0	10.0	10.0	0.0	10.0	29.6	43.3	57.3	66.7	78.4	92.1
Receivables	92.5	91.8	100.0	107.2	0.0	107.2	111.4	114.7	126.2	133.8	141.8	150.3
Inventory	59.2	76.3	76.1	76.8	0.0	76.8	78.8	76.9	78.7	83.4	88.4	93.7
Other Current Assets	5.0	5.0	5.0	5.0	0.0	5.0	5.0	5.0	5.0	5.0	5.0	5.0
Current Assets	166.7	183.1	191.1	198.9	0.0	198.9	224.7	240.0	267.2	288.9	313.6	341.1
PP&E - Net	185.0	191.0	196.0	200.0	0.0	200.0	201.0	203.0	205.0	207.0	209.0	211.0
Goodwill	0.0	0.0	0.0	0.0	135.2	135.2	131.9	128.5	125.1	121.7	118.3	115.0
Total Assets	351.7	374.1	387.1	398.9	135.2	534.2	557.6	571.4	597.3	617.6	640.9	667.1
Accounts Payable	55.9	62.4	61.6	65.3	0.0	65.3	74.6	76.9	83.3	88.3	93.6	99.2
Accrued Expenses	20.0	20.4	21.6	22.9	0.0	22.9	24.8	25.5	28.0	29.7	31.5	33.4
Current Liabilities	75.9	82.8	83.2	88.2	0.0	88.2	99.4	102.4	111.3	118.0	125.1	132.6
Bank Revolver	0.0	0.0	0.0	0.0	0.0	0.0	0.0	0.0	0.0	0.0	0.0	0.0
Bank Term Loan	0.0	0.0	0.0	0.0	231.0	231.0	211.0	186.0	151.0	106.0	56.0	0.0
Total Senior Debt	0.0	0.0	0.0	0.0	231.0	231.0	211.0	186.0	151.0	106.0	56.0	0.0
Subordinated Debt	0.0	0.0	0.0	0.0	63.0	63.0	71.8	81.9	93.3	106.4	121.3	138.3
Total Funded Debt	0.0	0.0	0.0	0.0	294.0	294.0	282.8	267.9	244.3	212.4	177.3	138.3
Deferred Taxes	20.0	22.0	24.0	26.0	0.0	26.0	28.0	30.0	32.0	34.0	36.0	38.0
Common & Retained	255.8	269.3	279.9	284.8	(158.8)	126.0	147.4	171.2	209.6	253.2	302.5	358.2
Ttl. Liabs. & Equity	351.7	374.1	387.1	398.9	135.2	534.2	557.6	571.4	597.3	617.6	640.9	667.1

Exhibit 5
XYZ Manufacturing Inc. Sensitized Case

FYE 12/31/xx
Millions $

WORKSHEET ASSUMPTIONS & RESULTS

	Historical				Sensitized Projected					
	1986	1987	1988	1989	1990	1991	1992	1993	1994	1995
OPERATING ASSUMPTIONS										
Sales Growth	10.0%	2.0%	6.0%	6.0%	8.0%	0.0%	4.0%	4.0%	4.0%	4.0%
Cost of Goods Sold	65.0%	68.0%	67.0%	67.0%	67.0%	68.0%	68.0%	68.0%	68.0%	68.0%
Operating Expenses	18.0%	18.5%	18.5%	18.3%	18.0%	18.5%	18.5%	18.5%	18.5%	18.5%
Margins:										
EBITDA	16.2%	13.5%	14.5%	14.7%	15.0%	13.5%	13.5%	13.5%	13.5%	13.5%
EBIT	13.2%	10.4%	11.4%	11.6%	11.4%	9.7%	9.6%	9.4%	9.3%	9.2%
Net Profit	7.9%	6.2%	6.8%	6.9%	3.5%	2.6%	2.8%	3.0%	3.2%	3.4%
Interest - Bank Debt	n/a	n/a	n/a	n/a	11.0%	11.0%	11.0%	11.0%	11.0%	11.0%
Interest - Sub Debt	n/a	n/a	n/a	n/a	14.0%	14.0%	14.0%	14.0%	14.0%	14.0%
Tax Rate	40.0%	40.0%	40.0%	40.0%	40.0%	40.0%	40.0%	40.0%	40.0%	40.0%
WORKING CAPITAL										
Receivable/Sales	18.5%	18.0%	18.5%	18.7%	18.0%	18.0%	18.0%	18.0%	18.0%	18.0%
Inventory/COGS	18.0%	22.0%	21.0%	20.0%	19.0%	20.0%	20.0%	20.0%	20.0%	20.0%
Accounts Payable/COGS	17.0%	18.0%	17.0%	17.0%	18.0%	18.0%	18.0%	18.0%	18.0%	18.0%
Accrued Expenses/Sales	4.0%	4.0%	4.0%	4.0%	4.0%	4.0%	4.0%	4.0%	4.0%	4.0%
Receivable Days	67	65	67	67	65	65	65	65	65	65
Inventory Days	65	79	76	72	68	72	72	72	72	72
Payable Days	61	65	61	61	65	65	65	65	65	65
KEY RATIOS										
EBIT / Total Interest	n/a	n/a	n/a	n/a	2.16	1.96	2.11	2.30	2.55	2.86
EBITDA / Total Interest	n/a	n/a	n/a	n/a	2.85	2.72	2.98	3.31	3.70	4.21
EBITDA-CAPEX/ Tot. Int.	n/a	n/a	n/a	n/a	2.24	2.00	2.16	2.36	2.60	2.92
EBITDA/Cash Interest	n/a	n/a	n/a	n/a	3.92	2.98	3.56	4.93	8.95	15.75
EBITDA-CAPEX/Cash Interest	n/a	n/a	n/a	n/a	3.07	2.90	3.13	4.51	6.30	10.85
Fixed Charge Cov. Ratio	n/a	n/a	n/a	n/a	1.46	1.24	1.13	1.06	1.06	1.06
Total Funded Debt/EBITDA	n/a	n/a	n/a	n/a	3.05	3.21	2.88	2.55	2.23	1.90
Senior Debt/EBITDA	n/a	n/a	n/a	n/a	2.27	2.23	1.81	1.38	0.94	0.49

Exhibit 6
XYZ Manufacturing Inc. Sensitized Case

FYE 12/31/xx
Millions $

INCOME STATEMENT	<----- Historical ----->				Sensitized Projected <-------------------------->					
	1986	1987	1988	1989	1990	1991	1992	1993	1994	1995
Sales	500.0	510.0	540.6	573.0	618.9	618.9	643.6	669.4	696.2	724.0
Cost of Goods Sold	329.0	346.8	362.2	383.9	414.6	420.8	437.7	455.2	473.4	492.3
Gross Profit	171.0	163.2	178.4	189.1	204.2	198.0	206.0	214.2	222.8	231.7
(%)	34.2%	32.0%	33.0%	33.0%	33.0%	32.0%	32.0%	32.0%	32.0%	32.0%
Operating Expenses	90.0	94.4	100.0	104.9	111.4	114.5	119.1	123.8	128.8	133.9
EBITDA	81.0	68.9	78.4	84.2	92.8	83.5	86.9	90.4	94.0	97.7
(%)	16.2%	13.5%	14.5%	14.7%	15.0%	13.5%	13.5%	13.5%	13.5%	13.5%
Depreciation	15.0	16.0	17.0	18.0	19.0	20.0	22.0	24.0	26.0	28.0
Amortization	0.0	0.0	0.0	0.0	3.4	3.4	3.4	3.4	3.4	3.4
EBIT	66.0	52.8	61.4	66.2	70.5	60.2	61.5	63.0	64.6	66.4
(%)	13.2%	10.4%	11.4%	11.6%	11.4%	9.7%	9.6%	9.4%	9.3%	9.2%
Interest Expense	0.0	0.0	0.0	0.0	32.5	30.7	29.1	27.3	25.4	23.2
EBT	66.0	52.8	61.4	66.2	37.9	29.5	32.4	35.7	39.2	43.1
Provision for Inc. Taxes	26.4	21.1	24.6	26.5	16.5	13.1	14.3	15.6	17.0	18.6
Net Income	39.6	31.7	36.8	39.7	21.4	16.3	18.1	20.0	22.2	24.5
(%)	7.9%	6.2%	6.8%	6.9%	3.5%	2.6%	2.8%	3.0%	3.2%	3.4%

Exhibit 7
XYZ Manufacturing Inc. Sensitized Case

FYE 12/31/xx
Millions $

CASH FLOW STATEMENT (1)	Historical				Sensitized Projected					
	1986	1987	1988	1989	1990	1991	1992	1993	1994	1995
Net Income	39.6	31.7	36.8	39.7	21.4	16.3	18.1	20.0	22.2	24.5
Adjustments to Reconcile Net Income to Cash:										
Depreciation	15.0	16.0	17.0	18.0	19.0	20.0	22.0	24.0	26.0	28.0
Amortization	0.0	0.0	0.0	0.0	3.4	3.4	3.4	3.4	3.4	3.4
Deferred Taxes	2.0	2.0	2.0	2.0	2.0	2.0	2.0	2.0	2.0	2.0
Non-Cash Interest	0.0	0.0	0.0	0.0	8.8	10.1	11.5	13.1	14.9	17.0
(Increase) Decrease in Working Capital	1.5	(9.5)	(7.6)	(2.9)	5.0	(4.3)	(3.8)	(4.0)	(4.1)	(4.3)
Cash Flow from Operating Activities	58.1	40.2	48.2	56.9	59.6	47.5	53.1	58.5	64.3	70.6
Cash Flow from Investing Activities:										
Capital Expenditures	(22.0)	(22.0)	(22.0)	(22.0)	(20.0)	(22.0)	(24.0)	(26.0)	(28.0)	(30.0)
	(22.0)	(22.0)	(22.0)	(22.0)	(20.0)	(22.0)	(24.0)	(26.0)	(28.0)	(30.0)
Cash Flow from Financing Activities:										
Bank Term Loan Amortization	0.0	0.0	0.0	0.0	(20.0)	(25.0)	(35.0)	(45.0)	(50.0)	(56.0)
Bank R/C Draw / (Paydown)	0.0	0.0	0.0	0.0	0.0	0.0	5.9	12.5	13.7	15.4
Common Dividends	(36.1)	(18.2)	(26.2)	(34.9)	0.0	0.0	0.0	0.0	0.0	0.0
	(36.1)	(18.2)	(26.2)	(34.9)	(20.0)	(25.0)	(29.1)	(32.5)	(36.3)	(40.6)
Excess Cash	0.0	0.0	0.0	0.0	19.6	0.5	0.0	0.0	0.0	0.0
Beginning Cash Balance	10.0	0.0	0.0	0.0	10.0	29.6	30.1	30.1	30.1	30.1
Plus Excess Cash Generated	0.0	0.0	0.0	0.0	19.6	0.5	0.0	0.0	0.0	0.0
Ending Balance Sheet Cash	10.0	0.0	0.0	0.0	29.6	30.1	30.1	30.1	30.1	30.1

(1) For presentation purposes, the 1989 cash flow does not reflect the sources and uses of the proposed transaction.

Exhibit 8
XYZ Manufacturing Inc. Sensitized Case

FYE 12/31/xx Millions $	Historical			Pre-Closing 1989	Closing Adjustments	Post-Closing 1989	Sensitized Projected					
	1986	1987	1988				1990	1991	1992	1993	1994	1995
BALANCE SHEET												
Cash & Mkt. Securities	10.0	10.0	10.0	10.0	0.0	10.0	29.6	30.1	30.1	30.1	30.1	30.1
Receivables	92.5	91.8	100.6	107.2	0.0	107.2	111.4	111.4	115.9	120.5	125.3	130.3
Inventory	59.2	76.3	76.1	76.8	0.0	76.8	78.8	84.2	87.5	91.0	94.7	98.5
Other Current Assets	5.0	5.0	5.0	5.0	0.0	5.0	5.0	5.0	5.0	5.0	5.0	5.0
Current Assets	166.7	183.1	191.1	198.9	0.0	198.9	224.7	230.6	238.4	246.6	255.0	263.8
PP&E - Net	185.0	191.0	196.0	200.0	0.0	200.0	201.0	203.0	205.0	207.0	209.0	211.0
Goodwill	0.0	0.0	0.0	0.0	135.2	135.2	131.9	128.5	125.1	121.7	118.3	115.0
Total Assets	351.7	374.1	387.1	398.9	135.2	534.2	557.6	562.1	568.5	575.3	582.4	589.8
Accounts Payable	55.9	62.4	61.6	65.3	0.0	65.3	74.6	75.8	78.8	81.9	85.2	88.6
Accrued Expenses	20.0	20.4	21.6	22.9	0.0	22.9	24.8	24.8	25.7	26.8	27.8	29.0
Current Liabilities	75.9	82.8	83.2	88.2	0.0	88.2	99.4	100.5	104.5	108.7	113.1	117.6
Bank Revolver	0.0	0.0	0.0	0.0	0.0	0.0	0.0	0.0	5.9	18.3	32.0	47.4
Bank Term Loan	0.0	0.0	0.0	0.0	231.0	231.0	211.0	186.0	151.0	106.0	56.0	0.0
Total Senior Debt	0.0	0.0	0.0	0.0	231.0	231.0	211.0	186.0	156.9	124.3	88.0	47.4
Subordinated Debt	0.0	0.0	0.0	0.0	63.0	63.0	71.8	81.9	93.3	106.4	121.3	138.3
Total Funded Debt	0.0	0.0	0.0	0.0	294.0	294.0	282.8	267.9	250.2	230.7	209.3	185.7
Deferred Taxes	20.0	22.0	24.0	26.0	0.0	26.0	28.0	30.0	32.0	34.0	36.0	38.0
Common & Retained	255.8	269.3	279.9	284.8	(158.8)	126.0	147.4	163.7	181.8	201.8	224.0	248.6
Ttl. Liabs. & Equity	351.7	374.1	387.1	398.9	135.2	534.2	557.6	562.1	568.5	575.3	582.4	589.8

inventory accounting systems, as well as the introduction of new technologies to the manufacturing process, is currently under way; management believes that this will shorten inventory turns to approximately 61 days by 1992 (compared to 79 days in 1987). Capital expenditures, which were more than adequate over the past few years, are maintained just slightly above straight-line depreciation.

These operational forecasts result in the generation of strong EBITDA margins and a swing back to more normalized working capital levels. As is evidenced by the cash flow statement (Exhibit 3), cash flows from operating activities are more than adequate to service annual working capital uses, capital expenditures, and scheduled term loan principal payments (normally, excess cash flows are recaptured during the period and applied towards the early retirement of debt). EBITDA-CAPEX/Cash Interest ratio measures in at a strong 3.64X in 1991 and improves thereafter; notice the considerable difference between EBITDA-CAPEX/Total Interest and the EBITDA-CAPEX/Cash Interest ratios, displaying the importance between income statement analysis and cash flow analysis. Fixed charge coverage is satisfactory at 1.42X in 1991, displaying sufficient cash flows to service XYZ's most important cash outflows (Exhibit 3). Expected cash flows fully amortize scheduled principal payments under this scheme (Exhibit 3).

Taking into consideration many different factors, the Management Case should now be sensitized ("Sensitized Case"). A conservative approach must include a scenario that incorporates many possible negative factors such as increased competition, technological obsolescence, etc.

Therefore, conservatism makes 1991 a flat year for sales with zero real growth thereafter. COGS and SG&A, as a percentage of sales, will be forecasted at their worst historical levels (1987), which allow for no realization of benefits from Management's cost reduction programs (Exhibit 5). Inventory management, which proved a problem in 1987, has displayed considerable improvement over the past few years. Nonetheless, a measurable decline in demand could quickly impact inventory levels; accordingly, project inventory days at their approximate historical average of 72 days.

In analyzing the Sensitized Case cash flow statement, it can immediately be seen that there exists cash flow for debt service shortfalls in years 1992 through 1995 (Exhibit 7). Keeping in mind that this is a projected worst case scenario, these cash deficiencies are not as alarming as they seem. First, working capital and CAPEX needs, the bare minimum, are easily funded through cash from operating activities. Second, there exists some balance sheet cash as well as a $60 million revolver which can (and usually will) be utilized to temporarily fund the principal payment shortfalls (based on monthly working capital projections, the term loan amortization is scheduled during periods of full revolver availability). Third, the refinancing risk is mitigated given strong asset coverage. Allowing 85% eligibility for receivables and 50% for inventory, a 12/31/95 borrowing base of $160.0 million covers the 12/31/95 $47.4 million revolver balance by more than 3.3X. Overall, under this scenario the bank debt is in fact reduced by nearly 80% of the original balance, again mitigating the refinancing risk.

The Sensitized Case provides a good downside view of XYZ, with 1991 through 1995 cumulative cash flow from operating activities approximately 27% lower than the Management Case. EBITDA-CAPEX/Cash Interest coverage remains at more than adequate levels throughout the life of the loan, while fixed charge coverage stays noticeably close to the 1:1 level during the latter years of the loan (Exhibit 5). It is important that a company can at least cover interest out of cash flow, because under a worst case scenario there may be a refinancing alternative if the amortization schedule becomes overly burdensome. However, refinancing is a risk, particularly when the company has not met scheduled principal payments. Accordingly, refinancing and asset sales as a secondary source of repayment must be analyzed as part of the investment process.

The cash flow analysis is one of the most important tools utilized during the credit process. Though the balance sheet and income statement provide the creditor with data needed to measure the financial and operational condition of a company, the cash flow statement is crucial in assessing the ability of a borrower to repay debt. Without such information—as well as the ability to analyze it—the creditor risks extending financing to an unworthy borrower or, at the opposite end of the spectrum, foregoing an attractive return on a senior bank debt investment.

Contingent Risks

The credit analysis must extend to identifying any contingent risks that may exist. These contingent risks may be the result of direct or indirect business operations of the company and are usually reflected in the footnotes accompanying the audited financial statements. While many contingent risks exist, the following are general categories of contingent risks:

- environmental

- pension fund liability

- litigation

- interest rate risk

- foreign currency risk

Environmental risk is an increasing concern to many companies. Acute public awareness and stricter laws and enforcement have elevated this risk. Monetary penalties for violation of environmental requirements can have a severe impact on cash flow. In particular, toxic-related environmental issues are of significant concern and should be reviewed accordingly. Proper due diligence would require an acceptable environmental audit.

Underfunded pension liabilities can result in a negative cash flow for the company and thus result in pressuring debt service capability. Recently, there has been increased scrutiny over the status of corporate pension fund liabilities. Analysis should review what liabilities, if any, the company may have towards its pension fund.

Third party litigation activity against the company should be closely reviewed and the seriousness of any claims assessed. Much of the outstanding litigation may not have a material impact on the financial condition of a company, an opinion many times offered by management. However, the circumstances and issues contained in the litigation should be identified. It would be prudent to discuss with counsel any litigation against the company that appears serious or unusual in order to measure the degree of potential severity. Litigation can result in large and unforeseen cash outlays by the company.

Bank debt borrowings are primarily a floating rate cost to the company. Accordingly, as interest rates increase, so do the company's interest costs. A company's interest rate exposure can significantly increase in certain rate environments. The assessment of a company's interest rate exposure includes determining its interest costs during different rate scenarios. The company may hedge its rate exposure through interest rate swaps or other derivative products such as caps and floors. Analysis should conclude the degree of exposure, and, what the impact is on cash flow under a worst case rate scenario.

Credit analysis also measures a company's foreign exchange exposure to determine the impact of changing currency prices. Companies with foreign operations most likely depend on foreign earnings to be repatriated for debt service requirements. Therefore, the weakening of a foreign currency may reduce the level of dollars available for debt service, regardless of stable or increased foreign operating profits. Determining the company's level of foreign exchange exposure and what, if any, hedging techniques are being used by the company to mitigate this risk, are a necessary part of the overall analysis.

SECONDARY SOURCE OF REPAYMENT

Senior bank financing relies on operating cash flow as the primary source of repayment. However, unforeseen events may occur that negatively impact a borrower's cash flow and, consequently, the ability to repay its obligations in a timely manner.

In order to satisfy the position of a senior secured creditor, the borrower will then be compelled to seek a secondary source of funds as a method of repayment. Therefore, the investor should also assess the secondary means of repayment, which can be sourced through asset sales and/or refinancing.

A company can raise needed funds selling subsidiaries, divisions, or specific current assets (receivables and inventory) and noncurrent assets (sale-leasebacks, etc.). A company can also be sold in its entirety, if conditions warrant.

The analysis of the secondary source of repayment assesses the company's potential to sell assets at a value necessary to retire the senior bank debt facility. A good measurement of this value or secondary coverage is the Senior Bank Debt/EBITDA ratio. This ratio will indicate what cash flow multiple the company needs to be sold for, in its entirety, to make the senior lenders whole at any point during the life of the loan. A division by division or segment by segment valuation can also be performed, as well as appraisals on owned properties.

Another available secondary source of repayment is refinancing. This generally involves a lender or institution providing funds to a company so that it may repay its current debt obligations. Refinancing the senior debt facility will most likely result in lower interest costs and increased flexibility for the company depending on the circumstances.

The recognition and analysis of secondary sources of repayment are important to the overall investment analysis. Secondary sources of repayment provide additional means for investment protection. This is another advantage for senior bank creditors, who receive priority payments resulting from asset sales or refinancing activity.

COVENANTS

During the documentation process of a bank credit facility the inclusion of covenants pertaining to the obligor's current and future financial operating status is extremely important. Covenants are a vital part of the credit agreement. They provide the lender with the tools to monitor closely the obligor's financial and operating status and provide a legal basis to accelerate the credit facility should one of the covenants be breached. The covenant provisions in a credit agreement give the lender the legal right to determine whether or not to accelerate a credit facility prior to the further deterioration of the obligor's operating and financial condition.

A covenant is essentially a legal commitment by the obligor that certain acts will be strictly followed and other acts will be prohibited. The specific acts, as described below, are defined by the lender and agreed to by the obligor. These acts cover a wide range of activity and normally depend on the obligor's capital structure at the time the credit agreement is executed and what the predicted capital structure most likely will be going forward. Generally, the more highly leveraged a company is, the more restrictive the covenants.

Covenants are divided into two categories: affirmative covenants and negative covenants. Affirmative covenants are acts which the lender has stated the obligor is required to perform. Negative covenants are acts, defined by the lender, which are legally prohibited by the obligor. Although the grace period permitted to remedy a breach of a certain affirmative and negative covenant varies, if the obligor violates a covenant then the lender has the legal right to accelerate its credit facility and demand payment and/or termination of the credit agreement. The breach of a covenant is called an event of default.

The main purpose of covenants in a credit agreement is to set guidelines for the operations of the borrower's business to ensure that the borrower will conduct its business so as to remain credit worthy during the period of the credit agreement.

Affirmative Covenants

Affirmative covenants are actions which are required by the obligor. The intention of affirmative covenants is to require the company to continue operating as a going business concern in a similar fashion as when the credit agreement was executed. These covenants require that the company maintain accurate financial accounting which is then reported to the lender in a timely manner. Although by no means an exhaustive list, typical affirmative covenants identified by the lender and placed in the credit agreement are presented below.

Financial Statements. The obligor must send its financial statements to the lender. The financial statements are prepared in accordance with Generally Accepted Accounting Principals (GAAP) and are usually on a consolidated basis. The financial statements include the balance sheet, income statement, cash flow statement and capitalization statement. Depending on the situation, a lender may require to see the financial statements on a subsidiary or divisional consolidating basis. Again, depending upon the situation, these may be required on a monthly or a quarterly basis. There is always some limitation on time, such as 45 days following the end of the month or quarter, by which the company must send to the lender the financial statements.

The financial statements issued at the end of the fiscal year must always be audited by an independent certified public accounting firm acceptable to the lender. These should be reported without qualification arising out of the scope of the audit.

Certificates. Certificates are statements by both the independent certified public accountants and the responsible financial officer that the company has not breached any covenants or other provisions in the credit agreement and has performed to all the terms and conditions contained in the credit agreement. These certificates, which are testimony that there are no events of default, are normally sent to the lender concurrently with the financial statements.

Conduct of Business and Maintenance of Existence. The company agrees that it will continue to engage in business of the same general type as it is conducting during the time that the credit agreement is executed. It agrees to maintain corporate existence and take all reasonable action to maintain this corporate existence going forward.

Notices. This particular affirmative covenant is quite important to the lender because it requires the obligor to promptly or within a specified period of days notify the lender that the company has violated one of the terms and conditions in the credit agreement as well as a violation of any of the company's other contractual obligations. The company must notify the lender on a wide range of possible areas. This protects the lender in that it puts the responsibility with the obligor to closely monitor its ongoing business.

Foremost, the company must give notice of the occurrence of any event of default pertaining to the credit agreement and any other contractual obligation of the company. Other areas may include notifying the lender of the following: litigation, potential occurrence of an event of default, and any material adverse change in the business.

Use of Proceeds. The lender may request that the use of the particular credit facility be for a specific purpose. Typical uses include general corporate purposes, back-up liquidity support for a commercial paper program, capital expenditure programs, etc.

Negative Covenants

Negative covenants are acts which are prohibited by the obligor. These acts are specified by the lender and agreed to by the obligor. They differ from affirmative covenants in that they primarily focus on the obligor's current and future operating and financial position. While affirmative covenants require the obligor to perform certain acts with respect to reporting and requirements, negative covenants prohibit the obligor from engaging in certain acts such as increasing its indebtedness or merging with another company.

Important in the negative covenant section are the provisions located under the subsection of financial covenants. Financial covenants act as a barometer for the lender to continually gauge the ongoing financial performance of the obligor against specified targets. These targets such as interest coverage tests and debt/equity tests are set at the time of execution of the credit agreement and cover the life of the credit agreement. The obligor must meet these targets normally on a monthly or quarterly basis. If the company fails to meet these targets then there is an event of default and the lender will have the option to accelerate the credit facility.

As with affirmative covenants, negative covenants are negotiated between the lender and the obligor. Negative covenants vary widely among credit agreements. Normally a company which has a high debt-equity ratio will be in a weaker negotiating position and have to accept more restrictive financial covenants than a company that has a lower debt-equity ratio. While not an exhaustive list, the following outlines the most commonly found negative covenants in the credit agreement.

Financial Covenants. As mentioned above, financial covenants are based on the company's current financial statements and projected forward during the life of the credit agreement. Financial covenants protect the lender in that they set up credit parameters around which the lender is willing to keep the credit facility outstanding. If the company fails to meet the financial covenants then the company begins to take on a different creditworthiness than the lender had originally intended. The lender then has the option whether or not to accelerate its credit facility. For discussion purposes take the case of Company XYZ credit facility and refer to Exhibits 1 through 8 for financial information.

Based on historical and projected financial information the financial covenants are constructed. The following summarizes the major financial covenants typically required by senior bank lenders:

Interest Coverage Ratio: This covenant allows for an event of default if the obligor does not meet the agreed upon ongoing interest coverage tests. The Interest Coverage Ratio would be defined in the definition section of the credit agreement. Here it is defined as earnings before interest, taxes, depreciation and amortization (EBITDA) divided by the cash interest expense. For purposes of this example, a lender may require the following: maintain an Interest Coverage Ratio as of the end of each fiscal quarter for the immediately preceding twelve-month fiscal period at least the ratios specified in the following schedule:

> For fiscal quarters ending
> through December 31, 1991:   1.5X
>
> For fiscal quarters ending
> through December 31, 1992:   2.0X

For fiscal quarters ending through December 31, 1993:	2.5X
For fiscal quarters ending through December 31, 1994:	2.5X
For fiscal quarters ending through December 31, 1995:	2.5X

Fixed Charge Ratio: The Fixed Charge Ratio test is similar to the Interest Coverage Ratio test in that it commonly will use EBITDA as the numerator of the ratio. The denominator is a combination of the debt service expense with the other fixed charge obligations of the company. These most common fixed charge obligations relate to capital expenditures and to long-term lease arrangements.

In this example, the Fixed Charge Ratio is defined as EBITDA divided by the cash interest expense plus scheduled principal payment plus capital expenditures plus the lease expense. The obligor must maintain a Fixed Charge Ratio as of the end of each fiscal quarter for the immediately preceding twelve-month fiscal period at at least the ratios specified in the following schedule:

For fiscal quarters ending through December 31, 1991:	1.1X
For fiscal quarters ending through December 31, 1992:	1.2X
For fiscal quarters ending through December 31, 1993:	1.3X
For fiscal quarters ending through December 31, 1994:	1.4X
For fiscal quarters ending through December 31, 1995:	1.5X

Funded Debt to Cash Flow: This is a leverage test which prohibits the company from placing to much debt in its capital structure vis-a-vis its cash flow levels. The lender wants to ensure that the obligor can continue to support its debt service. The lender can protect itself with the inclusion of this funded debt to cash flow test. In this case, funded debt to cash flow ratio is defined as total funded debt divided by EBITDA. In this case the company would be prohibited to have such a ratio higher than the following schedule:

> For fiscal quarters ending
> through December 31, 1991:   3.3X
>
> For fiscal quarters ending
> through December 31, 1992:   3.0X
>
> For fiscal quarters ending
> through December 31, 1993:   2.7X
>
> For fiscal quarters ending
> through December 31, 1994:   2.4X
>
> For fiscal quarters ending
> through December 31, 1995:   2.1X

Maintenance of Net Worth: Although it may be categorized as a type of leverage test, this financial covenant protects the lender against erosion of the capital base of the company. A company could meet the interest coverage test and the debt to total capital test and be losing the value of its net worth. This is the lender's cushion and when it decreases so does the creditworthiness of the company. A lender needs to closely monitor this cushion with the option of accelerating the credit facility if it is decreasing to an unacceptable level. In this case Net Worth is defined as assets minus liabilities and would have the following schedule:

> For fiscal quarters ending
> through December 31, 1991:   160,000,000
>
> For fiscal quarters ending
> through December 31, 1992:   180,000,000

For fiscal quarters ending
through December 31, 1993:   200,000,000

For fiscal quarters ending
through December 31, 1994:   220,000,000

For fiscal quarters ending
through December 31, 1995:   240,000,000

Summary of Financial Covenants: Financial covenants vary greatly depending upon the particular credit facility and the company which is the obligor. There are many ways a lender may hold a company in check and the above represent only some of the more commonly found financial covenants. These set up parameters around which a lender is willing to keep its credit facility outstanding at the agreed upon terms and conditions. During the negotiation process the lender is always looking for more restrictive covenants while the obligor would prefer to have none at all in order to have ultimate financial flexibility.

Limitation on Indebtedness. The lender would like to prohibit the amount of debt that the obligor is able to place next to its credit facility. At the least, a lender should know how much debt the obligor is able to put on its balance sheet pari passu with the lender or even below in a subordinate position. This covenant clearly states the additional debt that the obligor is able to borrow.

Limitation of Liens (Negative Pledge). If the credit facility is partially secured or unsecured then the lender wants to prohibit the obligor from attempting a new credit facility that is secured by unencumbered assets. This covenant prohibits the obligor from allowing liens on its assets for any reason. It is normal, though, for certain assets to be "carved out" of this provision, such as equipment, on which the obligor could undertake a sale/leaseback. All proceeds from such a financing would typically go towards repayment of the existing senior bank facility. All issues concerning the possibility of future liens on assets are raised and agreed upon by the obligor and lender at the time of the establishment of the senior bank credit facility.

Limitation on Sale of Assets. This covenant prohibits the obligor from selling, leasing, assigning, transferring or otherwise disposing of any of its property, business or assets whether now owned or hereafter acquired. Normally there is a specified list of assets that the company may consider to sell in the future and accordingly these may be carved out of this covenant. If the company would like to sell other assets it is prohibited unless the lender agrees to it.

Consolidations, Mergers, etc. This covenant prohibits the company from merging with, or into, or consolidating with, any other person. Person is normally defined in the definition section of the credit agreement as any entity other than the obligor itself. This protects the lender in that the company will maintain its current business existence and not dramatically change through some type of buyout or consolidation.

Change of Ownership. This covenant further clarifies the point that the company cannot be acquired by another entity. The obligor must maintain its current ownership structure and any violation of this will result in the lender having the option to accelerate its credit facility.

The borrower's failure to comply with a covenant is usually a sign that it is in financial difficulty. Depending on the terms of the credit agreement, the borrower's breach of a covenant is either a default or an event of default. Upon the occurrence of an event of default, the bank has the right to exercise all the remedies provided for in the credit agreement.

Typically, these remedies include termination of the bank's obligation to make additional loans and the immediate repayment in full of all outstanding loans. In most cases, the credit agreement gives the borrower a period of time, commonly referred to as a cure or grace period, to correct its breach of a covenant. If a default is not cured by the end of the grace period, then the default becomes an event of default, then the bank can permanently terminate its obligation to make loans and demand repayment in full of all outstanding loans.

Waivers and Amendments

When an affirmative and negative covenant are violated this does not necessarily mean that the lender will accelerate or terminate the credit facility. If an event of default appears likely or actually does occur the lender may choose to waive or amend the particular covenant in order to keep the credit facility outstanding.

Waiver. A waiver is the action of allowing the obligor to violate one of the terms and conditions of the credit agreement, including the covenants. A waiver may occur prior to an event of default or after an event of default is recognized. The lender may believe that the company will violate a particular covenant during a specified period but ultimately the company will be able to meet the covenant. For example, if the company's Interest Coverage Ratio will be below the covenant test for one quarter due to very specific one time events, then the lender may choose to waive this covenant test for the quarter. After the quarter the covenant at the same level will again be effective.

Amendment. An amendment to one of the terms and conditions of the credit agreement results in the permanent change of the terms and conditions of the credit agreement. A waiver is on a temporary basis while the amendment permanently effects the credit agreement.

There are many examples for why a credit agreement may be amended. For example, if the lender is looking to make a large acquisition for which it needs to borrow a substantial amount of debt, the lender may approve this and agree to amend the financial covenants and other terms and conditions to allow this acquisition to proceed.

Any waiver or amendment of covenant terms and conditions in the credit agreement must be agreed to by a predetermined percentage of the senior bank creditors. Changes to the credit agreement that effect interest, principal or security usually must be agreed to by all of the senior bank creditors.

SECURITY

A credit facility is designed to either be on a secured basis or an unsecured basis. A secured basis is where there is some type of asset which backs up the credit facility. Typical assets include the following: accounts receivable, inventories, property, plant and equipment, subsidiary stock, trademarks, etc. The value of the assets is normally higher than the amount of the credit facility. These assets may be the final resort for the lender to be made whole in the case that the obligor is unable to make total repayment. The security must be carefully outlined in the credit agreement and liens on these assets by the lender must be perfected.

Conditions Precedent

The assets which constitute the agreed upon security for the credit agreement are initially outlined in the Conditions Precedent section of the credit agreement. This section describes the mechanisms by which the lender will perfect its liens on these specified assets. The following will describe the typical documentation processes which are used to perfect the security interests for the lender. These agreements are appendixes to the credit agreement and are between the lender and the obligor.

Security Agreement. This agreement focuses on the current assets of the company. It grants to the lender the security interest in the agreed upon lender's current assets such as accounts receivable and inventory. The agreement outlines how the obligor will maintain its current assets. It also prohibits the obligor from granting any other interests in these assets.

Real Property and Equipment Security Agreement. Often the security for a credit facility may be the fixed assets of the company. These assets may include the equipment contained in a manufacturing facility as well as the real estate which is owned by the company. This agreement between the lender and the obligor grants to the lender the perfected security interest in the agreed upon fixed assets.

The agreement normally contains a clause that there have been unqualified Uniform Commercial Code (UCC) financial filings with the respective governmental agency. In order to aviod confusion, a governmental agency will record liens which are placed on fixed assets. Through a filing one can determine if there are already existing liens on the fixed assets. The lender protects itself by filing the UCC because it knows that it has the sole lien on the particular asset. Also if there is a subsequent filing by another party then the lender will be notified. UCC filings are highly recommended and are normally a condition precedent to executing the credit agreement.

Contained in the Real Property and Equipment Security Agreement is the manner by which the obligor will maintain the shape and value of the assets. It also prohibits the obligor from granting liens to any other potential lender.

Pledge Agreement. The pledge agreement is used to perfect the interest in the stock of the company or of the company's subsidiaries. This is used in the case where the security of a credit facility is the stock of the obligor or the obligor's subsidiaries. This agreement prohibits the company from pledging the stock to a third party.

Chapter 7

Bank Loans in a Bond Market Context: Nominal Yields and Default Patterns

STEVEN C. MILLER
ANALYST
LOAN PRICING CORPORATION

This chapter discusses the return of broadly syndicated commercial loans in a bond market context. The first part looks at the nominal yields of bank term loans as measured by fixed-rate equivalents and compares

Portions of this chapter were originally published in *The Loan Pricing Report*, Volume 4, Number 4, April, 1991. The author would like to thank Christopher L. Snyder, Jr., and Floyd A. Loomis for their direction and feedback in conducting the research and analysis covered in this chapter. Mike Sepesi provided invaluable fact-checking and feedback which helped maintain the accuracy of this research. Also, Christopher Bumcrot provided guidance in developing techniques we used to calculate the yield-to-maturity of bank term loans.

them to the subordinated debt of the same issuer. The following section presents a summary of some of our initial findings on default rates.

BOND EQUIVALENTS

Looking at bank loans in the context of the bond market and other capital markets is clearly a necessary, though difficult, exercise if commercial loans are to be packaged and sold outside the banking industry on a large scale. Banks are struggling to redefine their roles as financial intermediaries. Several factors, including the rise of savings vehicles outside the banking industry, the growth of pension and mutual funds as repositories for consumer deposits, and capital adequacy guidelines, have helped to undermine the position of banks.

Today, institutional investors provide capital directly to companies through the private placement and public capital markets. Banks are looking to institutional investors as a potential source of capital for commercial lending. However, in order to make a compelling case for bank loans to institutional investors, either directly through the sale of assignments or indirectly through the sale of shares in a securitized pool, banks must: (1) speak a language institutional investors are accustomed to (i.e., yield-to-maturity and spread over Treasuries) and (2) offer a product palatable to nonbank institutions.

In building a bridge between bank loans and other investments, we have developed a yield-to-maturity (YTM) calculation method, which is discussed later in this chapter. This calculation is designed to provide a sense of the nominal return of bank loans in a bond market context. The implied YTM can be used as a translator between the LIBOR spreads understood by banks and the yields used by non-cash flow based investors.

Tenor and Implied Bank Loan Yields

Most bankers agree that term loans are rarely repaid on schedule. Generally, bank loans are either repaid early or refinanced at a lower coupon if the financial condition of the company improves, or extended if the company's cash flow becomes tight. The former is generally referred to as a positive refinancing, while the latter is a negative refinancing. Because of the prepayment option allowed in most bank loans, it is impossible to swap floating-rate for fixed-rate payments and thereby derive a true YTM. However, swapping floating-rate LIBOR payments for a fixed-rate equivalent over Treasuries gives a market view of the expected interest levels at each maturity date. This can service as a market-based proxy for expected yield.

Looking at a generic bank loan priced at LIBOR plus 250 basis points with an expected average life of four years, it becomes clear how the secondary pricing level and a loan's average life affect expected yield. If an investor purchases the loan at 100 basis points in upfront fees, or 99, and the initial repayment schedule is adhered to, the loan would generate a yield of 12.51%.

Exhibit 1 shows the expected yield different purchase prices would generate given a one to five year average life. It is clear that as the discount to par increases, the yield increases sharply as average life extends. When the discount is lower, the overall yield may actually increase as the average life extends because the base Treasury and swap rates, which are used in the YTM model to approximate the expected coupon, are higher. In this example, the yield derived at a four-year average life may be somewhat understated because the difference between the three- and four-year Treasury rate was 14 basis points. Other year-to-year increases are more dramatic.

Nominal Yield Comparisons: Senior Secured and Subordinated Debt

Bank loans and bonds are clearly two very different types of instruments with their own unique characteristics. Even within the universe of bank loans and bonds, discreet types of agreements exist. In general, bonds are publicly registered, fixed-rate instruments written with bullet maturities and specific call provisions. Typically, issuers report financial performance every three months through public disclosures. Bonds may have negative pledges to insure that the company does not offer assets as security to a new creditor; however, the covenants generally provide the borrower with a great deal of flexibility to undertake corporate and financial initiatives. Bank loans, by contrast, are generally floating-rate instruments priced at a spread over LIBOR. These instruments are, for the most part, the most senior debt in the capital structure. The bank creditor typically receives monthly updates of a company's performance. This information is not in the public domain, meaning that banks are privy to insider information. Bank loans typically allow borrowers the option to prepay at quarterly interest payment dates with little or no penalty. HLT and non-investment grade bank credits generally are secured with assets

Exhibit 1
Implied Yield-To-Maturity at Different Price Levels and Average Half Life

This exhibit shows the expected yield different purchase prices would generate on a bank term loan priced at LIBOR plus 250 basis points given a one- to five-year maturity. The yields are derived by swapping floating-rate LIBOR for a fixed-rate spread over Treasuries. It is clear that as the discount-to-par increases, the yield declines sharply as average life extends. When the discount is lower, the overall yield may actually increase as the average life extends because the base Treasury and swap rates, which are used in the YTM model to approximate the expected coupon, are higher. In this example, the yield derived at a four-year average life may be somewhat understated because the difference between the three- and four-year Treasury rate was 14 basis points. Other year-to-year increases are more dramatic.

Average Life

Purchase Price	One Year	Two Year	Three Year	Four Year	Five Year
99	12.18%	12.18%	12.33%	12.51%	12.67%
98	13.38%	12.82%	12.78%	12.85%	13.19%
97	14.60%	13.45%	13.23%	13.21%	13.72%
96	15.82%	14.10%	13.68%	13.58%	14.26%
95	17.09%	14.76%	14.15%	13.95%	14.81%

Date: March 1990.

of the company and hold restrictive covenants which force the borrower to prepay loans with excess cash flow or proceeds from asset sales.

Key Comparisons

Despite these clear differences, the YTM calculation provides at least a theoretical way to measure the expected nominal returns of bank loans against subordinated bonds. Looking at the bank loan and public debt markets as of the first quarter of 1991, some striking comparisons can be seen. Exhibit 2 lists the expected yield and secondary market prices on the senior and subordinated issues of four borrowers. Though this chapter does not purport to be an investment advisory or make any representations about the value of one investment versus another, several examples provide a compelling case for bank loans in the context of the public bond market.

For example, RJR Nabisco's four-year, $3.5 billion term loan (RJR I) was confirmed to have traded in March 1991 at 275 basis points in upfront fees, or a purchase price of 97.25. At the time of the trade, this loan would have generated an implied YTM of 11.6%. RJR's $2.25 billion recapitalization term loan (RJR II), issued in 1990 in order to refinance some of the company's original issue, high-yield bonds, has been quoted in the market at 98.5, or an implied YTM of 12.2%. The spread over average Treasuries of these loans was about 370 basis points for RJR I and 410 basis points for RJR II. The difference can be attributed to the difference in average life, since the RJR I facility pays in full before the first principal payment on the six-year loan kicks in.

Publicly traded RJR bonds trade at a variety of levels, based on their position in the capital structure. The company's pre-existing 9.25% senior notes, due in 1995, trade at 97, or a YTM of 10.25%. This translates to a 270 basis points spread over applicable Treasuries. These notes are considered *pari passu* to bank loans. The company's 13.5%, senior subordinated bonds, which were issued as part of the 1989 leveraged buyout transaction, trade at 104.38, or a YTM of 12.71. This translates to a spread over Treasuries of 470 basis points.

Fort Howard, Georgia Gulf, and Kroger Co., are other examples of how close in yield, measured by the spread over Treasuries, the senior secured and subordinated debt of a single borrower can trade in the secondary market. The next section of this chapter addresses the ultimate yield of bank loans and subordinated debt of the same issuer in a liquidation scenario.

Exhibit 2
Yield Comparisons: Senior Secured and Subordinated Debt

	Credit Class	Stated Coupon	Indicated Quote (% of Par)	Stated Maturity	Implied YTM	Spread Over Avg T-rate (bps)
RJR Nabisco[1]	Term Loan (I)	L+250	97.50	12/31/94	11.50%	360
	Term Loan (II)	L+350	98.25	09/30/96	12.20	410
	Sr Nts[2]	9.25%	96.38	05/01/95	10.25%	270
	SF Deb	8.38	77.63	05/15/17	11.00	275
	Sub Deb	13.50	104.38	05/15/01	12.71	470
Fort Howard	Term Loan	L+225	99.50	12/31/96	9.38	272
	Sub Deb	12.38%	98.50	11/30/97	12.71	484
Georgia Gulf	Term Loan	L+250	99.75	12/30/97	10.82	346
	Sr Sub Deb	14.10%	104.50	04/30/00	14.10	608
Kroger Co.	Term Loan	L+125	100.00	12/31/96	8.87	181
	Sr Sub Deb	12.88%	105.50	01/15/99	11.83	383

[1]RJR was refinanced in November 1991.
[2]Pre-acquisition debt. Considered *pari passu* to the bank loans.
Sources: All yield calculations and pricing for bank term loans provided by Loan Pricing Corp., bond information on RJR Nabisco provided by Continental Bank (Chicago), all other bond pricing data supplied by Salomon Brothers. Date: April 1, 1990.

In making the yield comparisons, it is important to note that it has become increasingly attractive to equity holders or potential acquirers to repurchase subordinated debt of a highly leveraged company at market prices. This is because subordinated debt can often yield between 15-25% at secondary market prices, while bank debt accrues at about 11%. Therefore, the price of some subordinated debt issues increased dramatically during the second half of 1990 and the first quarter of 1991. This has been particularly true for "brand name" borrowers, such as RJR Nabisco, Supermarkets General, R.H. Macy & Co., and Fort Howard, which have repurchased subordinated debt at discounted levels.

An Arbitrage Opportunity

In theory, it appears that a perfect arbitrage play would be to go long the bank debt and short the subordinated debt of select issuers, because the risk of loss is clearly higher for subordinated debt while the yields are comparable. In reality, this type of arbitrage scheme could break down if the company is acquired or announces a bond repurchase program. Even though the bank debt may come out whole while the subordinated debt is repurchased at a discount to par, as the next section of this chapter shows, this could still represent a loss on the arbitrage play because the difference between the market price and the ultimate purchase price may be far wider in the subordinated debt market than the bank market.

Key Examples

For example, Tonka Corp.'s bank debt had been quoted in the 85-90 range in late 1990 during the depth of the company's financial problems. During the same time period, the company's subordinated debt had been quoted in the 45-50 range. Hasbro offered to acquire the toy maker in a deal worth 100 cents on the dollar to bank creditors and 75-80 on the dollar to subordinated debtholders. If an investor had shorted the subordinated and taken a long position in the bank debt, he would have suffered a significant loss as a result of the buyout. Though this is an extreme example, this type of movement can occur because senior secured debt tends to trade at, or close to, par.

Fort Howard's 12.375% subordinated debt increased in price from 77 cents on the dollar during the third quarter of 1990 to 94 by February 1991 on the strength of a $250 million equity infusion and a debt repurchase program. Over the same period of time, indicative quotes for the bank debt increased from 98 to 99.5. Similarly, RJR Nabisco's 13.5% subordinated bonds have increased in price on the secondary market by over 10% during the first quarter of 1991, while the company's bank debt has risen from about 95.5 cents on the dollar to 98.5, or about 3.15%.

While these examples provide pause to investors looking at senior to subordinated debt arbitrage, the fact remains that in many highly leveraged situations the senior secured and subordinated debt can be extremely close in yield, even on a nominal basis. Based on the senior secured status of bank loans, a case for bank loans can begin to be made, particularly in view of the ultimate returns discussed in the next section.

Applying Yield-To-Maturity to Bank Loans

The YTM calculation gives commercial banks two key tools. One is a way to compare the yield of bank loans based on their stated coupon, repayment schedule, and fee income, with the public debt of comparable borrowers. This comparable analysis can also be used in comparing bank loans to privately placed instruments. Second, the YTM calculation can be sued in syndication or selling loans to non-bank institutions as a starting point for a nonbank to judge the nominal yield of a potential investment.

There are a number of weaknesses inherent in the yield-to-maturity calculation. First, bank loans generally allow optional prepayments and leveraged loans call for mandatory prepayments tied to events. This makes the stated repayment schedule of a bank loan tentative. Therefore, it is impossible to swap the floating interest payments associated with bank loans for a fixed rate equivalent through the financial market. Another problem is that the yield-to-maturity calculation is basically an internal rate of return (IRR) figure, which assumes that repayments can be invested at the initial coupon rate. Despite these problems, the IRR is a starting point, offering investors a sense of nominal return, but does not incorporate the risk of default.

Yield-To-Maturity Calculation

Our yield-to-maturity analysis consists of several elements. First, the term loan is divided into payment strips. Second, floating-rate LIBOR is converted to a fixed rate equivalent, or a bond equivalent yield (BEY), at each payment date using the applicable Treasury rate and swap spread. The model computes an average BEY for the loan as a whole, weighted by the amount outstanding at each payment date and the length of the strip in terms of time outstanding. Then, the discount—defined in most cases as the upfront fee passed along to a secondary investor—is amortized over the life of the loan in order to derive an implied YTM. As previously mentioned, substantial early repayments or extension of the repayment schedule can have a profound effect on a loan's return and therefore YTMs are quoted as implied.

DEFAULT AND REPAYMENT PATTERNS FOR BANK LOANS

Overall Return Comparisons in Liquidation and Reorganization: Senior and Subordinated Debt

Though no broad statistics exist, several reorganizations completed or proposed during the fourth quarter of 1990 and first quarter of 1991 suggest that while the nominal rates of bank loans are substantially lower than that offered by subordinated debt, the ultimate yield may be substantially higher. Exhibit 3 outlines how different classes of debtors fared in the acquisition of three large corporate borrowers.

Key Examples

In February 1991, Cinema General announced plans to acquire Harcourt Brace Jovanovich; Hicks Muse & Co. purchased MorningStar Foods; and Hasbro Inc. acquired Tonka Corp. In all three cases, the bank loans were made whole prior to, or as a result of, the acquisition. Using an internal rate of return (IRR) method, the banks loans averaged a return of about 10.5-11.0%, using an average LIBOR rate of 8%. The original issue bonds issued as part of the initial LBO and recapitalization transactions of these debtors were paid out at various percentage of face value. Exhibit 3 shows the annualized yield of the bonds.

- **Harcourt Brace Jovanovich:** The company underwent a recapitalization in 1988. It has five classes of original issue high-yield bonds outstanding. General Cinema purchased its 13% senior notes, issued in 1988, at 93% of par. This translates into an annual yield of 2.8%. An issue of 14% senior subordinated was acquired at 77 cents on the dollar or a yield of 2.32%. HBJ subordinated

Exhibit 3
The Effect of Recovery Values on Ultimate Yields

	Issue Date	Assumed Restructuring Date	Coupon	Recovery Rate	Estimated IRR
MorningStar					
Term Loan	1/30/88	3/30/91	L+250	100.0	10.75%
Sr Sub	1/30/88	3/30/91	13.00%	52.0	-1.35
Tonka					
Term Loan	12/30/86	3/30/91	L+250	100.0	11.20%
Sub Deb A	12/30/86	3/30/91	16.25%	80.0	2.95
Sub Deb B	3/30/87	3/30/91	17.25	75.0	2.96
HBJ					
Term Loan	12/30/86	3/30/91	L+250	100.0	10.50%
Sr Nts	12/30/87	3/30/91	13.00%	93.0	2.80
Sr Sub	12/30/86	3/30/91	14.00	77.0	2.32
Sub Deb	6/30/86	3/30/91	14.25	48.5	-1.00
Sub Disc Deb	6/30/87	3/30/91	14.75	32.4	-6.41

Source: Loan Pricing Corporation

debt was repurchased at 42%, this generates an IRR of negative 1%. The subordinated discount bonds generated a negative 6.4% based on the current tender offer.

- **Tonka Corp.:** Hasbro purchased the company in a transaction worth 80 cents on the dollar for its Series A 16.25% bonds, 75 for its Series B 17.25% bonds, and 100 cents on the dollar to its bank creditors. Tonka floated the A and B series of bonds to finance its 1987 LBO. Based on the current tender offer, these bonds would generate an IRR of 2.95% and 2.96%, respectively.

- **MorningStar Foods:** MorningStar was recapitalized in a transaction involving two of its bank creditors and equity investor Hicks Muse & Co. The original bank group came out whole. Subordinated debt, issued as part of its 1988 spin off from Southland Corp., will be repurchased at 52% of face value. Based on this tender offer, and its 13% coupon, the issue would generate an annualized IRR of negative 1.35%.

Reorganization: How do Different Creditor Classes Fare?

Most current distressed restructurings are not as clean as the three discussed above. Exhibits 4 and 5 show how different classes of creditors stand in the restructuring of three large corporate bankruptcies. The essential concession banks are being asked to make in the reorganization of troubled, non-retail companies is a more liberal repayment schedule. In some cases, however, where asset values and cash flow have deteriorated, banks are also asking for equity in exchange for debt forgiveness. The Zapata example is evidence of this trend (see Exhibit 5).

QUANTIFYING DEFAULT RATES ON HLT BANK LOANS

Repayment and default rates for broadly syndicated bank loans are clearly difficult to measure. Analysis of highly leveraged bank loans originated in 1987 and 1988 reveals some interesting patterns. In the 1987 and 1988 cohort, $10.85 billion and $26.65 billion of highly leveraged term loans were originated and funded.

Exhibit 4
The Southland Restructuring Plan

Creditor Class	Initial Commit.	Current Claim	Offer/Concession
Secured			
Bank Term Loan	$2,500	$1,299	Under the proposal, the bank agreed to:
Bank Revolving Credit		215	(1) allow the proceeds of stock sales not to be used to repay the term loans, (2) eliminate the limitations on the revolving credit and letter of credit, (3) lossen cash flow and other financial covenants in line with current projections, and (4) release capital stock pledged as collateral.
Unsecured			Received the following package for each $1,000 of principal amount tendered:
Senior Reset Nts	$593	$593	(1) $475 of 12% Sr Nts, due 12/15/96, (2) 86.5 shares of common stock, (3) $57 in cash, (4) a warrant stock.
Sr Sub Nts	395	395	(1) $650 of 5% first priority Sr Sub debt due 12/15/2003, (2) 40.5 common shares, and (3) warrant.
Sr Sub Disc Nts	392	392	(1) $555 of first priority debt, (2) 35 shares of common stock, (3) warrants to purchase 6.5 shares.
Sub Deb	592	592	(1) $500 of 4.5% second priority Sr Sub Deb due 6/15/2004, (2) 28 shares of common stock, (3) warrant stock.
Jr Sub Deb	50	50	(1) $257 of 4% second priority Sr Sub Deb due 6/15/2004, (2) 11 shares of Common Stock, (3) warrant stock.
Equity			
Cumulative Preferred Stock			Received one share of common stock for each share tendered. The Thompson family, who founded Southland and took the company private in the 1987 leverage to a 5% ownership interest in the company. This interest will be diluted if warrants are exercised.

Exhibit 5
Zapata's Bank Debt Structure

Tranche	Original Amount ($ Mil.)	Current Outstanding ($ Mil.)	Type	Purpose	Coupon	Maturity	Offer/Concession
A	$ 45.0	$ 13.0	RC	WC	P	9/30/96	The banks received a $138 million cash disbursement, and common stock equal to an 85% equity stake in the company, and convert their additional claim of $115 million to a senior, secured note. The note repays over a six-year period, with final September 30, 1997.
B	299.9	301.4	TL	Refin.	P+75		
C	125.0	145.7	TL	Refin.	8.7%	9/30/96	
D	125.0	60.0	TL	Refin.	8.7	9/30/96	

Exhibit 6 shows the repayment and default rates of the 1987 and 1988 loan groups. This type of analysis is extremely new to banks because traditionally, bank loans did not default, they became nonperforming and were generally restructured until they were gradually repaid and/or written off. However, with the growth of the subordinated debt market, many distressed situations have both a layer of bank debt and subordinated claims. This has complicated the restructuring process from the standpoint of senior secured lenders because, unlike dividends on common stock, which can be cut or eliminated when a company's financial performance deteriorates, subordinated creditors can force a company into default.

Default Incidence

The incidence of default among the 1987 and 1988 bank term loans was 15% of the 71 broadly syndicated loans reviewed. This number was skewed by the large number of retail companies that defaulted. The default incidence among retail transactions originated in 1988 was 35%. Default incidence is the number of defaulted loans as a percentage of the original sample set. The default rate is the amount of a loan which goes into default as a percentage of the original commitment amount. The overall default rate found on the 1987 and 1988 loans was 8%. Once retail transactions are factored out, the rate of defaults is 2.5%.

The default incidence among highly leveraged transactions originated in 1987 and 1988 which had both senior secured bank debt and subordinated bonds outstanding was 33% lower for senior secured bank debt than for subordinated debt of the same issuer. This means that for every three debtors that defaulted one had already repaid its bank debt in full. Further, the default rate among these transactions was 45% higher in the bank loan market than in the subordinated debt market. In other words, the collections prior to default on the 1987 and 1988 set of loans was about 55%, while collections on the subordinated debt was negligible.

Retail Industry

Over three quarters of the 1988-originated highly leveraged bank loans we have reviewed that have subsequently defaulted were retail-industry related. Big name retail defaults, including Allied Stores, Ames Department Stores, Federated Department Stores, Best Products, Amdura, and

Exhibit 6
Repayment and Default Rates

Broadly Syndicated Highly Leveraged Loans Originated in 1987 and 1988

	Year One	Year Two	Year Three
Repaid	24.16%	36.00%	62.97%
Outstanding			
Current	68.28%	53.00%	17.82%
Technical Default[1]	7.56%	7.00%	13.00%
Payment Default	0.00%	4.00%	6.21%

[1]Loans are in violation of covenants but still pay interest to banks.
Sample loans: large corporate HLTs of borrowers with sales over $250 million originated in 1987 and 1988.
Sample size: 71 transactions with total dollar volume of $36 billion.
Source: Loan Pricing Corporation (Loan Investor Services)
Date: April 1991

Interco, Inc., have mounted in recent months as consumer spending tailed off and real estate prices continued to slump.

A review of LPC's Public Deals database shows that of the 2,316 highly leveraged loan facilities negotiated by banks in the five years ended December 31, 1990, 121 were retail industry related. Transaction volume of retail issues was $19.3 billion, out of a total universe of 2,316 transactions negotiated with a total deal volume of $416 billion. Though retail bankruptcies are front page news today, these transactions represented only a fraction of the total volume of HLT loans.

Retail industry transactions were typically based on high cash flow expectations. This is because many of the transactions took place during the consumer spending binge of the 1980s and most retail companies are asset-poor and cash-flow rich. Further, the primary assets of most retailers—outside of their name franchise—are inventories, which are pledged to trade creditors; leases, which have declined in value as vacancy rates have increased; and real estate. As consumer spending slows, many highly leveraged retailers lose their key value, cash generation. While this is true for non-retailers, most of these companies have salable assets which can be seized and liquidated in a default.

CONCLUSION

While default incidence is up among broadly syndicated commercial loans, the examples cited in this chapter present a strong case for senior bank debt as a more secure and better yielding form of debt than unsecured bonds. Clearly, much of the HLT secured bank loans have stood up in the restructuring of troubled debt and often are fully or substantially recoverable through collections prior to default and recoveries following default. In fact, the total return generated by the broadly syndicated bank term loans originated in 1987 that we reviewed was significantly in excess of the base LIBOR rate. This is based on cash flows, defaults, recovery levels, and first quarter 1991 trading prices and is exclusive of initial origination fees and amendment fees.

Chapter 8

Basic Analytical Tools for Valuing HLT Bank Loans

CHRISTOPHER REGIS RYAN
VICE PRESIDENT
LOAN PRODUCT MANAGER
LEHMAN BROTHERS

INTRODUCTION

One of the most exciting aspects of the emerging market for highly leveraged transaction (HLT) bank loans is its breadth. Because of the tremendous number of borrowers which have bank loans outstanding, the opportunistic investor may "beat the market" by identifying attractive loans that other investors overlook. Investors able to establish absolute valuation parameters for bank loan investments will capitalize on these market opportunities. They will evaluate an array of loans and continually reexamine their conclusions. Investors having a view as to the "worth" of certain loans will manage their portfolios by comparing the market values of those loans to their perceived "worth."

New investors will enter the HLT market when they believe that bank loans offer superior relative value to the assets they already buy. Intermediaries must be able to make a case for HLT's *vis-à-vis* the customer's investment of choice. Bank loans are attractive to some investors because they offer an alternative investment vehicle in the capital structure of companies with which they are familiar. Because the crossover between bank loan and bond and equity investors is small, there is no market mechanism to create efficiency between the prices of bank loans and the prices of bonds and equity of comparable credits (or even the same company). Therefore, some bank loans may be relatively "cheap" when compared with other investment opportunities having similar risk characteristics.

To determine the attractiveness of a loan on an absolute or relative basis, the investor must develop an opinion of the value of the loan and compare it to the expected purchase price. The valuation of any financial asset is labor intensive and bank loans are no exception. In fact, certain aspects of HLT bank loans require a higher level of scrutiny than that required to value other corporate indebtedness or equity. However, by establishing a basic framework for valuing HLT's, investors may streamline this process.

Like the valuation of other financial assets, the valuation of an HLT bank loan utilizes several different techniques, each of which provides evidence to support the ultimate conclusion. The various pieces of evidence will rarely point to a single answer. Each piece must be weighed according to the applicability of the analysis that produced it. This is what makes valuation an art. The valuation tools described in this chapter will help the investor gather evidence. It is up to the investor to interpret this evidence, weigh it, and draw conclusions.

Similarity to Valuing Corporate Debt Securities

HLT's are senior loans to leveraged corporate issuers. Given this, it should not be surprising that HLT valuation techniques are similar to those techniques used to value high yield and high grade corporate bonds. For example, traditional credit analysis is an important part of the valuation process for all three asset categories. The basic creditworthiness of the underlying borrower is the most critical aspect of HLT valuation. The analysis of the borrower in an HLT valuation is identical to that performed for the bonds of the same issuer and guarantors. This chapter will not address the framework for traditional securities credit analysis and valuation.[1] Rather, it will focus on the specific tools most applicable to valuing HLT bank loans.

Bank loans are different than most corporate securities in many ways. They usually pay interest on a floating rate basis. They are generally senior and often secured. Holders of bank loans sometimes bear unique legal risks because of their status. Many bank loans include revolving credit or letter of credit facilities, in which the lender has ongoing funding obligations. These qualities make HLT's an interesting investment class, but they also require the investor to modify the traditional securities analysis.

Analytical Tools

The analytical tools addressed in this chapter are:

Intrinsic Value. Determines the basic asset values available to cover the loan. Requires a thorough analysis of the left and right hand side of the balance sheet, as well as all "off-balance sheet" assets and liabilities.

Collateral Value. Determines the extent to which a loan's security interests exceed or are less than the amount of the loan. Requires a complete understanding of the collateral pool and its worth. Also requires a detailed study of the legal validity of the HLT's liens and any collateral sharing arrangements. The investor must apply a common sense approach to the importance of the collateral to the ongoing health of the business. This is the most technical of the analytical tools which are outlined in this chapter. Investors may require legal help.

Expected Recovery Value. The investor must attempt to predict the future. What will the borrower's cash flow from operations be under various assumptions? Do expected cash flows cover expected cash needs? How likely is a restructuring? What are the potential outcomes and the probabilities of each?

---

[1] There is a substantial body of work which addresses basic credit analysis for corporate borrowers/issuers. See Jane Tripp Howe, "Credit Analysis for Corporate Bonds," Chapter 22 in Frank J. Fabozzi and Irving M. Pollack (eds), *The Handbook of Fixed Income Securities* (Homewood, IL: Dow Jones-Irwin, 1987). Also see Roger H. Hale, *Credit Analysis: A Complete Guide* (New York, NY: John Wiley & Sons, 1983).

Relative Value Compared With Alternative Investments. Qualitative comparisons: creditworthiness of borrower and guarantors; security interests and collateral; seniority; covenant protection and ability to enforce rights. Quantitative comparisons: current yield; discount margin; yield to maturity (current basis); yield to maturity (swapped basis); intrinsic value; expected recovery value. These tools enable the investor to compare a HLT to a benchmark loan or security with a market price. They allow investors to determine the relative attractiveness of a loan compared with alternative assets

Legal Risks and Analysis

Holders of bank loans are subject to many legal risks, particularly in credits where the interests of other security holders or creditors may be impaired. Because of their superior position in the typical leveraged capital structure, HLT's have the most to lose. Risks include the loss of seniority or security interests. Liens may be attacked as fraudulent transfers or preferences. Loans to leveraged transactions may be attacked because of the nature of the transactions themselves (e.g., fraudulent conveyance). If the lenders behave like owners rather than creditors, their loans may be subordinated to the claims of other creditors. A framework for the analysis of these risks is beyond the scope of this chapter, but their significance should not be minimized.

HLT's are governed by a credit agreement and supporting ancillary documentation, which constitute a contractual arrangement between the banks in the loan syndicate and the borrower. In addition to interest rates, maturity, amortization schedules and covenants, the loan agreement will detail a number of other important considerations, including defaults, representations of the borrower and lender, the structure and documentation of any security interests, and terms and conditions under which the loan may be sold. This chapter will not explicitly address the analysis of loan documentation. However, implementation of the analytical techniques described will require such analysis.[2] Credit agreements are roughly analogous to bond indentures. Investors may choose to seek legal advice with respect to reading and interpreting the loan documentation of any given loan.

---

[2] For a concise overview of the fundamentals of loan documentation, see Robert H. Behrens and James W. Evans, *Fundamentals of Commercial Loan Documentation* (Rolling Meadows, IL: Bank Administration Institute, 1989).

INTRINSIC VALUE

Overview

HLT bank debt offers the investor/lender a rate of return that reflects the perception of the buyer and seller of the likelihood of default and impairment. As the likelihood of an eventual payment default on a loan increases, the yield to maturity required to induce a new investor to make the same loan also rises. Because yield to maturity calculations are based upon the *stated* interest and amortization schedule, at some level of default risk yield to maturity becomes moot. One alternative method of analysis that is more applicable to riskier loans is intrinsic value (asset value) analysis.

An intrinsic value analysis determines the value of a loan as a claim against the pool of assets of the borrower and any other guarantors (i.e., the estate). This requires three basic steps. First, one must determine the value of the assets against which the lender may have a claim. Second, one must determine the extent to which the intrinsic value must be shared. Senior claims may have a prior right to the asset value. Junior claims may require some portion of the asset value in order to permit the HLT lenders to realize the value to which they are entitled. Finally, the investor must estimate the cost to the estate (time value and monetary cost) that must be incurred before values are realized. Generally, investors will pay a price that is a discount to the intrinsic value of the loan they acquire to provide a return on such an investment commensurate with the risk involved.

Determine Asset Value of Borrower

The techniques involved in determining the asset value of an HLT borrower are no different than those used to determine enterprise value *en route* to a fairness ("valuation") opinion or a stock recommendation. The investor must determine going concern, third party sale, and liquidation values of the borrower. One must also analyze the value of any guaranties that may have been provided by entities other than the borrower. Finally, the investor must understand and quantify all operating liabilities (on or off the balance sheet).

While a detailed look at the basics of business valuation would be a digression, it seems in order to mention of a few of the subtleties of valuing HLT borrowers.

Do not assume that a third party sale premium can be realized. While a sale of assets or the business as a whole may be the way to maximize value to the estate, it is very difficult to get all parties involved to agree upon a sale. Once a business (difficult to value) is turned into cash (easy to value), implementation of an absolute priority reorganization becomes easier. Junior claims and equity interests (which usually control the company) are the parties most hurt by absolute priority. Hence, third party sales are rare.

Do not assume that this year's results will predict next year. Companies on the verge of financial difficulty will almost invariably experience deteriorating results. Do not believe projections that were made prior to the company's problems. Treat any new projections with healthy skepticism.

Expect the unexpected. When analyzing the nonfinancial liabilities of the borrower, the investor should assume that any and all problems will come home to roost (and consequently must be settled) before value may be realized by the lenders. Look for potential sources of liability like litigation, employee benefit obligations and environmental or product liability. Other restructuring candidates can provide ideas for problems that may arise involving the business being analyzed.

Determine Loan's Position Relative to Other Obligations

Generally, bank loans are senior indebtedness of the borrower. Many borrowers have other senior indebtedness (usually incurred before the bank loans), which may be *pari passu* with the bank debt. It is important to determine the amount of debt that has an equal ranking to the bank debt. Other things being equal these obligations will share in the asset value of the estate proportionally with the bank loans.

Most highly leveraged transactions involve subordinated debt. These obligations are of lower priority than the bank loans, but their magnitude and relative rights are critical. While absolute priority would indicate that senior obligations be repaid in full before junior claims receive anything, few financial restructurings are accomplished on this basis. Determining the share of the asset value that "belongs" to the subordinated debt is an important step in the analytical process.

Understanding the ownership structure of the borrowing entity is critical. While technically a loan may be a senior obligation of the borrower, the borrower may only have a junior claim on the underlying assets of the business. In this way, a loan may be structurally subordinated to other claims in the borrowing entity. (See Exhibit 1.)

In Exhibit 1, the trade obligations and senior unsecured debt of XYZ Manufacturing are structurally senior to the bank loans of XYZ Holdings. The Senior Secured Bank Loan has a claim on the operating assets of XYZ only through its security interest in the stock of XYZ Manufacturing. Hence, the bank lenders have an equity claim on XYZ Manufacturing assets which has lower priority than all direct claims against XYZ Manufacturing. It is common for bank loans borrowed by a holding company to be guaranteed by the operating subsidiaries on a senior basis. Absent such guaranties, holding company bank debt is structurally subordinated to operating company obligations with respect to the assets of such operating company.

Security interests play an important part in determining a bank loan's position in the borrower's capital structure. Many HLT's are secured, but the collateral will vary. The investor must determine what the collateral is, how much it is worth, and if it is shared. (See Collateral Value). Generally, senior debt incurred pre-HLT is protected by a "negative pledge" covenant, which restricts the imposition of liens against the assets of the borrower without securing the senior debt on an equal and ratable basis. HLT credit agreements are generally written to give the lenders as much access to the collateral as possible given the negative pledge covenant in the pre-HLT indenture. Some credit agreements secure assets not specifically covered by the covenant, some stop short of securing the assets to avoid triggering the covenant, and some simply trigger the covenant.

Exhibit 1
Structural Subordination

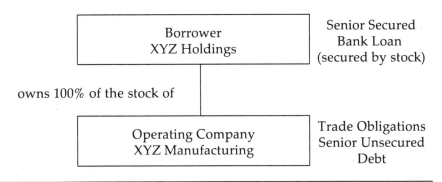

Borrowers often incur indebtedness that is specifically secured by certain assets. Mortgage notes on individual facilities are an example. Some asset specific debt will have a guaranty from the borrower or a subsidiary of the borrower. Intrinsic value analysis requires the investor to understand the relative rights and priority of all asset specific debt.

Estimate Settlement Costs

Settlement costs include legal fees, financial advisory fees and time value. If the restructuring involves significant impairment of the borrower's obligations (i.e., the borrower is insolvent), these costs can be substantial.

Example

Suppose that Acme Diversified was acquired by Acme Holdings in a leveraged buyout. Acme Diversified through its wholly-owned subsidiaries operates in the cable television, contract drilling and forgings businesses as outlined in Exhibit 2. Exhibits 3 and 4 reflect the ownership and capitalization of Acme Holdings and its affiliates.

To determine the intrinsic value of the Acme Diversified Term Loan (emboldened in Exhibit 4), the investor must first calculate the value of the assets in the Acme estate available to the holders of the Term Loan. Exhibit 5 shows the value of each of Acme Diversified's operating subsidiaries net of any obligations which have a prior claim on such assets. The investor must then determine how the net asset value should be shared among Acme's various parties at interest. In Exhibit 6, the in-

Exhibit 2
Acme Diversified Business Mix (Dollars in millions)

Segment	Cash Flow	Estimated Value*
Cable Television	$20	$160
Contract Drilling	10	200
Forgings	8	40
Totals	38	400

*Net of nonfinancial liabilities.

Exhibit 3
Ownership Structure

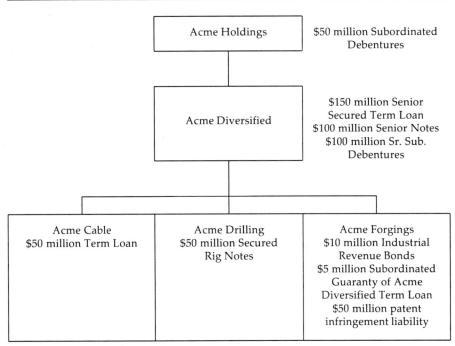

NB – All subsidiaries are 100% owned.

vestor provides for a sharing of value among the equity owners and creditors of Acme Holdings, the subordinated debt holders of Acme Diversified and the senior creditors of Acme Diversified. The value "belonging" to the Acme Diversified senior debt is then shared between Senior Notes and the Term Loan. Typically, loans to distressed borrowers are expressed on a cents per dollar of principal basis.

Arriving at Conclusions and Interpreting Those Conclusions

Intrinsic value analysis requires the investor to make numerous assumptions about relative standing of various claims in the borrower's estate and then actually quantify expected recoveries for various obligations. The actual outcome of any restructuring often takes years to actually

Exhibit 4
Acme Holdings and Consolidated Subsidiaries
Capitalization Summary (Dollars in millions)

10% Secured Rig Notes (Pre LBO)	$50	Acme Drilling. Secured by all drilling equipment. No other guarantors.
Term Loan	150	Acme Diversified. Secured by the stock of the operating subsidiaries. $5 subordinated guaranty from Acme Forging. LIBOR + 250.
6% Senior Notes (Pre LBO)	100	Unsecured. Negative pledge (omitted stock of subsidiaries). Otherwise pari passu w/Term Loan.
Cable Term Loan (Pre LBO)	50	Unsecured. Prohibits incurrence and guaranty of other indebtedness. LIBOR + 250.
Industrial Revenue Bonds (6%)	10	Acme Forgings. Secured by plant and machinery.
13.5% Senior Subordinated Debentures	100	Subordinated obligations of Acme Diversified.
15% Subordinated Debentures	50	Pay in Kind. Subordinated guaranty of Acme Diversified.
Total	$510	

occur and thus may be determined by factors that are unknowable at the time of investment. While no one can predict the future, it is possible to make educated guesses.

Research each asset and liability. Each assumption requires a detailed analysis of the legal rights and obligations of the borrower and its affiliates with respect to each of its liabilities. Much of the basic information needed will be obtainable from the original financing prospectuses and merger proxies, credit agreements, indentures and contingent liabilities discussions in the borrower's public filings.

Keep up with reorganization case law and out of court settlements. No two cases are the same, but it is not uncommon for the same issues to arise in more than one situation. If the circumstances surrounding two cases are close enough, it is possible that the parties involved may act similarly. By the same token, certain court decisions may be precedential.

Exhibit 5
Net Asset Value Calculation (Dollars in millions)

Acme Cable	$110	$160 business value, less $50 Acme Cable Term Loan. (Structurally Senior.)
Acme Drilling	150	$200 business value, less $50 Secured Rig Notes. (Asset Specific Debt.)
Acme Forgings	5	$40 business value, less $10 IRB's, less assumed settlement of patent infringement judgement of $20, less $5 subordinated guaranty of Acme Diversified Term Loan.
Net Asset Value Available*	265	

*Acme Diversified Estate.

Such decisions increase the likelihood that cases with similar fact patterns will be resolved in a similar manner.

Solicit legal advice. Restructurings are resolved within the context of the rights, obligations, and risks of the various parties at interest under the Bankruptcy Code, the securities acts, common law, and various state and local commercial laws. Understanding all of the various laws, their interplay and their relative applicability to a particular case is often beyond the investor's capability. Bankruptcy and securities lawyers can be extremely helpful in "forecasting the outcome" of a restructuring by identifying potential legal issues, using directly applicable experience, following other cases, and being able to interpret language in a credit agreement or an indenture.

Intrinsic value analysis is most applicable when the loan being analyzed is impaired. In such cases, investors will rarely pay the full intrinsic value of a loan. Rather, a return will be sought by acquiring the loan at a discount to its asset value. The magnitude of the discount will be a function of the buyer's confidence in the underlying values and the expected timing for recovery of such values.

If the available asset value of the estate exceeds the amount of the loan in question, it is useful to determine how much so. The greater the intrinsic value coverage of a loan is, the lower a "new money" investor's required return for that loan will be.

Exhibit 6
Value Sharing (Dollars in millions, except per $ of loan amounts)

Net Asset Value Available	$265	
Recovery for Acme Holdings	(35)	For equity and 15% Debentures. $30 plus $5 in costs
Net Asset Value Available to Acme Diversified Debt	230	Must cover $345 of obligations[a]
Less: Recovery for Sr. Subs.	(45)	$0.40/$ recovery plus $5 in costs
Available for Acme Diversified Senior Debt	185	Must cover Term Loan and Senior Notes
Term Loan Valuation		
Recovery From Acme Diversified	109	Assumes *pari passu* treatment of Term Loan and Senior Notes[b]
Recovery From Acme Forgings	5	
Total Term Loan Recovery	114	
Estimated Value Per $ of Loan	$0.76	$114/$150. A purchaser would pay a discount to this amount

[a] $100 Senior Notes, plus $100 Senior Subordinated Debentures, plus $145 Term Loan ($150 less $5 covered by Acme Forgings guaranty).

[b] The security interests of the Term Loan would likely command a superior recovery for the Term Loan over the Senior Notes but are assumed to be *pari passu* for conservatism.

COLLATERAL VALUE

Property security interests are one of the most important aspects of HLT bank loans. Security interests are established by agreement between lender and borrower, a security agreement. In a security agreement, the borrower grants a security interest in certain specified assets to assure repayment of the loan in exchange for some consideration (usually the loan proceeds). If a loan is in default, the lender may have the right to claim the collateral to recover amounts owed. If the borrower files for bankruptcy protection, secured creditors are treated much differently (in some cases, continuing to receive or accrue interest during the bankruptcy) than unsecured creditors.[3] Lenders are undersecured when the value of their collateral is less than the amount they are owed. Their loans are secured only to the extent of the collateral value of their loan. The deficiency portion is generally treated as an unsecured claim. Outside of bankruptcy, the negotiating leverage of a bank lender with the borrower and with other creditors will largely hinge upon whether or not the loan is adequately secured. Before investing in an HLT, the investor must understand the extent to which the loan is protected by liens against the assets of the borrower and any guarantors.

Analyzing security interests is a difficult and often highly technical process. The investor must develop a basic framework for determining the collateral value of HLT bank loans. Such framework should consider the following factors:

- The type of collateral

- The value of the collateral

- The importance of the collateral to the ongoing viability of the borrower

- The ability of the lender or bondholder to foreclose on the collateral

- The validity of the liens

- The standing of the security interests

While the investor can make a preliminary assessment of a loan's collateral value, it may be helpful to seek legal advice with respect to certain factors. Experienced bank loan investors obtain advice most frequently to confirm the validity and standing of the security interests.

---

[3] See Benjamin Weintraub and Alan N. Resnick, *Bankruptcy Law Manual* (Boston, MA: Warren, Gorham & Lamont, Inc., 1990).

Types of Collateral

HLT loans may be secured by virtually any asset of the borrower or the guarantors. The types of collateral available to lenders will vary according to the business of the borrower. Generally, assets that can be recovered most easily and are the most liquid make the best collateral. Some commonly secured assets are outlined in Exhibit 7.

Valuing Collateral

Determining the value of any given collateral will depend upon the type of assets involved. More liquid collateral like cash and receivables is easier to value; less liquid collateral like intellectual property and subsidiary stock is more difficult to value. Generally, it is appropriate for the investor to consider the realizable value of the collateral under the most likely means of realization. Going concern value may also be considered. Exhibit 8 outlines selected valuation alternatives for common types of collateral.

Exhibit 7
Common Forms of Collateral

Type of Collateral	Advantages	Disadvantages
Cash and Marketable Instruments	Highly liquid Value is easily determinable Lender usually takes possession	
Receivables	May be liquid Becomes cash on collection	Subject to credit of payor
Inventory	May be remarketable Critical to ongoing viability	May not be remarketable Difficult to track
Fixed Assets	Critical to ongoing viability	Rarely remarketable
Intellectual Property and Other Intangibles	Critical to ongoing viability	Difficult to value Often loses value quickly May not be transferable
Stock of Subsidiaries	Better than no collateral Conduit for cash to holding company	Junior to direct claims on assets Difficult to value

Exhibit 8
Valuing Collateral

Type of Collateral	*Selected Valuation Alternatives*
Cash and Marketable Instruments	Not controversial
Receivables	Face value less doubtful accounts (subject to a discount reflecting credit of customer base) Sale of portfolio
Inventory (subject to discount for possible obsolescence)	Raw material—refund value or cost Work in progress—varies (cost, cost plus value added, zero) Finished goods—liquidation value or cost (subject to discount)
Fixed Assets	Liquidation value
Intellectual Property and Other Intangibles	Third party sale value, if transferrable
Stock of Subsidiaries	Value of equity of business (liquidation or going concern)

In choosing which valuation alternatives to consider, the investor should take a common sense approach. As mentioned above, collateral value is important to the lender because it affords negotiating leverage over the borrower and other creditors. That leverage is strongest if the loan is oversecured, even under the most conservative methodology.

All lenders must be vigilant with respect to the value of their collateral on an ongoing basis. Collateral value may be reduced in many ways. Commodity collateral (e.g., raw materials like copper) may lose value because of changes in the marketplace for that collateral. Fixed assets may be lost to damage or fire if not properly insured. Inventory may be lost, stolen, or miscounted. Collateral may become obsolete (e.g., a technology or fashion product). The investor should be satisfied that the value of the collateral is being maintained before buying a secured loan.

Importance of Collateral to the Business

If collateral is vital to the ongoing health of the business or the preservation of the value of the business in a liquidation, it is more valuable to the borrower and the other creditors. In such cases, the security interest against such collateral may have incremental value to the lender above its realizable value. If collateral is not important to the business (e.g., a closed warehouse facility), the lender's security interest may have little or no incremental value above liquidation.

Forecloseablilty

The bankruptcy laws provide for an automatic stay of foreclosure of encumbered assets of the borrower. The automatic stay can prevent a lender from actually receiving title to collateral while the debtor reorganizes and attempts to pay its creditors. While the automatic stay is helpful to a borrower in danger of losing operating assets to a secured lender, the bankruptcy laws also prevent the borrower from paying other obligations of the estate including trade vendors and advance purchase customers desiring refunds. Bankruptcy can have a tremendous negative impact on a business and its relationships with vendors, customers, employees and investors. Some businesses can withstand bankruptcy. Others fare poorly. If a business is likely to be hurt by a bankruptcy, the borrower's access to the automatic stay may be limited. This makes security interests against such borrower more valuable.

Validity of the Liens

All security interests granted in commercial loan transactions must be established in accordance with state commercial law (e.g., Uniform Commercial Code, Article 9) in the state where the borrower has its principal place of business and where the collateral is located. An enforceable lien is established in two steps, attachment and perfection. Attachment is achieved through a consensual agreement between lender and borrower. Several other tests must be met to have a valid attachment. Perfection protects the lien holder's rights to collateral against other creditors and requires certain further steps to be taken by the lender. To the extent that a security interest is defective, the collateral value of the loan may be considerably reduced. It is critical that the investor determine that a secured loan has valid, enforceable liens against the collateral of the borrower. If the security interests are faulty, the loan's value should be discounted to reflect such defects. Commercial law is a very specialized area (lawyers often defer to specialists). It is difficult for a lay investor to make conclusive judgement about the validity of security interests. Many experienced loan buyers retain commercial law specialists to help with this exercise.

Standing of Security Interests

Even if security interests are properly attached and perfected, the loan may not have the exclusive right to certain collateral. It is not uncommon for competing liens to be secured by the same collateral. Security interests may be subject to a hierarchy. Liens are only valuable to the extent that they are supported by collateral value that does not belong to a competing security interest. It is critical for the investor to understand the priority of the security interests of the loan in question.

EXPECTED RECOVERY VALUE

Overview

All financial instruments may be evaluated as a stream of expected cash flows. The investor can determine the present value of that cash flow stream by applying a qualitative, risk-based discount rate. This analysis will provide an expected recovery value for an HLT. Under certain circumstances, the expected cash flows from a loan will vary from those contractually mandated by the credit agreement. Expected recovery analysis requires the investor to project the stream of cash flows from a bank loan and its corresponding present value under various environmental (e.g., business, economic, interest rate, etc.) alternatives. The likelihood of each alternative is used to establish probability weightings. Finally, the investor will calculate probability weighted composite net present value (expected recovery value) for the loan.

Expected recovery analysis allows the investor to quantitatively factor recovery risk into the evaluative process. It also gives the investor the opportunity to examine the best case and worst case scenarios and develop return expectations under each. It requires the investor to assign probabilities to those scenarios. Expected recovery analysis enables investors to determine the price at which the upside potential is worth the downside risk.

Expected recovery analysis also requires the investor to make numerous assumptions about the borrower and the environment in which the borrower will operate. Any conclusions derived from the analysis will only be as good as the underlying assumptions. This makes expected recovery analysis the least empirical of our methodologies.

Defining Alternative Scenarios and Assigning Probabilities

The performance of any business will be affected by the environment within which it must operate. HLT borrowers generally have little room for comfort because of the financial leverage imposed upon them. The investor must establish a set of alternative operating environments, each of which define a set of expectations for the business in the future.

Many factors will affect each scenario. Industry conditions, macroeconomic conditions, capital market conditions and company-specific conditions must all be considered. The base factors that underpin the analysis should be general enough so that the investor understands them and can assess their likelihood. For example, when evaluating a contract drilling concern, choose scenarios based upon oil and gas prices rather than specific day rates. Investors will be more familiar with oil and gas prices providing the analysis with a firm foundation. Day rate scenarios may then be derived from these base assumptions. Every credit will demand that a different set of factors and perhaps different number of scenarios be considered.

Each scenario represents a point in a probability continuum. While the likelihood of any one scenario occurring is small, the investor can estimate the probability of an outcome occurring within a range established around a specific scenario.

In Exhibit 9, it is unlikely that either our base or our downside case may occur. However, we may be able to assume that the probability of a case worse than our downside case is 30% and the probability of a case better than our upside case is 20%. This will give us probability weightings for our expected recovery calculations.

Determine Expected Cash Flows From the Loans

Once we have defined our scenarios and the related probabilities, we may begin the process of determining expected cash flows from the loan. **Project Cash Flows for the Underlying Business Based Upon Operating Scenarios.** While starting from a foundation with which the investor is comfortable (e.g., oil and gas prices), each scenario should build to assumptions from which projections may be derived (e.g., day rate

Exhibit 9
Assigning Probabilities

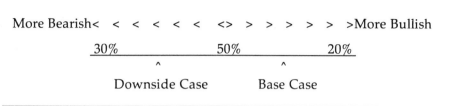

and utilization estimates for contract drilling rigs). The assumptions required to develop the projections should be explicitly noted.

Establish Payment Outcomes for Each Set of Operating Cash Flows.
The operating cash flows should be compared to cash needs. If cash
flows plus available liquidity are insufficient to cover cash requirements,
restructuring is likely. The investor must consider the implications of a
potential restructuring on the expected stream of cash flow paid to the
bank loan. It may be necessary to consider more than one restructuring
scenario for each operating scenario. In this case, a probability matrix
should be developed as in Exhibit 10. The horizontal axis shows business
environment scenarios that correspond to the continuum in Exhibit 9.
The vertical axis provides alternative restructuring outcomes for each
scenario.

For each box, a set of expected cash flows for the loan should be
established. Those cash flows will be determined by the outcome of restructuring negotiations between the borrower and the various credi-
tor/lender groups. The treatment of the bank loans will be a function of
their standing within the capital structure of the borrower (see Relative
Value Compared With Alternative Investments, *Qualitative Measurements*). Many bank loan investors find it helpful to discuss alternative
restructuring outcomes and probabilities with a bankruptcy lawyer. Prepayments will be determined by the ability of the borrower to generate
excess cash flow and the likelihood that such excess cash flow will be
used to repay bank debt.

Calculate Risk Adjusted Present Value. Once expected cash flow
streams are projected for the loan under various alternatives, the investor
should discount each stream back to the present using a discount rate
reflecting the perceived risk of the investment. The discount rate should

Exhibit 10
Probability Matrix

	Worse than Downside (30%)	Median (50%)	Better than Base (20%)
Bull	Payment on Schedule (5%)	Moderate Prepayment (10%)	Complete Refinancing (0%)
Base	Moderate Restructuring (15%)	Payment on Schedule (35%)	Moderate Prepayment (10%)
Bear	Severe Restructuring (10%)	Moderate Restructuring (5%)	Payment on Schedule (10%)

equal the return that the investor requires in order to make an investment of the same riskiness as the loan.

Calculate Probability Weighted Estimate. Each present value calculation represents an estimate of the value of the loan under one (or more) scenario. As those scenarios have been assigned probabilities, the investor may now calculate a simple probability weighted average (i.e., expected recovery value).

Example

Consider a term loan made to Acme Diversified with the characteristics shown in Exhibit 11. Suppose Acme Diversified was operating under conditions reflected in the probability matrix shown in Exhibit 12.

As reflected in Exhibit 12, we have assumed that four potential outcomes for the term loan exist. The investor must estimate cash flows to the term loan for each outcome as shown below and in Exhibit 13.

Severe Restructuring. Interest payments stop after one year. Reorganization after four years. Banks receive $0.25 in cash and $0.50 of a three year, LIBOR + 250 note (Assumed to swap into 11.10% fixed).

Exhibit 11
Acme Diversified Term Loan

Seven Year Term Loan (No Amortizations*)
Interest at LIBOR + 250 (Swapped for 7 years into 11.10%)
Cost to Unwind Swap in Prepayment Case of 2 points
Investor's Hurdle Rate is 16% for this Loan

*Few HLT's have bullet maturities. This assumption is chosen for simplicity.

Moderate Restructuring. Interest payments stop after two years. Reorganization after three years. Banks receive $1.00 of a new four year note. LIBOR flat for year four. LIBOR + 50 for years five through seven. LIBOR + 250 assumed to swap into 11.10%; LIBOR flat assumed to swap into 8.60%; LIBOR + 50 assumed to swap into 9.10%.

Payment on Schedule. Seven year bullet. LIBOR + 250 (Swapped to 11.10%).

Moderate Prepayment. Loan prepaid after five years. Two point swap unwind cost.

Exhibit 12
Probability Matrix

	Worse than Downside (30%)	*Median* (50%)	*Better than Base* (20%)
Bull	Payment on Schedule (5%)	Moderate Prepayment (10%)	Complete Refinancing (0%)
Base	Moderate Restructuring (15%)	Payment on Schedule (35%)	Moderate Prepayment (10%)
Bear	Severe Restructuring (10%)	Moderate Restructuring (5%)	Payment on Schedule (10%)

Exhibit 13
Loan Cash Flow Assumptions (Percent of original principal amount)

Quarterly Period	Severe Restructuring	Moderate Restructuring	Payment on Schedule	Moderate Prepayment
1	2.78%	2.78%	2.78%	2.78%
2	2.78	2.78	2.78	2.78
3	2.78	2.78	2.78	2.78
4	2.78	2.78	2.78	2.78
5	0.00	2.78	2.78	2.78
6	0.00	2.78	2.78	2.78
7	0.00	2.78	2.78	2.78
8	0.00	2.78	2.78	2.78
9	0.00	0.00	2.78	2.78
10	0.00	0.00	2.78	2.78
11	0.00	0.00	2.78	2.78
12	0.00	0.00	2.78	2.78
13	0.00	2.15	2.78	2.78
14	0.00	2.15	2.78	2.78
15	0.00	2.15	2.78	2.78
16	50.00	2.15	2.78	2.78
17	0.69	2.28	2.78	2.78
18	0.69	2.28	2.78	2.78
19	0.69	2.28	2.78	2.78
20	0.69	2.28	2.78	100.78
21	0.69	2.28	2.78	
22	0.69	2.28	2.78	
23	0.69	2.28	2.78	
24	0.69	2.28	2.78	
25	0.69	2.28	2.78	
26	0.69	2.28	2.78	
27	0.69	2.28	2.78	
28	25.69	102.28	102.78	

The investor must then discount each stream of cash flows at the appropriate hurdle rate given the riskiness of the loan (in this case, 16%). The resulting net present value for each assumed outcome is reflected in Exhibit 14.

Each outcome must then be weighed according to its likelihood of occurrence, per Exhibit 11. As shown in Exhibit 15, the result of the weighted average calculation is the expected recovery value.

RELATIVE VALUE COMPARED WITH ALTERNATIVE INVESTMENTS

Overview

The principles underpinning relative valuation are simple. First, investors must establish the relative riskiness of the an HLT bank loan *vis-à-vis* a universe of other assets, which have values that are known or that can be determined. Once they understand the relative status of the HLT and the values of assets in the comparable universe, investors may gather valuation data based upon direct comparisons with such other assets.

The first step in relative valuation process is the choice of comparable assets. Generally, four or five good comparables is enough. If more exist, use them. If fewer exist, use as many as possible. The best comparables have:

- The same obligor and guarantors

- Similar ranking (e.g., Senior Secured Notes as comparables to a Senior Secured Term Loan)

Exhibit 14
Net Present Value Calculation

Severe Restructuring	Moderate Restructuring	Payment on Schedule	Moderate Prepayment
49.17%	69.40%	80.83%	83.47%

Exhibit 15
Probability Weighted Average Calculation

Severe Restructuring (10%)	Moderate Restructuring (20%)	Payment on Schedule (50%)	Moderate Prepayment (20%)
4.9%	13.9%	40.4%	16.7%

Weightings

Severe Restructuring	$0.05
Moderate Restructuring	0.14
Payment on Schedule	0.40
Moderate Prepayment	0.17
Expected Recovery Value	$0.76

- Similar payment characteristics (e.g., Floating Rate Notes as comparables to a Floating Rate Term Loan)

- A well established trading market to determine their absolute value

Since all of these criteria will not be met, the investor must choose assets coming closest to the HLT in question. Some differences will be qualitative (different underlying obligor and guarantors), others will be quantitative (fixed rate versus floating rate). By establishing techniques for overcoming the differences between HLT Bank Loans and comparable assets, investors will add to the arsenal of data at their disposal to establish absolute value and to choose between alternative investment opportunities.

Qualitative Measurements

It is vital to understand the sources of credit that stand behind an HLT and any other asset with which the HLT may be compared. Ideally (and rarely), the two assets will have the same borrower and guarantors. Absent that, the investor must determine the relative creditworthiness of the underlying obligors. Assets in the same capital structure make good comparables even if the obligor and guarantors are different. Choose liabilities of other leveraged companies in the same industry next. If the universe is still too small, consider credits that will improve or deteriorate under the same macroeconomic circumstances (e.g., furniture manufacturers and appliance manufacturers).

Security interests in the assets of the borrower and other guarantors can provide HLT Bank Loans with significant qualitative benefits over unsecured obligations. The extent of these benefits will be a function of the following factors, which are more fully discussed above (see Collateral Value):

- **The type and value of the collateral.** Liquid collateral (e.g., receivables) is usually better. The more that the value of the loan's interest in the collateral exceeds the face amount of the loan, the more important the security interests will be.

- **The importance of the collateral to the ongoing viability of the borrower.** If the collateral is integral to the operation of the business as a going concern, the loan's security interest in that collateral is more significant.

- **The ability of the lender or bondholder to foreclose on the collateral.** If the borrower can easily seek bankruptcy protection to stay foreclosure without affecting the underlying business, the security interests are less beneficial to the lender. For example, if a loan is secured by the stock of a borrower's operating subsidiaries but not the assets of those subsidiaries, it may be possible for the borrower to stay the foreclosure of the stock while business continues as usual at the operating subsidiaries.

- **The validity of the liens.** To the extent that liens are attached or perfected with faulty documentation or may be attacked as preferences or fraudulent conveyances, they are less valuable. The prospective investor must assess the risk that the security interests securing an HLT may be deemed invalid.

- **The standing of the security interests.** If collateral is shared, it is important to determine which liens have priority. Security interests are only valuable to the extent that they are supported by *available* collateral value.

The investor must understand the loan's ranking within the relevant capital structure. This means establishing the priority of the obligations of the obligor as well as any guarantors. Usually, HLT bank loans are senior obligations of the borrower. The investor must determine if there is a significant amount of *pari passu* indebtedness or if any debt is "structurally senior" as previously discussed. The greater the amount senior and *pari passu* debt, the lower the standing of the bank loan. This analysis should be applied separately to each obligor and each guarantor. (See Intrinsic Value Analysis, *Determine Loan's Position Relative to Other Obligations*.)

HLT credit agreements typically provide comprehensive covenant protection for the lender. Financial covenants enable the bank lenders to monitor the performance of the borrower and take remedial action if necessary. Typical financial covenants include cash flow, interest coverage, net worth and debt to equity tests. If the borrower fails to meet these tests, it will be forced to seek waivers from the banks or risk acceleration of the loans. This provides the bank group with a forum in which to negotiate with the borrower. Lenders are often able to improve their position in the capital structure or lower their exposure in exchange for providing waivers. Negative covenants restrict the borrower from taking actions which will impair the creditworthiness supporting the bank loans. Typical negative covenants include restrictions on dividends, acquisitions, asset sales, change of business, change of ownership and change of management. Affirmative covenants require the borrower to take certain actions which maintain the lender's position and ability to monitor that position. Typical affirmative covenants include financial reporting requirements, maintenance of insurance and upkeep of collateral.

Quantitative Measurements

The investor must compare loans to other assets quantitively in order to come to relative value conclusions (i.e., which assets are cheapest). The unique financial characteristics of HLT's can make comparisons more difficult. By understanding an array of alternative methods, the investor will be able to choose those techniques most applicable to the assets being evaluated.

Current yield is calculated by dividing the current interest rate being paid to the holder of an asset by the assumed purchase price. Exhibit 16 shows current yield calculations for an HLT (Example 1) and a senior note (Example 2).

Exhibit 16
Current Yield Calculations

Example 1

> HLT Bank Loan bearing interest at LIBOR + 250 basis points
> Assumed Purchase Price: 96.5% of face value
> LIBOR assumed to equal 6.75%

LIBOR	6.75
+250	2.50
Current Interest Rate	9.25
Divided by:	
Assumed Purchase Price	96.5%
Current Yield	9.59%

Example 2

> Senior Note bearing interest at 7%
> Assumed purchase price: 83% of face

Current Interest Rate	7.00
Divided by:	
Assumed Purchase Price	83%
Current Yield	8.43%

While providing an easily calculated comparison between the loan and the note, current yield has several shortcomings, which Exhibit 16 illustrates. Current yield understates the benefits of buying an asset at a discount to face value. In Example 1, the investor in the loan will earn 3.5 points of gain at maturity (100 – 96.5). In Example 2, the investor in the senior note will earn 17 points. While the loan provides 116 basis points of incremental current yield, the note may provide more total return because of the larger discount (depending on the maturity of each instrument).

Although current yield may be calculated for both fixed and floating rate instruments, the results are not comparable. The calculations do not provide for interest rate fluctuations on a loan as LIBOR changes. Fixed rate assets are inherently riskier than their floating rate cousins because their value changes with general changes in interest rates. This is why holders of floating rate assets may increase their current yield by purchasing an interest rate swap. Current yield has no means to reflect the presence or absence of interest rate risk.

Discount margin ("DM") analysis is used to compare floating rate notes of similar maturity.[4] Some of the shortcomings of the current yield analysis are solved by DM. DM attempts to take into account the variability of future interest payments over the life of the asset and any discount purchase of that asset. The result of a DM calculation is a margin over the interest index. DM can not be applied to fixed rate assets. It also fails to provide for sinking fund payments, amortizations or prepayments. One may construct a rough proxy for the DM of a bank loan by calculating an average life and assuming no unscheduled prepayments. In this way, DM can be used to compare the loan to other floating rate assets (albeit, roughly) but not to fixed rate assets.

Yield to maturity ("YTM") or internal rate of return is the traditional yardstick for measuring the relative value of debt and equity instruments. Applying a yield to maturity analysis to a bank loan enables the investor to compare the loan to fixed rate debt instruments. Yield to maturity solves many of the problems that current yield and discount margin ignore. YTM provides meaningful results and comparative data for virtually any purchase price and maturity. Thus, a discount instrument may be compared to one trading near par and long dated assets may be compared to shorter dated assets (ignoring reinvestment risk). The principal difficulty with calculating YTM for a bank loan is predicting the interest rate.

Two methodologies are commonly used to forecast the interest rate for the loan. The first assumes that the current rate will remain in effect for the life of the loan. The second uses the interest rate swap market to calculate a fixed rate equivalent for the floating rate. An illustration of each methodology is shown below. Consider the loan described in Exhibit 16 (Example 1):

Interest Rate:	LIBOR + 250
Assumed Purchase Price:	96.5
LIBOR:	6.75
Final Maturity:	7 years from purchase date
Quarterly Amortizations:	8 equal amortizations beginning in the fifth year

[4] See Kenneth E. Jaques, "Evaluating Floating Rate Notes," Chapter 9 and David Muntner, "Evaluating Floating Rate Notes: II," Chapter 10 in Frank J. Fabozzi (ed), *Floating Rate Instruments* (Chicago, IL: Probus Publishing Company, 1986).

Yield to Maturity (Current Rate Method). First the investor must determine a stream of cash flows for the loan. This may be done by assuming that LIBOR remains constant at 6.75 for the life of the loan. Exhibit 17 demonstrates the cash flow stream under a constant LIBOR assumption. Here the "coupon" rate on the loan is 9.25% per annum (6.75% + 250 BP).

Using the cash flows established in Exhibit 17, the investor may calculate yield to maturity as a semiannual equivalent internal rate of return. This calculation is demonstrated in Exhibit 18.

Yield to Maturity (Swapped Method).[5] In order to establish an assumed stream of cash flows from the loan, the investor must first segregate the loan into eight floating rate notes each corresponding to a principal amortization as illustrated in Exhibit 19. Assume that the total amount outstanding is 100.

The investor must determine the equivalent fixed interest rate for each floating rate note using the interest rate swap market. The investor determines the fixed rate into which a stream of LIBOR payments of a given duration may be swapped. The LIBOR spread is then added to that fixed rated to determine the fixed rate equivalent for a floating rate note of a given maturity. That calculation for the seven year note is illustrated in Exhibit 20.

The investor must repeat the same process as shown in Exhibit 20 for the other seven floating rate notes. Exhibit 21 shows the result of these calculations.

Using these interest rates, the investor must calculate projected quarterly interest payments for each note. The payments must then be compiled for all the notes together. As illustrated in Exhibit 22, the quarterly cash flows will be the sum of the interest on all of the unmatured notes plus any maturing principal. The investor may then use these cash flows to calculate an internal rate of return (yield to maturity) based upon an assumed purchase price.

YTM (Swapped) allows the investor to compare HLT's to fixed rate debt on a rate of return basis without ignoring the interest rate risk difference. This methodology assumes that the loan will be repaid as scheduled. However, most loans permit (in fact, encourage) prepayments at par. This is the main shortcoming of YTM (Swapped). The failure of this

---

[5] See Paul H. Ross, Dennis G. Dolan, Christopher R. Ryan and James B. Windle, *HLT Bank Loans: A New Market for Relative Value Investors* (New York, NY: Salomon Brothers Inc, 1990).

Exhibit 17
Cash Flow Stream

Quarterly Period	0	1–20	21	22	23	24	25	26	27	28
Principal		0.0	12.5	12.5	12.5	12.5	12.5	12.5	12.5	12.5
Interest		2.3	2.3	2.0	1.7	1.4	1.2	0.9	0.6	0.3
Total Cash Flow		2.3	14.8	14.5	14.2	13.9	13.7	13.4	13.1	12.8
Remaining Principal	100.0	100.0	87.5	75.0	62.5	50.0	37.5	25.0	12.5	0.0

Exhibit 18
Internal Rate of Return Calculation

Quarterly Period	0	1–20	21	22	23	24	25	26	27	28
Cash Flow	−96.5	2.3	14.8	14.5	14.2	13.9	13.7	13.4	13.1	12.8

Semiannual IRR: 10.10%

Exhibit 19
HLT as a Series of Floating Rate Notes

Period	5 yrs., 3 mos.	5 yrs., 6 mos.	5 yrs., 9 mos.	6 yrs.
Principal Amount	12.5	12.5	12.5	12.5

Period	6 yrs., 3 mos.	6 yrs., 6 mos.	6 yrs., 9 mos.	7 yrs.
Principal Amount	12.5	12.5	12.5	12.5

Exhibit 20
Fixed Rate Equivalent Calculation

Seven year swap vs. LIBOR:	8.60%	(7 yr Treasury note + 63bp)
Plus 250 Basis Points	2.50	Spread over LIBOR
Fixed Rate Equivalent	11.10%	

Exhibit 21
Fixed Rate Coupons

Note	5y, 3m	5y, 6m	5y, 9m	6y	6y, 3m	6y, 6m	6y, 9m
Fixed Rate Equiv.	10.85%	10.88%	10.92%	10.95%	10.99%	11.02%	11.06%

analysis to account for prepayment risk is mitigated if the loan is acquired at a discount to par value. In that case the prepayments will in fact accelerate the recognition of gain to the extent of the discount. It is also possible to forecast prepayments based upon expected cash flows, asset sales, or refinancings. A YTM (Swapped) calculation may be performed for a revised amortization schedule in the same way as for the contractual amortization schedule.

Intrinsic value and expected recovery value (see Intrinsic Value and Expected Recovery Value) may also be used for relative comparisons, particularly for loans to insolvent borrowers. For each asset in the comparative universe, calculate the percentage of intrinsic value or expected recovery value for that asset's purchase price. This percentage will provide a benchmark which may be compared to the same statistic for the HLT in light of the qualitative differences. For example, an investor

Exhibit 22
Cash Flow Compilation

Note	Quarterly Cash Flows (Interest Only)	Final Cash Flow (Interest and Principal)
5 yrs., 3 mos.	.3391	12.8391
5 yrs., 6 mos.	.3400	12.8400
5 yrs., 9 mos.	.3413	12.8413
6 yrs.	.3422	12.8422
6 yrs., 3 mos.	.3434	12.8434
6 yrs., 6 mos.	.3444	12.8444
6 yrs., 9 mos.	.3456	12.8456
7 yrs.	.3469	12.8469

Price: 96.5   YTM: 11.96%

Exhibit 23
Qualitative Measurements Summary

Methodology	*Comments*
Current Yield	Easiest method to calculate. Does not work well with discount or floating rate debt.
Discount Margin ("DM")	Floating rate note technique. Does not apply to fixed rate debt. Hence, no fixed v. floating comparisons.
Yield to Maturity (Current)	Ignores the absence of interest rate risk in the floating rate paper. Allows fixed v. floating comparisons.
Yield to Maturity (Swapped)	Captures the absence of interest rate risk in floating rate paper. Can not factor in prepayment risk. Best methodology for "par" and "near par" loans.
Intrinsic Value	Loans to distressed credits.
Expected Value	Loans to distressed credits.

would be unlikely to buy a loan for 75% of its intrinsic value if another loan with better qualitative attributes (e.g., better security interests) is available at 60% of intrinsic value.

PART III
Securitization

Chapter 9

Collateralized Loan Obligations

PETER J. CARRIL, JR.
SENIOR VICE PRESIDENT
DAIWA SECURITIES AMERICA INC.

FRANK J. FABOZZI, PH.D., C.F.A.
VISITING PROFESSOR OF FINANCE
SLOAN SCHOOL OF MANAGEMENT
MASSACHUSETTS INSTITUTE OF TECHNOLOGY

Collateralized loan obligations (CLOs) are securitized investment products which are formed by the pooling of assets, specifically, senior bank loans. The collateral is financed by liabilities structured and tranched to produce a unique and customized security to fit the particular needs of institutional investors. The concept of cash flow tranching is equivalent to that utilized in the mortgage-backed securities market in the structuring of collateralized mortgage obligation (CMO) structures. However, the underlying collateral is senior bank loans originated from highly-leveraged transactions (HLT), rather than mortgage loans or pass-through mortgage securities.

CLOs are usually structured in two or three tranches, with the top tranche usually receiving a triple-A rating from one of the rating agencies. This portion is approximately 75% to 85% of the transaction. The triple-A rating is due to the collateral, the subordination underneath the top layer, any arbitrage reserve buildup, if present, and secondary insurance. The middle tranche is subordinated to the top tranche and usually represents approximately 15% of the total capitalization of the transaction. The return on this class depends on the amount of subordination below this tranche. Finally, the bottom equity layer, which can be 4% to 8% of the transaction, is similar to a CMO residual. The return on this tranche depends heavily on the structure of securities senior to that layer, the original spread on the collateral, the pricing on the tranches above it, and any incidence of default. This equity tranche produces a wide-ranging return pattern.

The purpose of this chapter is to discuss the basic characteristics of CLOs: structure, investment considerations, credit support, and cash flow mismatch. At the end of this chapter, considerations in the marketing of the subordinated tranches is discussed. Appendix A of this chapter lists the CLOs that have been done to date and Appendix B provides a sample term sheet. The characteristics of the collateral—senior bank loans—has been discussed in Chapter 1. In the next chapter, an in-depth explanation of the rating of CLOs is provided.

CLO STRUCTURE

The issuer of the CLO is often a *special purpose vehicle* (SPV). The transfer of assets—in this case, senior bank debt—is accomplished through the creation of a SPV. In particular, the SPV must be distinct and separate enough from the originator (or depositor) of the assets to garner true sale of assets treatment. Failure to achieve true sale of asset treatment will raise issues of consolidation, which usually renders the deal uneconomical.

The legal form selected by the structuring agent for the issuer of the CLO is determined by the same guidelines and considerations used when structuring generic asset-backed securities such as credit card and automobile securitizations. These possible choices include, but are not limited to, a corporation and a partnership.

Corporate forms require a capital structure comprised of both debt and equity. The equity is often referred to as a residual interest or an income appreciation note. The structure needs a sufficient percentage of supporting equity to provide the more senior tranche investors comfort regarding debt versus equity tax treatment. Like any taxable corporation, the entity is subject to tax payments. Often, these types of corporate issuers are domiciled in an offshore geographic locale that offers favorable corporate tax treatment.

Partnership structures require the designation of a general partner and a limited partner. It is often difficult to find an entity willing to accept the role of the general partner due to the unlimited liability feature. The general partner can itself be formed as a corporation. The limited partners participate in the economic upside as would an equity holder under the corporate structure. Of note is the difficulty some accounts have with purchasing limited partnership interests. This is one reason why many CBO structures have joint obligors. The issuer is both a partnership and a corporation, with the general partner of the partnership being a corporation.

The format of a CLO involves exceedingly complex tax and accounting issues which affect all classes of investors. For offshore corporations, this involves providing senior tranche investors sufficient comfort that there is little likelihood of a withholding tax problem and what, if any, are the provisions available to rectify these problems. In addition, the domicile of the equity holders, or owners, of the structure may affect the determination of the domicile of the corporation. In conclusion, the same care used with all asset-backed securitizations applies to the structuring of CLOs.

Tranche Allocation

Securitization involves the division and tranching of the available cash flow generated by the collateral which supports the deal and any credit enhancement that may be present. The process begins by finding a buyer for the bottom tranche of the structure. It is the successful placement of the equity which drives the direction of the transaction, and, in effect, prices the other tranches as one moves up the capital structure.

Most deals are comprised of three or four tranches. The top tranche can comprise up to 75% to 85% of the capitalization. This tranche can be structured with a one, two or five year reinvestment period during which all cash flow is reinvested in "like" collateral. Certain over-collateralization (O/C) and interest coverage (I/C) tests must be satisfied in order for additional collateral to be purchased.

The middle tranche can be rated or unrated. It can represent 15% of the capitalization. The bottom tranche represents a strict equity tranche, and equals 4% to 8% of the capitalization. It can have a yield of over 20% depending on the leverage. Finally, of most importance, is to realize that the CLO can have as many tranches as needed to meet the investment demands and criteria of the perspective buyers and insure a swift closing of the transaction.

Liquidation/Continuous Life

CLOs can be structured to be self-liquidating or to be professionally managed by an asset manager over a predetermined period of time. The introduction of an asset manager is often done as a by-product of a structuring need. A revolving period (or reinvestment period) is structured into the transaction to increase the average life of the tranches. The longer the reinvestment period, the longer the average life. The longer the average life, the greater the potential return on the equity as the arbitrage profits have more time to build up. However, if it is necessary to purchase more collateral, and if an active sector/industry rotation is mandated, then a qualified, proven asset manger is needed. The asset manager must initially choose the collateral as well as perform the on-going credit due diligence. The fee for this can vary between 25 and 100 basis points per year.

With a liquidating transaction, there can be a very short reinvestment period. Prepayments of the collateral that are accelerated greater than mandated in the credit agreement required by each individual loan can be invested in a suspense account and then passed along to the investors as dictated in the CLO placement memorandum. The selection between a liquidating and managed SPV is usually a function of investor demand.

INVESTMENT CONSIDERATIONS FOR ISSUANCE

Balance Sheet Restructuring

The benefits and motivating factors surrounding the issuance of a CLO can often be pinpointed toward the specific financial condition presented by a seller's balance sheet. For example, commercial banks in the United States as well as those in the international banking community must comply with the new risk-based capital guidelines. This capital adequacy issue is forcing many regulated institutions to transfer a portion of their loan portfolios off their balance sheets.

By reducing the amount of loans carried on a financial institution's balance sheet, its overall asset base decreases and the required capital that must be set aside to support these activities is reduced. As the secondary market for loans has matured, both outright, whole loan sales as well as securitized loan products have become easier to accomplish.

Risk Re-allocation

Many structured transactions, including collateralized mortgage obligations and collateralized bond obligations, are brought to market to capture an arbitrage profit. In particular, when the spread between where the supporting collateral can be purchased in the secondary market is *wide* relative to where the securities issued by the SPV can be priced, then an arbitrage situation exists. The "cheap" collateral can now be purchased and structured into a product and sold into a relatively "rich" or expensive market.

In effect, what occurs is best described as an exploitation of the credit preferences of investors. When the yield at which the investor is willing to purchase highly-rated securities (i.e., investment grade) is low relative to the yield of the subordinated collateral, a structured transaction can be instituted. If the investor has no yield preference between triple A and single B securities, then most deals could not be brought to market. The wider the credit spread, the higher the return on the equity. Thus, the purchaser of the equity usually serves as the motivating force for the creation of CLOs.

INVESTMENT CONSIDERATIONS

The various tranches of any securitized product offers an investor a wide-range of investment opportunities tailored to the specific risk profile sought. An investor who desires safety of principal and a more stable return profile would choose the top tranche of a CLO. An investor who is able to withstand a higher return volatility may look to invest in the bottom layer of the CLO. An investor seeking a blended return profile can look to invest in the middle tranche of the CLO.

Virtually any risk/return pattern situated within the context of stability and durability of risk (i.e., the ability of the structure to withstand defaults) can be produced by mixing non-proportionate combinations of tranches. For example, the investor could purchase one portion of tranche A, two portions of tranche B, and one-half portion of equity so that the portfolio produces a single mode return pattern.

The following descriptions outline the investment considerations for the various individual tranches.

Tranche A/Senior Class. The tranche A securities, if rated triple A, have historically been priced at between 25 and 75 basis points over three-month LIBOR. Double-A rated securities would have a pricing range of anywhere between 75 and 125 basis points over three-month LIBOR. They are often overcollateralized by a factor of 1.2 times, and can withstand a high degree of default incidence before the payment of principal and interest is affected. This can range from 40% to 50%, cumulative, depending on the structure.

The securities can be either registered or bearer, and are often listed on a non-U.S. exchange such as the Luxembourg Stock Exchange. The securities are not SEC registered.

Tranche B/Senior Subordinated. The middle tranche of these transactions has no deep historic pricing benchmark. This tranche is more sensitive to the performance of the subordinate layers, which in turn, is sensitive to the default incidence, reinvestment of proceeds, and adherence to the scheduled amortization of the underlying loans. The pricing can range from 250 to 400 basis points over three-month LIBOR. Both principal and interest payments due to the holder of tranche B securities are subordinate to payments due the tranche A securities.

These securities can, depending on the amount of the equity tranche, price of the collateral, and issuance expenses, be 1.1 times overcollateralized. Tranche B securities can withstand a set percentage of defaults, and thus represents an interest in a seasoned, diversified pool of senior loans.

Equity. The lower tranche has a return pattern similar to an equity class. The return can vary, but can easily exceed 20% if only the *bottom* layer is purchased. It is often purchased as part of a strip combined with more senior tranches to give the investor some potential for upside appreciation while enjoying an above market rate of return. Its required repayment of principal and interest is subordinate to both the tranche A and tranche B securities.

CREDIT SUPPORT

Through the structuring process, the top layer will need some form of credit enhancement to achieve a triple, double, or single A rating.

The decision to add external credit enhancement through the use of a third-party credit agency (such as FGIC, FSA or CapMAC), or to structure the transaction with the enhancement added through over-collateralization by the addition of a subordinated layer depends upon several factors. These factors include:

- The cost of the external credit enhancement.

- The cost of internal credit enhancement. That is, what is the interest rate on the subordinated layer(s).

- The appetite of the investor for third-party guaranteed paper.

- The flexibility of terms and conditions of the provider of the credit enhancement.

- The reality of successfully placing the subordinated layer, and the conditions (excluding price) required by the purchaser.

These factors will result in a choice which will combine the lowest cost (both absolute paid to the enhancer and absolute demanded by the purchasers) as well as the fewest structuring difficulties.

From the standpoint of a prospective purchaser, the exact and detailed credit support needs to be examined. In particular:

- Is principal the only component guaranteed, or are timely interest payments included in the guarantee?

- What is the financial condition of the external insurer?

- Will the insurer's parent provide catastrophic financial support?

- What type and percentage of capital does the provider have (i.e., hard capital/soft capital)?

- If subordinated credit enhancement is chosen, can the subordinate owners block any interest payment above them?

- Under what conditions can the subordinated owners force a liquidation of the collateral?

These considerations need to be structured into the transaction which
will result in the lowest interest cost to the deal and produce the safest,
most durable structure.

CASH FLOW MISMATCH

As explained in the discussion of senior bank debt in Chapter 1, each
individual borrower has as its own option the standard index from
which to peg its borrowing. The borrower can choose the prime rate as
its index and thereby avoid any prepayment and/or break-funding penalty. The borrower can also choose between one, three or six-month
LIBOR. The borrower will choose the options which best fits its internal
financing requirements.

In contrast, the CLO in our example will issue securities that pay
either quarterly or semiannually and are priced off three-month LIBOR.
There can be a temporary cash flow mismatch or basis risk. For example,
suppose that the yield curve between one and three-month LIBOR is
very steep. This condition may prompt borrowers to shift their borrowings to one-month LIBOR. However, the liabilities of the CLO still are
indexed off of three-month LIBOR. As such, a basis mismatch could result between the supporting collateral and the securities issued. There are
two possible remedies: employing an interest rate basis swap or creating
a reserve account.

An interest rate basis swap can be structured to remove this basis
risk.[1] The cost of this swap will depend on the prevailing swap curve, as
well as the ease or difficulty involved in swapping a potentially dynamic
cash flow. The swap is senior to the subordinated tranches and their cash
flows.

The other structuring technique is to create a reserve account from
which to debit any negative basis mismatch as it may occur. The amount
of this reserve account can be calculated by estimating the relative vola-

---

[1] In an interest rate swap, one party pays a fixed rate and receives a floating rate; the
counterparty pays a floating rate and receives a fixed rate. In an interest rate basis, or
floating-to-floating rate swap, both parties pay floating rate. The floating-rate
benchmark for each party is different.

tilities of the asset and liability cash flows, the practicality of the borrowers switching their borrowing choices,[2] and the actual dating of the cash flows of the collateral. The reserve fund can also serve as a means of repayment for the senior tranche, and if never utilized, can provide the equity holder with an incremental return component.

As always, the lowest cost to the structure as well as investor desire and comfort will usually influence the decision as to the use of a swap or reserve account.

MARKETING THE SUBORDINATED TRANCHES

The key to a successful closing of any CLO is the ability to place the bottom tranche at a price/yield level which is within the confines of the cash flow that is available to this residual. This, in turn, depends on the correct structure matched with the purchaser's investment criteria of yield, default durability, diversification, manager requirements (if applicable), and assumptions on recoveries and their timing.

Investors in subordinated tranches of a CLO are receiving an instrument with the following characteristics:

- floating-rate return of LIBOR

- senior secured collateral

- diversification by industry, issuer, seller

- manager performance (if applicable)

Identifying the Buyer

Identifying the universal subset of possible purchasers earlier on in the process can save significant time and aggravation. The following outlines potential purchasers along with any relevant investment features.

Asset/Liability Matching Accounts. Due to the floating rate nature of the collateral, and hence return of the equity tranche, investors will match fund their assets to lock in the spread on their investment. Fund-

---

[2] Indeed, one must ascertain the allowability and penalties involved as detailed in the credit agreement.

ing with LIBOR significantly reduces the investor's basis mismatch between the collateral repricing and the investor's borrowing index.

Commercial Banks. These financial institutions are likely candidates for this product as they are the originators of the underlying collateral. However, regulatory accounting treatment for these buyers (RAP accounting) introduces the concept of retained subordination into the banks capital picture. That is, were a bank to sell loans into the CLO and purchase (retain) the bottom layer, this could be deemed a recourse transaction. The bank would be forced, under RAP guidelines, to set capital aside for not only their "hold" position but for the amount of colateral submitted to the transaction. Finally, the non-liquid nature of the equity is problematic for commercial bank portfolios. This by no means suggests that commercial banks do not own these products nor does it imply that they are poor investments for commercial banks.

High-Yield/Hedge/Arbitrage Accounts. Select yield-driven accounts purchase these layers. However, a steep yield curve will often not provide enough absolute yield for these accounts. The nature of the CLOs underlying collateral adds immediate diversity and stability to the portfolio. Unfortunately, the lack of liquidity and the managed product (i.e., lack of control) aspect of the CLO seem to be the common points of contention with these accounts.

Insurance Companies. Historically, these financial institutions have purchased this product, and will continue to be likely candidates. A desire among many portfolio mangers is to swap the yield from floating to fixed. Asset/liability matching as well as loan-for-equity swaps are items which are important to these institutions.

Corporations. Whether they are utilities requiring earnings enhancement, cash-rich corporations, tax-advantaged institutions, or trust managers, all these entities have historically been purchasers of this product. Here, identifying accounts that already own loans will reduce the education process down to the structuring of the product itself. Indeed, holders of the loans themselves can swap out of a portion of their loans into the CLO subordinated tranches and achieve a significant yield pick-up with no loss in diversity.

Non-U.S. Accounts. These purchasers, European and Asian banks, corporations, finance and trading companies are all potential candidates. CLOs provide yield and help match fund their dollar assets. Many of these accounts hold and actively manage individual loan pools. Non-U.S. purchasers could determine the domicile of the "owner" of the SPV necessitating other structuring pecularities.

The list of potential purchasers would also include endowments, the Prime funds, the several structured CLOs currently outstanding in the marketplace, and private trusts.

Sensitivity Analysis

The subset of returns of the subordinated tranches is a collective function of the assumptions used to perform the cash flow analysis. As such, each assumption can be sensitized to help the potential customers analyze their investments.

To illustrate, we will use a CLO model that has the following indicatives and assumptions:

LIBOR Margin:	LIBOR + 250 basis points
Price:	$99.50
Stepdowns:	Yes; 5% of portfolio
Recovery:	90%, lagged 12 months
Default:	1.0% per annum

Leverage. The returns on the subordinated tranches can vary between LIBOR plus 300 basis points to LIBOR + 2500 basis points due to structural and market factors. The yield on subordinated tranches is impacted by the level of subordination and the all-in pricing of the senior liabilities. The two capital structures in Exhibit 1 illustrate this point.

The equity in capital structure B is more leveraged and produces higher returns at lower default rates but non-linear lower returns at high default rates. This structure is said to have (relatively) low default durability. The important point to note is that the structurer has the flexibility to dynamically design the transaction around the yield constraints of the buyer.

Stepdowns. Certain of the loan interests will contain contractual interest margin stepdowns that are based on the borrowers' achieving positive operating conditions such as reduced leverage ratios or reduced total in-

184   Carril/Fabozzi

Exhibit 1
Two Capital Structures and Associated Return Matrixes

	Capital Structure	
	A	B
Senior	80%	80%
Senior subordinated	0	10
Equity	20	10

Equity Return Matrix

Annual Defaults						Annual Defaults				
	0%	1%	2%	3%	4%		0%	1%	2%	3%	4%
IRR	13%	11%	9%	7%	6%	IRR	18%	9%	2%	0%	NA

debtedness. Such loan interests may not restrict the margin stepdowns by reference to specific dates. For illustrative purposes, three different sets of average stepdown assumptions shown in Exhibit 2 have been simulated. Assumptions have been held constant as 1.0% upfront default with recoveries of 90%.

Collateral Price. Loans may be purchased at par, discount, or premium. The effect on return can be seen in Exhibit 3. As can be seen, the effect of purchasing the collateral at a discount will be to increase the yield for the subordinated tranche holders while purchasing at a premium will decrease the yield. It has a very significant effect on the subordinated tranche returns but the floating rate nature of the collateral helps to reduce volatile price movement.

Exhibit 2
Results of Average Annual Stepdown Assumptions

Collateral Average Annual Stepdown	Expected Equity Yield over LIBOR
0 basis points	575 basis points
5	500
10	425

Exhibit 3
Effect of Collateral Purchase Price on Yield

Collateral Average Purchase Price	Expected Equity Yield over LIBOR
100.0%	375 basis points
99.5	500
99.0	625

Recoveries and Defaults. The creation of a CLO involves the input of several variables into the overall transaction. Some of these variables are set upon the loan collateral entering the portfolio, namely the initial dollar price of the loan collateral and the initial LIBOR margin. Other variables, such as the coupon stepdowns, are subject to change. However, the default and recovery variables are those which potential equity investors are most often concerned. Investors can use historical default rates for a given average portfolio rating to help set a base case for the default rates. However, there is less historical data for recovery rate assumptions. The effect of a change in recovery rates is significant. Exhibit 4 shows for our hypothetical portfolio how combinations of annual default rates and recovery rates produce approximately the same equity yields.

The secured nature of the underlying CLO collateral supports an argument for higher recovery rates when determining an investor's base case return.

Exhibit 4
Combinations of Annual Default Rates and Recovery Rates that Produce Approximately the Same Equity Yields

Annual Default	Recovery (lagged 12 months)
6%	87.50%
5	85.00
4	81.25
3	75.00
2	62.50
1	25.00
0	N.A.

APPENDIX A: CLO TRANSACTIONS

Representative HLT Securitization

Issuer	Structure	Amount (millions)	Rating	Maturity	Initial Pricing	Investment Banker
Friends I B.V.	Class A Secured	120	BBB	12/31/96	L+80	Continental
	Class B Notes	20	NR	12/31/96	Residual Formula	Continental
Friends II B.V.	Class A1-Notes Secured	297	A1	12/97	L+75	Continental
	Class A-2 Notes	12	BBB	12/97	NA	
	Class B Notes	34	BB	12/97	NA	
After B.V.	Class A Secured	500	A1	2/15/98	L+25	BNP Capital
	Class B Notes	50	N/R	2/15/98	L+75	
	Class C Notes	55	N/R	2/15/98	NA	
	Class D Notes	20	N/R	2/15/98	NA	
Rosa B.V.	Senior Secured Notes	300	AAA		L+30	Nomura
	Secured Sub Notes	500	A3		L+75	
	Residual Income Notes	200	N/R		NA	
Prospect St Senior Loan Portfolio, L.P.	Senior	N/A	AAA		C.P.	Citibank
	Sub	N/A				
	Partnership Equity	N/A				
Freedom Finance I						IBJ, Mellon, Barclay's
Freedom Finance II						IBJ, Mellon, Barclay's

APPENDIX B: SAMPLE TERM SHEET

International CLO I

$500 Million Collateralized Loan Obligation
Summary of Proposed Terms

Issuer: International Collateralized Loan Obligation I, a special purpose entity created for the sole purpose of purchasing senior secured bank debt and issuing collateralized loan obligation securities ("CLOs").

Issue: $150 million Triple-A Rated, Secured Senior/Floating Rate Notes
$250 million Single-A Rated Senior Subordinated Floating Rate Notes
$100 million Unrated Subordinated Notes

Portfolio Manager: N.A.

Placement Agent: Daiwa Securities America Inc.

Collateral Profile: Type: Senior Secured Bank Debt
Index: CD, LIBOR, Prime
Reset: Overnight, 1, 2, 3 and 6 months
Number of Loans: 25–40
Loan Size: Avg – 15MM, Range – $5–20MM
Interest Margin: Avg – 250 bps, Range – 200–275 bps
Interest Stepdowns: 40% of loans, # of stepdowns unlimited
Rating: Ba3 initial weighted average
Pool Diversity: 4% issuer, 8% industry
Asset Coverage: 122.8% initially; 112.5% ongoing test
Interest Coverage: 144% initially; 125% ongoing
Interest Reserve: .75%

Interest: Senior Notes: 3-month LIBOR +75 bp
Senior Subordinated Notes: 3-month LIBOR +150 bp
Subordinated Notes: Approximate Yield
                                             13.5–16.0%

	(Payable quarterly, commencing three (3) months from issuance)
Maturity:	Seven (7) years from issuance.
Principal Payment:	No principal repayments during the reinvestment period; thereafter principal will be amortized based on collateral principal collections and distributed to holders by priority class.
Covenants:	Will include, but not limited to, an interest coverage test of 125.0%, an asset coverage test of 112.5%, maintenance of at least a Ba3 average collateral rating, and a weighted average margin differential test of 1.75%.
Rating:	As a condition of issuance, the Senior Notes must be rated at least Aaa and the Senior Subordinated Notes A3 by Moody's.
Credit Support:	Overcollateralization.
Trustee/Paying Agent:	To be determined.

Chapter 10

Rating Debt Securitized By Bank Loans

Linda K. Moses
Structured Finance Group
Moody's Investors Service

OVERVIEW

Collateralized loan obligations (CLOs) evolved from preceding types of structured securities to provide an investment-grade vehicle for securitizing bank loans. CLOs are usually backed by highly diversified pools of speculative-grade bank loans, although they may be supported by investment-grade loans, loans to companies in a single industry, or even a single loan. Cash flows from bank loans support the promised payment of principal and interest on the CLO. The first CLO was originated in 1988; three were issued in both 1988 and 1989, and five others in 1990. The

The author adapted portions of this chapter from articles previously written with Noel E. D. Kirnon, Douglas J. Lucas, and Kimberly O. Rhodes.

volume of newly rated CLOs decreased between 1988 and 1989, but tripled in 1990 as shown in Exhibit 1. These 11 transactions have a wide array of structures, ratings, and collateral.

A CLO can be structured in several ways to enhance the probability that the investor will receive full and timely payment of principal and interest. Most commonly, CLOs are issued in a number of classes ranking in payment priority and lien position. In these structures, senior class holders are protected by the subordinated status of junior class holders. Should any shortfall in cash flows from the underlying bank loans occur, credit losses will be absorbed first by the subordinated classes. The seniority of claims to the collateral cash flows strengthens the credit quality of the top tranches, but at the same time increases the credit risk associated with the subordinate tranches.

CLOs may be structured to pay principal simultaneously to all classes or, more commonly, to pay principal sequentially, retiring one class after another in order of lien position. Triggering mechanisms, usually based on overcollateralization and interest coverage ratios, are frequently used to divert cash flow from subordinate classes. Diverted cash flow either may be funnelled into a reserve fund account where it can be drawn upon in the future to make payments to senior classes or may be used immediately to pay senior class principal. Multiclass structures may

Exhibit 1
Rated CLO Volume by Year

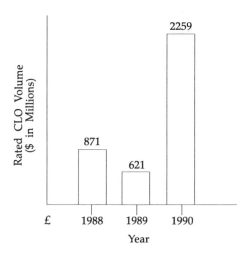

also have additional external third-party credit support, such as letters of credit, surety bonds, or liquidity facilities. Senior classes carry less credit risk and usually offer investors lower expected yields than that of the underlying bank loan portfolio. Conversely, subordinated securities have more credit risk and offer higher expected yields than the bank loan portfolio.

In "arbitrage" CLO transactions, bank loans are purchased from third parties unassociated with the issuance of the CLO. In "portfolio" transactions, a single seller of collateral initiates the CLO transaction in order to adjust the asset side of its balance sheet. A CLO can also be structured with either a managed or a passive collateral portfolio. With a managed portfolio, underlying bank loan principal payments are reinvested in new bank loans subject to specific standards of loan quality and diversity. In passive structures, underlying bank loan principal payments are used to retire outstanding CLOs.

Because a CLO relies on cash flows from the underlying bank loans and not on their market value, the CLO sponsor is usually not obligated to add more collateral to the structure should the price of the collateral decline. The rating of a CLO is based on the sufficiency of the cash flow generated by an underlying portfolio of bank loans. Investors will receive timely payment of principal and interest as long as actual portfolio defaults do not overrun the protections against default that are built into the structure. Changes in the market value of the collateral, with the exception that it may indicate a higher level of default risk, are usually not important to the CLOs.

Moody's credit ratings are designed to provide a simple and globally consistent framework for investors to use in analyzing credit risk. A Moody's rating is an opinion regarding the credit quality of a specific security. As such, a rating provides an estimate of the level of risk associated with a security's promise of timely payment of principal and interest and serves as an indicator of the comparative risk premium necessary to compensate investors for the risk of credit loss. Ratings are thus used by investors for a number of credit-related decisions; for example, in determining whether a particular security meets established credit guidelines and in estimating the level of risk premium needed to offset potential credit losses. Ratings are not intended to forecast protections against other investor concerns, such as market value risk (e.g., changes in price due to changes in interest rates, foreign exchange rates, and prepayment rates).

Bank loan defaults are the predominant credit risk in a CLO, and the first step in Moody's CLO credit analysis focuses on the credit quality of the bank loan portfolio. The default risk of the entire portfolio is based on the credit quality of each bank loan in the portfolio, and on the number and diversity of firms represented in the portfolio. The lower the credit quality and diversity of the collateral, the greater the portfolio's risk. The risk of the CLO bank loan portfolio is then compared with the safety of the CLO class being rated—usually the most-senior CLO class. The safety of a CLO class depends on the amount of subordination and other credit enhancement backing it and the conditions under which cash flow is diverted from subordinate classes to the CLO class in question.

The comparison of collateral risk to CLO structural safety is the fundamental quantitative task in rating a CLO. Moody's formally specifies the risk of the bank loan portfolio numerically as *portfolio credit risk,* which is a cumulative expected default rate on the underlying bank loans. The poorer the quality of the bank loans and the poorer the diversity of the portfolio, the higher the portfolio credit risk. Analogously, Moody's specifies the safety of a CLO class as the amount of cumulative defaults the CLO structure can sustain without causing the rated CLO class to default. That level of cumulative default, called the *structural credit protection,* is measured by cash flow models prepared according to Moody's specifications. Based solely on a quantitative perspective, a CLO's rating is determined by whether structural credit protection is at least equal to the underlying portfolio credit risk.

Paralleling the quantitative analysis is an evaluation of the transaction's legal and structural integrity. In addition, Moody's examines the various parties involved in the CLO transaction. The remainder of this chapter presents these four rating considerations as follows:

- Assessment of portfolio credit risk.

- Structural credit protection.

- Legal and structural integrity.

- Parties involved with the securities.

The calculation of portfolio credit risk is presented in the appendix.

ASSESSING PORTFOLIO CREDIT RISK

Average credit quality

The aggregate credit risk of a CLO portfolio is composed of the default probability and potential loss severity of each bank loan in the pool. That risk is explicitly addressed by the rating Moody's assigns or implies to each bank loan in the portfolio. Academic research and Moody's own studies show that an increased incidence of default accompanies a decrease in rating quality. Exhibit 2 presents average 10-year default rates for companies according to their senior unsecured rating, and includes defaults and distressed exchanges on more than 4,000 Moody's-rated companies from 1970 through 1990.

In assessing the credit risk of a portfolio, Moody's first calculates the average credit quality of the underlying bank loans, using the specific rating assigned to each asset in the pool. To calculate average ratings, Moody's has established numeric rating factors for each rating category. These are shown in Exhibit 3. Rating factors are then weighted by the par amount of the loan. If a portfolio has not been identified or if the CLO structure allows management, the issuer defines a rating factor as the lower bound for the portfolio's weighted average rating.

Moody's does not often rate bank loans; therefore, alternatives to pre-existing ratings are used. The easiest alternative is available if the bank loan obligor has rated debt of the same lien position as the bank loan

Exhibit 2
Ten-Year Company Default Rates of Senior Unsecured Debt

Rating	*Default Rate*
Aaa	1.0%
Aa	1.4
A	1.8
Baa	4.4
Ba	16.1
B	31.6

Exhibit 3
Rating Factor Equivalents

Rating of Debt Security	Rating Factor
Aaa	1
Aa1	10
Aa2	20
Aa3	40
A1	70
A2	120
A3	180
Baa1	260
Baa2	360
Baa3	610
Ba1	940
Ba2	1,350
Ba3	1,780
B1	2,220
B2	2,720
B3	3,490
Caa	6,500
Ca	10,000
C	10,000

included in the CLO portfolio. Alternatively, Exhibits 4 through 7 show how a rating may be implied to an unrated bank loan from the same company's Moody's-rated debt of a different lien position. In the case where the procedures in Exhibits 4 through 7 calculate different implied ratings, the lowest implied rating is used. The results of the procedures shown in Exhibits 4 through 7 may contain a conservative bias because they rely on generalizations of rating principles.

If no rated debt exists, a Caa rating may be implied if the borrower is not in reorganization or in other insolvency proceedings and if the bank loan is not in default. A B3 rating may be implied if the borrower meets the additional characteristics listed in Exhibit 8. As an alternative, Moody's may estimate a rating based on credit information furnished by

Exhibit 4
Senior Secured and Subordinated Debt Ratings Implied by Senior Unsecured Ratings

< ———————————	X ——————————— >	
Senior Secured Debt	*Senior Unsecured Debt*	*Any Type of Subordinated Debt*
Aaa	Aaa	Aa2
Aa1	Aa1	Aa3
Aa2	Aa2	A1
Aa3	Aa3	A2
A1	A1	A3
A2	A2	Baa1
A3	A3	Baa2
Baa1	Baa1	Baa3
Baa2	Baa2	Ba1
Baa3	Baa3	Ba2
Baa3	Ba1	Ba3
Ba1	Ba2	B1
Ba2	Ba3	B2
Ba3	B1	B3
B1	B2	B3
B2	B3	Caa
B3	Caa	Ca
Caa	Ca	C
Ca	C	C

either the CLO issuer or collateral manager. Rating estimates are made by Moody's industry specialists, who review the debt and assign a rating estimate for use in the CLO transaction. While these individual rating estimates are based on a limited review of the credit, they are useful in aggregate when calculating the weighted average rating of a bank loan portfolio. The guidelines in Exhibit 9 are usually met before analysts review the credit for inclusion in a structured security.

Additional estimation methods may also be used. For example, if a loan portfolio was underwritten by a single originator using a consistent

Exhibit 5
Senior Unsecured and Secured Debt Ratings Implied by Subordinated Ratings

< ————————————————————————— X	
Senior Unsecured and Secured Debt	*Highest Subordinated Debt*
Aaa	Aaa
Aaa	Aa1
Aa1	Aa2
Aa2	Aa3
Aa3	A1
A1	A2
A2	A3
A3	Baa1
Baa1	Baa2
Baa2	Baa3

Senior Secured Debt	*Senior Unsecured Debt*	*Highest Subordinated Debt*
Baa2	Baa3	Ba1
Baa3	Ba1	Ba2
Ba1	Ba2	Ba3
Ba2	Ba3	B1
Ba3	B1	B2
B2	B2	B3
Caa	Caa	Caa
Ca	Ca	Ca
C	C	C

internal credit rating scale, Moody's may be able to use the internal rating system to arrive at an estimation of credit quality. That method depends on a high correlation between the results of the internal rating system and Moody's own rating system. If an issuer wants to securitize a large number of loans and has relevant historical payment data available,

Exhibit 6
Senior Unsecured and Subordinated Ratings Implied by Senior
Secured Ratings

X ——————————————————————— >		
Senior *Secured Debt*	*Senior* *Unsecured Debt*	*Any Type of* *Subordinated Debt*
Aaa	Aa1	Aa3
Aa1	Aa2	A1
Aa2	Aa3	A2
Aa3	A1	A3
A1	A2	Baa1
A2	A3	Baa2
A3	Baa1	Baa3
Baa1	Baa2	Ba1
Baa2	Baa3	Ba2
Baa3	Ba1	Ba3
Ba1	Ba2	B1
Ba2	Ba3	B2
Ba3	B1	B3
B1	B2	B3
B2	B3	Caa
B3	Caa	Ca
Caa	Ca	C
Ca	C	C
C	C	C

Exhibit 7
Implying Ratings from Short-Term Debt

Short-Term *Rating*	*Equivalent Senior* *Unsecured Rating*
Prime-1	A2
Prime-2	Baa1
Prime-3	Baa3
Not Rated	No equivalent

Exhibit 8
Criteria for Estimating Ratings for Senior Secured Debt When No Debt Ratings Are Outstanding

Implied Rating	Necessary Criteria
Caa	• Borrower or affiliate is not in reorganization or other insolvency proceedings.
	• Debt is not in default.
B3	• Caa criteria.
	• Borrower or affiliates have not defaulted on any debt for the past two years.
	• Borrower has been in business for past five years.
	• Borrower is current on any cumulative preferred dividends.
	• Fixed-charge ratio exceeds 1.25 times in each of the past two fiscal years and in the most recent quarter.
	• Borrower had a net profit before tax in both the past fiscal year and most recent quarter.
	• Annual financial statements are unqualified and certified by a nationally accredited accounting firm, and quarterly statements are unaudited but signed by a corporate officer.

Moody's may also be able to apply a statistical approach based on historic default rates to determine credit quality as in other types of structured transactions, such as mortgage pass-throughs and credit-card receivables. The collateral quality rating approaches discussed here are useful when evaluating a large portfolio but may not be appropriate when evaluating individual unrated credits.

Exhibit 9
Guidelines For Reviewing Unrated Debt

Company Background	• Company is not currently in bankruptcy.
	• Company has five years of operating history.
	• Company, owner, or affiliate have not defaulted on debt during the previous five years.
Required Information For Each Debt Reviewed	• Description of company and, if available, the debt transaction, including a brief description of the security backing the debt and most recent compliance letter, including ratios.
	• Last three annual reports and last quarterly report.
	• Loan documents, including credit agreement, security documents, and participation agreement.
Monitoring Information, if Applicable	• Quarterly financial statements.
	• Audited annual statements.

Diversity

The default rate averages cited in Exhibit 2 do not reflect the variation in default rates that have occurred over different 10-year periods. For example, among companies rated **Ba** at the beginning of 1974, 6.1% defaulted over the next 10 years, compared with 21.2% over the 10-year period beginning in 1981. The magnitude of variations in these default rates suggests the presence of correlation, which means that if one company defaults there is a greater likelihood that others will default. Default correlation is only incidentally caused by one firm being the creditor of another; primarily, it is the result of individual companies being linked to one another through the general economy. In other words, to a certain extent, all companies suffer or prosper together.

The increased variability in default rates caused by correlation increases the credit protection a CLO needs to achieve an investment-grade rating. For example, suppose we know that on average a certain quality of bank loan will default 10% of the time. If defaults were uncorrelated, or independent, the default rate on a large portfolio of similar loans would not vary greatly from 10%. To protect the transaction against losses on such a portfolio, the structure would need only to be capable of absorbing losses from the approximate 10% of loans expected to default.

Suppose, however, that default correlation is so extreme that whenever one loan defaults all loans default. To be consistent with the 10% default rate, it must follow that 90% of the time none of the loans in the portfolio default and that 10% of the time all loans in the portfolio default. To fully protect against portfolio losses, the structure would have to be capable of covering losses when 100% of the loans default. The degree to which loans are default-correlated determines whether credit protection should be closer to 10% or to 100%.

Default correlation caused by general conditions in the national or international economy cannot be diversified by adding companies or industries to the portfolio. To varying degrees, all businesses are adversely affected at the same time, regardless of their specific characteristics, because of their sensitivity to the general economy. Correlation from the general economy is the base level to which default correlation from other sources must be added.

Default correlation, beyond that induced by the general economy, exists between firms in the same industry because of industry-specific economic conditions. Despite a favorable overall economy, 22 companies in the oil or oil service industry defaulted between 1982 and 1986. Other concentrations in defaults have centered on railroad conglomerates, which experienced one default in each year from 1970 through 1977; airlines, with three defaults in 1970 and 1971 and seven defaults from 1989 through 1991; thrifts, with 11 defaults in 1989; and casino/hoteliers, with 10 defaults in 1990. Default correlation also exists between companies in different industries that rely on the same production inputs and among companies that rely on the same geographical market. The 1986 oil price crash, for example, had a negative effect on a variety of companies doing business in Texas.

The next step in assessing the portfolio's risk involves the calculation of a diversity score, which measures how well the portfolio is diversified.

Moody's looks at both the number of firms in the collateral pool and their distribution among industry groups. A 32-industry classification system is used to measure intra-industry correlation (see Exhibit 10). More subtle sources of correlation, such as that caused by production inputs, markets, and geographical concentration, are then evaluated.

Adding companies to a portfolio lessens the chance of extreme outcomes and reduces portfolio credit risk. These benefits, however, are diminished to the extent that companies are correlated in terms of default and tend to survive or fail together. The phenomenon of companies tracking each other's performance is particularly apparent for firms in the same industry.

Correlation caused by the general economy is taken into account by the higher than historic default rate and loss severity assumed for the collateral. Moody's measures industry-related correlation by means of a Diversity Score, which penalizes the structure for having issuers in the same industry. For example, Exhibit 11 shows that the first firm in a particular industry earns the transaction a Diversity Score of 1. The second name in the same industry increases the Diversity Score in that particular industry to 1.5. The transaction's total Diversity Score is computed by summing the Diversity Scores of all industries in the portfolio. That methodology is adjusted to accommodate portfolios in which the par amounts per issuer are unequal.

It is industry practice to express concentration constraints by stating the maximum percentage of aggregate collateral to be held in any name or industry. To evaluate a diversity standard expressed this way, Moody's uses the lower of two diversity calculations. The first calculation assumes that the portfolio has the minimum number of names, the second calculation assumes the portfolio has the minimum number of industries. For example, if an issuer stated a diversity standard of 2% par per name and 5% par per industry, the fewest number of names would be 50. The 50 names would have to be spread over at least 25 industries; otherwise, the industry ceiling would be violated. Two names in each of 25 industries would yield a Diversity Score of 1.5 per industry and a total score of 37. The second computation assumes the fewest number of industries. For example, if the portfolio held only 20 industries each with 5% of aggregate portfolio par, each industry would have to contain three names; otherwise the name ceiling would be violated. Three names in each of 20 industries leads to a diversity index of 2 per industry, or a total of 40. Moody's would use the lower diversity score of 37.

Exhibit 10
Moody's Industry Classifications

1. Aerospace and Defense: Major Contractor, Subsystems, Research, Aircraft Manufacturing, Arms, Ammunition

2. Automobile: Automotive Equipment, Auto-Manufacturing, Auto Parts Manufacturing, Personal-Use Trailers, Motor Homes, Dealers

3. Banking: Bank Holding, Savings and Loans, Consumer Credit, Small Loan, Agency, Factoring, Receivables

4. Beverage, Food and Tobacco: Beer and Ale, Distillers, Wines and Liquors, Distributors, Soft Drink Syrup, Bottlers, Bakery, Mill Sugar, Canned Foods, Corn Refiners, Dairy Products, Meat Products, Poultry Products, Snacks, Packaged Foods, Candy, Gum, Seafood, Frozen Food, Cigarettes, Cigars, Leaf/Snuff, Vegetable Oil

5. Buildings and Real Estate: Brick, Cement, Climate Controls, Contracting, Engineering, Construction, Hardware, Forest Products (building-related only), Plumbing, Roofing, Wallboard, Real Estate, Real Estate Development, REITs, Land Development

6. Chemicals, Plastics, and Rubber: Chemicals (nonagriculture), Industrial Gases, Sulphur, Plastics, Plastic Products, Abrasives, Coatings, Paints, Varnish, Fabricating

7. Containers, Packaging and Glass: Glass, Fiberglass, Containers made of Glass, Metal, Paper, Plastic, Wood, or Fiberglass

8. Personal and Nondurable Consumer Products (Manufacturing Only): Soaps, Perfumes, Cosmetics, Toiletries, Cleaning Supplies, School Supplies

9. Diversified/Conglomerate Manufacturing

10. Diversified/Conglomerate Service

11. Diversified Natural Resources, Precious Metals, and Minerals: Fabricating, Distribution, Mining, and Sales

continued

Exhibit 10
Moody's Industry Classifications (*continued*)

12. Ecological: Pollution Control, Waste Removal, Waste Treatment, Waste Disposal

13. Electronics: Computer Hardware, Electric Equipment, Components, Controllers, Motors, Household Appliances, Information Service Communication Systems, Radios, TVs, Tape Machines, Speakers, Printers, Drivers, Technology

14. Finance: Investment Brokerage, Leasing, Syndication, Securities

15. Farming and Agriculture: Livestock, Grains, Produce, Agricultural Chemicals, Agricultural Equipment, Fertilizers

16. Grocery: Grocery Stores, Convenience Food Stores

17. Healthcare, Education and Childcare: Ethical Drugs, Proprietary Drugs, Research, Health Care Centers, Nursing Homes, HMOs, Hospitals, Hospital Supplies, Medical Equipment

18. Home and Office Furnishings, Housewares, and Durable Consumer Products: Carpets, Floor Coverings, Furniture, Cooking, Ranges

19. Hotels, Motels, Inns, and Gaming

20. Insurance: Life, Property and Casualty, Broker, Agent, Surety

21. Leisure, Amusement, Motion Pictures, Entertainment: Boating, Bowling, Billiards, Musical Instruments, Fishing, Photo Equipment, Records, Tapes, Sports, Outdoor Equipment (Camping), Tourism, Resorts, Games, Toy Manufacturing, Motion Picture Production, Theaters, Motion Picture Distribution

22. Machinery (Nonagriculture, Nonconstruction, Nonelectronic): Industrial, Machine Tools, Steam Generators

continued

Exhibit 10
Moody's Industry Classifications (*continued*)

23. Mining, Steel, Iron, and Nonprecious Metals: Coal, Copper, Lead, Uranium, Zinc, Aluminum, Stainless Steel, Integrated Steel, Ore Production, Refractories, Steel Mill Machinery, Mini-Mills, Fabricating, Distribution, and Sales

24. Oil and Gas: Crude Producer, Retailer, Well Supply, Service, and Drilling

25. Personal, Food, and Miscellaneous Services

26. Printing, Publishing, and Broadcasting: Graphic Arts, Paper, Paper Products, Business Forms, Magazines, Books, Periodicals, Newspapers, Textbooks, Radio, TV, Cable, Broadcasting Equipment

27. Cargo Transport: Rail, Shipping, Railroads, Railcar Builders, Ship Builders, Containers, Container Builders, Parts, Overnight Mail, Trucking, Truck Manufacturing, Trailer Manufacturing, Air Cargo, Transport

28. Retail Stores: Apparel, Toy, Variety, Drugs, Department, Mail Order Catalog, Showroom

29. Telecommunications: Local, Long Distance, Independent, Telephone, Telegraph, Satellite, Equipment, Research, Cellular

30. Textiles and Leather: Producer, Synthetic Fiber, Apparel Manufacturer, Leather Shoes

31. Personal Transportation: Air, Bus, Rail, Car Rental

32. Utilities: Electric, Water, Hydro Power, Gas, Diversified

Exhibit 11
Diversity Score Calculation

Number of Firms in Same Industry	Diversity Score
1	1.00
2	1.50
3	2.00
4	2.33
5	2.67
6	3.00
7	3.25
8	3.50
9	3.75
10	4.00
>10	Evaluated on a case-by-case basis

Summary and Example

Both the portfolio's quality, as measured by the bank loan's average rating, and the portfolio's diversity, as measured by its diversity score, determine the collateral's risk. The lower the credit quality and the diversity of the collateral, and the higher the requested rating, the greater the portfolio's risk.

Portfolio credit risk is expressed in terms of the percentage loss of underlying collateral the structure should be able to withstand without causing a default on the rated structured bonds the collateral supports. For example, to achieve various investment-grade ratings, a structured security supported by 30 **B2**-rated obligations from companies in 30 different industries should be able to withstand the percentage loss of the underlying collateral (after recoveries) without defaulting, this is outlined in Exhibit 12.

As a rough test of the adequacy of the above portfolio's credit risk numbers, it is useful to compare them with historic default experience. The 39% loss necessary to achieve a **Aa2** rating translates into a 55.7% default rate using a fairly conservative recovery estimate of 30%. As the average 10-year default rate for **B**-rated companies is 31.6%, and its stan-

Exhibit 12

Desired Rating	Portfolio Credit Risk (Net Loss After Recovery)
Aaa	51%
Aa1	41
Aa2	39
Aa3	37
A1	35
A2	34
A3	32
Baa1	31
Baa2	29
Baa3	26

dard deviation is 5.2%, the **Aa2** portfolio credit risk number represents the average historical default rate, plus 4.6 standard deviations. Furthermore, it should be noted that incremental losses exceeding the protection demanded by the portfolio credit risk would not have much of a negative effect on the structured bond's return, compared with the often catastrophic loss in value that a traditional corporate bond experiences following default.

In sum, the portfolio's relative credit risk is the result of the portfolio's credit quality and default correlation and the desired rating for the structured obligation. (See appendix for mathematical details.) Tables estimating portfolio credit risk under a sampling of different collateral and diversity assumptions are presented in Exhibit 13.

STRUCTURAL CREDIT PROTECTION

The analytical complement to portfolio credit risk is structural credit protection. Having determined the credit risk of the bank loan portfolio, Moody's then tests the proposed CLO structure to determine whether its resiliency to collateral losses is at least as high. The CLO's credit protections are quantified by the percentage of loss that can occur on the underlying bank loans without interrupting promised payments to the

Exhibit 13
Portfolio Credit Risk Tables

These tables show how collateral rating, portfolio diversity, and the desired rating on the structured security correspond to portfolio credit risk. The numbers in the matrices are the losses (defaults net of recovery) we look for a structure to withstand without causing a loss to the senior structured bonds. These numbers do not reflect certain qualitatively assessed factors that affect portfolio credit risk and are examined on a case-by-case basis. Portfolio risk numbers for transactions with low Diversity Scores are particularly open to qualitative adjustment based on the default correlation of the companies in the pool. Collateral Rating is the par-weighted average rating of the assets in the portfolio.

Structured Security Desired Rating: Aaa

Collateral Rating

Diversity Score	B3	B2	B1	Ba3	Ba2	Ba1	Baa3	Baa2	Baa1	A3	A2	A1	Aa3	Aa2	Aa1
									Evaluated Case-by-Case ⟶						
1															
2	100%	100%	100%	100%	100%	100%	85%	71%	57%	52%	49%	47%	45%	42%	39%
3	99	98	97	95	95	92	75	59	43	38	36	35	33	32	30
4	95	92	91	87	84	80	64	50	36	33	31	29	27	25	24
5	90	87	85	83	76	73	58	44	30	27	25	23	22	21	20
7	81	77	73	69	66	60	49	38	27	24	22	20	19	18	17
10	75	69	65	59	58	51	41	33	25	22	20	19	18	17	16
15	66	60	56	51	46	43	36	30	24	21	19	18	17	16	15
20	62	56	51	46	42	38	33	28	23	20	18	17	16	15	14
25	58	53	48	43	38	35	30	26	22	19	17	16	15	14	13
30	56	51	46	40	35	32	28	24	20	17	16	15	14	13	12
35	54	48	44	38	35	30	26	22	19	16	15	14	13	12	11
40	52	47	42	37	33	29	24	20	17	15	14	13	12	11	10

continued

Exhibit 13
Portfolio Credit Risk Tables (continued)

Structured Security Desired Rating: Aa2

							Collateral Rating						
Diversity Score	B3	B2	B1	Ba3	Ba2	Ba1	Baa3	Baa2	Baa1	A3	A2	A1	Aa3
						—Evaluated Case-by-Case————————————————→							
1	←												
2	91%	89%	86%	83%	80%	75%	55%	48%	46%	44%	42%	40%	36%
3	81	78	74	67	62	58	41	34	32	31	29	28	27
4	74	69	64	60	55	50	33	29	27	25	23	22	21
5	69	64	59	54	50	45	27	25	23	22	20	19	18
7	63	57	52	47	43	38	24	20	19	18	17	16	15
10	57	51	46	41	37	33	23	19	18	17	16	15	14
15	51	45	41	36	32	27	22	18	17	16	15	14	13
20	48	43	38	33	29	25	21	17	16	15	14	13	12
25	46	40	36	31	27	23	20	16	15	14	13	12	11
30	45	39	34	29	26	22	18	15	14	13	12	11	10
35	44	38	33	28	25	21	17	14	13	12	11	10	9
40	43	37	33	28	24	20	15	13	12	11	10	9	8

continued

Structured Security Desired Rating: A2

Collateral Rating

Diversity Score	B3	B2	B1	Ba3	Ba2	Ba1	Baa3	Baa2	Baa1	A3
	<					*Evaluated Case-by-Case*				>
1										
2	80%	77%	73%	68%	63%	55%	45%	41%	39%	35%
3	70	65	60	55	50	46	32	27	25	22
4	64	58	53	48	43	39	26	20	19	17
5	59	53	49	44	39	34	22	18	17	15
7	54	48	43	38	34	29	19	17	15	14
10	49	43	39	33	29	25	18	16	14	13
15	45	39	35	29	25	22	17	15	13	12
20	43	37	32	27	23	20	16	14	12	11
25	41	35	31	26	22	19	15	13	11	10
30	40	34	30	25	21	18	14	12	10	9
35	39	33	29	24	20	17	13	11	9	8
40	38	32	28	23	20	16	12	10	8	7

continued

Exhibit 13
Portfolio Credit Risk Tables (*continued*)

Structured Security Desired Rating: Baa2

Collateral Rating

Diversity Score	B3	B2	B1	Ba3	Ba2	Ba1	Baa3
				— Evaluated Case-by-Case —			→
1	←						
2	65%	59%	52%	46%	42%	38%	34%
3	56	50	45	39	33	29	21
4	51	44	40	34	30	25	16
5	47	41	37	31	27	23	14
7	44	37	33	28	23	20	13
10	40	34	30	25	21	17	12
15	38	32	27	22	19	15	11
20	36	30	26	21	17	14	10
25	35	29	25	20	17	13	9
30	34	29	24	20	16	13	8
35	34	28	24	19	16	12	7
40	33	28	23	19	15	12	6

rated CLO. A cash flow model that accurately portrays structural protections and Moody's modeling assumptions is fundamental to the analysis.

The credit protection of the CLO structure depends on several factors, including the amount of rated CLO issued, the level of subordination or other credit support, the interest rate spread between the bank loans and the CLOs, and the conditions under which cash flows are diverted from subordinated classes and used to protect the senior-rated CLOs. Diverted cash flows can be used to fund a reserve account or pay senior principal directly. Possible triggering mechanisms leading to the diversion of cash flow from subordinate classes include tests of interest coverage, asset coverage, portfolio defaults, and collateral credit ratings.

The structure's credit protection also varies by the assumption made regarding the timing of defaults. The longer the underlying obligations are outstanding before defaulting, the more interest income is generated by the defaulting debt and available to repay the structured bonds.

Moody's assumptions about the timing of losses are based on our default study of companies with speculative-grade ratings. About 66% of all the defaults that occur over 10 years happens in the first six years, with 35% of six-year cumulative defaults occurring in the first year. To ensure that our timing assumptions are more conservative than most actual historical loss patterns, Moody's added two standard deviations to these numbers. In that case, about 100% of 10-year defaults occur in the first six years; 50% in the first year. Accordingly, Moody's default scenario calls for 50% of all losses to occur in the first year, followed by 10% in each of years two through six. Furthermore, to protect against deterioration of credit protection at the end of the transaction, the structure is stressed by examining the losses it can sustain in its latter years.

Structural credit protection is usually significantly greater than the percentage of subordination present in the structure. The added capacity of the transaction to withstand losses is derived from the treatment of bank loan amortization in the cash flow model. In any year, defaults are based on the remaining principal outstanding, and prior principal payments are considered safe from default. Other factors that raise structural credit protection above the subordination percentage include the interest rate spread between the bank loans and CLOs and overcollateralization and interest coverage triggers which lead to the early diversion of cash flow from subordinate CLO classes to the senior-rated CLO class.

Additional modeling assumptions are made on a case-by-case basis to take into account risks unique to particular transactions; for example, those associated with floating-rate collateral, noncallable CLO debt, floating-rate structured debt, and certain interest-rate mismatches.

Miscellaneous cash flow considerations

Interest-rate mismatches and liquidity. Typically, bank loan collateral may reset at almost any time during a CLO payment period and may float off a number of indexes, including LIBOR, certificate of deposit, prime rate, and federal funds. Bank loans may also switch indexes and reset periods. Meanwhile, the CLO is likely to be based on one index that resets at regular intervals. Interest rate and interest payment date mismatches between the bank loans and the CLO must be addressed in the rating process.

Interest rate mismatches can be mitigated by obtaining an interest rate swap from an appropriately rated counterparty. Alternatively, the extent of interest rate mismatch may be sized through the use of a cash flow simulation model which assumes high interest rate volatility. If the second method is used, an interest reserve fund is sized to compensate for potential interest shortfalls throughout the life of a transaction. Timing mismatches may be addressed by a cash advance mechanism, provided either externally to the structure by an appropriately rated third party willing to make advances, or internally by a cash reserve fund.

Number of loans with interest stepdown provisions. Loans in CLO portfolios may allow stepdowns in interest rates if the borrower meets certain financial tests, which would narrow the interest spread between the bank loans and the CLOs. However, total portfolio cash flow is unlikely to be weakened by a high number of stepdowns at the same time that a large number of other loans in the portfolio default; it is unrealistic to treat the two risks as positively correlated. Nevertheless, Moody's determines whether a CLO structure can survive any reasonable scenario of interest-rate stepdowns if loans contain that provision.

Collateral accumulation. Prompted by a number of motivations, collateral managers have sought to purchase a portion of the collateral after the CLOs are sold. First, financing the purchase of the portfolio before the CLO is sold is expensive, particularly because bank loans are purchased in private transactions that can take months to complete. Second, as a market strategy, managers wish to purchase their portfolio at a slower pace and avoid a situation where sellers are aware that they must purchase their entire portfolio before their transaction closes. Therefore, additional mechanisms, such as ongoing compliance tests, are incorporated into CLO structures to help ensure that investors receive protection commensurate with the high ratings assigned to the senior classes of these securities.

Moody's is concerned that the final portfolio has the same characteristics as the portfolio presented for evaluation and modeled in the default stress test. CLO indentures for highly rated securities must contain detailed covenants that collateral managers must adhere to regarding the final characteristics of the portfolio.

Furthermore, Moody's is concerned about disruption in the collateral purchase procedure, perhaps because of an increase in collateral prices or a decrease in market liquidity. The collateral manager must demonstrate that at any time while collateral is being purchased the CLO will merit the original rating even if collateral purchase ceases. The structured securities should be able to withstand the appropriate level of loss, commensurate with the rating, taking into consideration collateral securities and uninvested cash. Again, ratings depend on detailed specification in indentures regarding how collateral is purchased during the collateral accumulation period. Moody's must also be confident that the trustee maintains a first-perfected security interest in the collateral throughout the collateral accumulation period.

Eligible investments. As with all structured transactions, eligible investments of collateral proceeds should be consistent with the rating of the transaction. Eligible investments are frequently used because CLOs receive principal and interest payments at any time during a structured security payment cycle. These receipts are reinvested in eligible investments until the structured security payment date or the date when new bank loans are added to the portfolio if appropriate.

Reserve funds also invest in eligible investments. In these cases, funds must be available in a timely manner to meet security holder obligations. Eligible investments are usually highly rated financial instruments, assuring that availability is consistent with the rating of the structured bonds.

LEGAL EVALUATION AND DOCUMENT CONTENT

Participation bank risks. Typically, CLOs can contain either loans purchased as assignments or as participations. Assignments establish a direct relationship between the borrower and the assignee. Under an assignment agreement, assignees assume a percentage of the originating banks' rights, benefits, and obligations created according to the loan agreement. However, most multibank loan agreements appoint an agent bank to receive payments from the borrower and to distribute them to the originating banks and assignees. Although these funds are not held in trust accounts, the loan agreement requires the agent to distribute its ratable share of each payment promptly to each assignee. As a practical matter, subsequent payments may be diverted around the agent bank because the loan agreement usually provides for replacement of the agent bank by a 66 2/3% vote of the originating banks and assignees. Assignments and credit agreements that provide for direct payments from the borrower to the assignee and originating bank eliminate such risk.

The inclusion of participations in a CLO may or may not affect the rating of the structured bonds. Participation loans carry the agent bank risk, along with three legal risks that involve credit exposure to the seller bank. The first problem with participations is that loan payments from the borrower flow through the seller bank, whose insolvency might interrupt payment. In a typical transaction, the participant buys a share of the benefits and obligations of the originating bank/seller created according to the loan agreement. The borrower and the participant have no contractual relationship. The originating bank retains all rights to administer the loan and make servicing decisions and provides the participants with information furnished by the borrower.

Second, if the seller bank becomes insolvent, a participation might be recharacterized as an unsecured obligation of the failed bank rather than as a true sale. If that should occur, the participant becomes a creditor of the seller bank and may not receive the incoming loan payments. That risk can be mitigated by the CLO issuer agreeing that each purchase of a participation must meet certain standards typical of a true sale. A participation may be considered a true sale if the participation agreement (1) indicates that the transfer of the interest in the loan is without recourse to the originating bank, (2) obligates the originating bank to remit payments to the participant only upon receipt of the corresponding payments from the borrower, and (3) identifies the interest sold (e.g., as a percentage of a loan).

A third participation risk exists if the seller bank becomes insolvent and borrower claims against the bank are set off against the loan, resulting in a reduction of the loan amount, including any participated amount. That risk may arise if the seller has an additional credit or a fiduciary relationship with the borrower. The seller usually discloses potential conflicts of interest to prospective participants to avoid charges of misrepresentation or omission of material fact. However, disclosure does not in itself reduce credit risk. That risk is difficult to either quantify or eliminate and becomes a factor in the participant's lending decision.

The likelihood of significant loss from these participation risks can be mitigated by either purchasing bank loans from highly rated sellers or adopting seller bank concentration limits. The lower a participant bank is rated, the fewer will be the participations from a particular bank that can be included in the portfolio of a highly rated CLO.

Other Legal Issues and Governing Documents. In addition to reviewing a proposed security's collateral portfolio and cash flow characteristics, Moody's reviews governing documents and possibly legal opinions before assigning a rating. Legal analysis and document review is an integral part of determining credit ratings for any structured security. As the facts of each transaction vary, the legal issues and their rating impact will vary as well. Moody's analysis necessarily evolves as new structures arise or as legal, legislative, or regulatory rules affecting structured finance change.

Specific concerns in this area include i) the bankruptcy-remote status of the issuer (including the likelihood of a judicial consolidation of the assets of the issuer with those of its parent in the event of the latter's insolvency), ii) the effectiveness of the transfer of loan collateral to the issuer, iii) the possibility of fraudulent conveyance of assets, iv) lender liability, v) effective subordination of tranches ranking below the most-senior of the notes, and vi) enforceability of the agreements.

i) Analyzing the Bankruptcy–Remote Status of the Issuer. In rating CLOs, Moody's evaluates the bankruptcy-remoteness of the issuer. An issuer in bankruptcy would likely cause delays in payment to the security holders, which would be inconsistent with the high investment-grade ratings enjoyed by most CLOs. Special-purpose corporations are the predominant legal vehicle used by sponsors of CLO transactions to achieve this bankruptcy-remote status.

When evaluating a special-purpose entity, Moody's looks for certain features and structural components, such as those described below, to help ensure that both the involuntary and voluntary filing of the issuer into bankruptcy is a remote possibility.

- **The risk of involuntary filings.** The existence of any third-party creditors other than rated security holders raises the possibility of an involuntary filing against the issuer. To mitigate that risk, an issuer's incorporation documents usually limit the corporation's purpose to issuing the structured debt and purchasing the collateral. In combination, these limitations severely restrict an issuer's ability to incur additional liabilities. The remaining liabilities that an issuer customarily *is* permitted to incur include accounting fees, trustee and paying agent fees, and other similar expenses. Moody's measures these projected expenses against the issuer's assets and cash flows to determine the risk of one of these parties not being paid and then possibly filing the issuer into bankruptcy. In addition, agreements by third parties that bar them from petitioning for bankruptcy until three months following the final payment of the rated CLO bonds further limits the risk of an involuntary filing against the issuer.

- **The risk of voluntary filings.** Prudent shareholders and boards of directors representing shareholders do not usually place an issuer into voluntary bankruptcy unless the issuer is unable to pay its debts when they are due. Since the possibility of a special purpose issuer of highly rated securities being unable to pay its debts is remote, the risk of a voluntary filing is arguably remote. Still, Moody's seeks further to minimize the risk of such an action. Mechanisms that reduce the risk of a voluntary filing by an issuer's shareholders or board of directors include the requirement that shareholders unanimously approve the bankruptcy petition *and* that the board of directors includes two independent directors whose approval is required for the filing of a voluntary petition.

- **Consolidation.** Even though an issuer may be bankruptcy-remote, the insolvency of the issuer's parent could give rise to an action by the parent's creditors seeking to consolidate the issuer's assets and liabilities with those of the parent. Consolidation is an equitable remedy that is highly dependent on the facts of each transaction. Such an occurrence could interrupt the business of the issuer and delay payments to the bondholders. In evaluating the risk of consolidation, consideration is given to whether (1) the issuer has established a separate business office, (2) at least one director, preferably two, has no affiliation with the parent company, (3) the issuer maintains separate corporate records and books of account, (4) the issuer's funds are not commingled with those of the parent company, (5) the issuer's board of directors holds meetings to authorize corporate actions, (6) the issuer observes all corporate formalities, (7) the parent, in dealing with its creditors, acknowledges the separate existence of the issuer, (8) the transaction has a legitimate business purpose, and (9) transactions between the parent and issuer are conducted on an arms-length basis. However, even when all these factors exist, nonconsolidation is not guaranteed. Other factors, such as the existence of loan guarantees between parent and issuer, may give rise to consolidation.

ii) Effective Transfer of Loan Collateral. Moody's also considers the effect of the insolvency of third parties, other than creditors, on a transaction, and seeks to minimize such risk to a level consistent with the requested rating. Customarily, third parties that must be evaluated include the seller of the loan collateral to the issuer and the issuer's parent company (often, the two are the same entity). In its evaluation, Moody's assesses the way in which the loans were transferred or sold to the issuer and the relationship of the issuer with its parent. In the event of the bankruptcy of the seller/transferor of assets to the issuer, a creditor of the seller may attempt to recharacterize the transfer as a secured financing instead of a true sale. If successful, the assets would be considered assets of the bankruptcy estate of the seller, and the automatic stay provisions of the bankruptcy code could apply.

In general, for a true sale to occur, the transferor must convey the future economic risks and benefits of ownership of the assets to the issuer. In determining whether a true sale has occurred, Moody's assesses the extent of recourse to the transferor, the level of subordination, and the control the transferor has over the assets. A legal opinion from independent counsel regarding the existence of a true sale may also be considered by Moody's.

In CLO asset transfers—particularly transfers of loan participations—the extent to which the transfers contain recourse provisions may raise true sale concerns. In a typical participation, the issuer buys a share of the originating bank/seller's benefits and obligations created under a loan agreement. The originating bank retains all rights to administer the loan and to make servicing decisions and provides the participants with information furnished by the borrower.

Some participation language may lead bank regulators or a court of competent jurisdiction to recharacterize the participation as a loan from the participating bank to the originating bank rather than as a true sale. For instance, participations that compel the seller to repurchase the loan in the event of a default or that subordinate the seller's share of the loan in relation to that of the participants could lead to a recharacterization. In addition, participations that have either (1) a shorter term than the originating bank's loan to the borrower, or (2) special payment arrangements that do not depend solely on payment from the borrower, could also lead to a recharacterization. If such a determination is made, the issuer would become a creditor of the originating bank. Moody's therefore examines the participation certificates and may also request legal opinions to confirm that experts consider the participations to constitute a true sale.

To help ensure that holders of the rated CLO securities benefit from the loan assets, the trustee, on behalf of the security holders, maintains a perfected-security interest in all the assets of the issuer. That interest provides additional protection in the unlikely event the issuer was rendered insolvent or the true sale was not respected. Such perfection is governed by state versions of the Uniform Commercial Code and usually requires (1) possession of assets if securities are certificated, and (2) registration in the name of the issuer or trustee for the benefit of the security holder by a financial intermediary if they are uncertificated (book-entry). Moody's may review a security interest legal opinion to confirm that all the necessary steps to convey and to perfect the security interest have been taken.

iii) Fraudulent Conveyance of Loans and Other Assets. If a loan borrower fails and if a court determines that the borrower (1) made such transfer with the actual intent to hinder, delay, or defraud its creditors, or (2) did not receive "reasonably equivalent value" for pledging its assets *and* was insolvent or became insolvent as a result of such transfer, the CLO trustee might lose its security interest in the borrower's assets. If that occurs, it would lower the expected recovery on the loan. To mitigate the risk of fraudulent conveyance, a thorough review of the loans purchased by the issuer is advisable. That procedure reduces but cannot in itself eliminate the risk of a fraudulent conveyance.

In the event of the seller's insolvency, its creditors may also attempt to retrieve assets from the CLO issuer's estate by claiming that a fraudulent conveyance occurred between the seller and the issuer (rather than between the seller and original borrower). The elements for establishing a fraudulent conveyance are the same as those described above. If the creditors are successful, a court could avoid the transfer and leave the security holders with no security interest in the collateral. In the event the issuer acquired the collateral from a single seller or from a limited number of sellers and the prices were determined in other than an arms-length manner, Moody's would closely study a fraudulent conveyance opinion, among other factors, to assess whether the seller received adequate consideration for the assets sold to the issuer.

iv) Lender Liability. A CLO security could be subject to allegations of lender liability, which may arise when a lender violates a duty of good faith and fair dealing with the borrower or assumes a degree of control over the borrower. That risk is partially mitigated in highly rated CLOs by examining the lending practices of each bank from which the CLO buys loans.

v) Subordination. When rating transactions with multiple tranches, a failure or payment delay in a subordinated, lower-rated tranche should not interfere with the priority of more senior, highly-rated tranches. Most commonly, lower tranches are structured as residual interests so that payments are due only to the extent that they are payable out of cash flows from the collateral. In such a case, the lower tranche securities may have payment-in-kind features and, even if payments are not made on the securities, a subordinated tranche security holder cannot take any action without the consent of the senior-most class of securities. In assessing whether the subordination is consistent with the rating, Moody's may also examine an opinion indicating that the subordination provisions are legal, valid, and binding.

vi) Enforceability of agreements. Moody's reviews legal enforceability opinions that address whether a transaction's governing documents and agreements are legal, valid, and binding against the relevant parties.

These opinions are typically furnished by the counsel of each entity upon whose performance the security holders and/or the issuer rely.

PARTIES INVOLVED WITH THE SECURITIES

Many structured securities, including CLOs, depend greatly on the underwriting, servicing, and administrative abilities of various parties to a transaction. Because CLOs are issued through special-purpose entities, it is often the parent company or independent third parties who perform these functions. As a result, the credit quality and/or performance of these parties is often material to the CLO rating.

The loan originator. CLOs are backed by loans that are usually originated by commercial banks; however, they are also originated by investment banks and insurance companies. The quality of the loan originator's underwriting standards is normally reviewed before rating the structured securities because standards for loan underwriting and documentation may affect the subsequent performance of the collateral. The financial strength of the loan originator is particularly important if the originator is an agent bank or if it originates participation loans. In such cases, monies are usually repaid to the agent or participating bank by the borrowers and are then forwarded to the CLO issuer.

The placement agent. A CLO placement agent usually structures a transaction by weighing the needs of the seller/loan originator, the nature of the collateral, the demands of investors, and the rating desired. The placement agent prepares cash flow models that simulate how the transaction will work if a high number of defaults occur. The placement agent also determines the impact of various changes in the bank loans, such as reductions in loan interest rates due to interest stepdowns.

The credit enhancer/liquidity provider. Some CLOs are partially supported by third-party credit enhancers that either cover losses up to a predetermined amount or provide cash advances for temporary shortfalls. The rating of these credit enhancers is usually critical to the rating of the CLO. If the rating of an enhancer is downgraded and the enhancer is not replaced or financially supported within a predetermined amount of time, then the rated structured securities face the likelihood of a downgrade.

The swap counterparty. If a swap is used to eliminate interest rate mismatches, the swap counterparty's rating is crucial to the rating of the structured CLO because a CLO default could occur if a swap payment is not made as promised.

The collateral manager. Collateral managers are usually affiliated with the loan originator or the placement agent. They may also be an independent third-party that selects collateral for inclusion in a transaction. A collateral manager's duties typically include (1) tracking the performance of the loan portfolio to determine whether it complies with certain standards set out in the transaction documents, (2) selling, trading, and purchasing new loans if the structure allows this option, and (3) periodically submitting collateral status reports to the trustee. On behalf of the trust or corporation, the manager also votes on changes in individual bank loan agreements.

The trustee. CLO bondholders rely on the trustee to act on their behalf in administering a transaction. The trustee tracks the collateral status and prepares periodic reports that are ultimately used to determine the amount of principal and interest that each class of bondholders is entitled to be paid. Because the monitoring of transactions can be intricate, sponsors of highly rated transactions usually seek an investment-grade trustee with previous, relevant experience.

The paying agent. The paying agent in a CLO distributes principal and interest payments to bondholders according to the schedule calculated by the trustee. The role of paying agent may be performed by the trustee or an independent party. The credit quality of the paying agent and the form of bank accounts that is set up help determine whether investors will be paid in a timely manner.

The custodian. As with the role of paying agent, the trustee may double as custodian or the role may be fulfilled by another third party. In any event, the duties of a custodian are to hold the loan documents comprising the collateral. By holding the documents, a custodian makes loan administration easier because the documents are in one place. This segregation of documents also helps perfect the security interest in the loans.

The accountants. Before the closing date, accountants typically verify the CLO cash flows to ascertain compliance with transaction documents. On an ongoing basis, the accountants verify information and calculations furnished by the collateral manager and trustee to ensure that investors are paid correctly.

The legal counsel. The lawyers involved in a CLO obviously play a role in providing guidance and may supply legal opinions regarding specific aspects of the transaction. In addition, the banking department of a law firm may review individual bank loan documents and focus on participation risks. They help ensure that each loan conforms with pre-established criteria.

APPENDIX: CALCULATING PORTFOLIO CREDIT RISK

Moody's uses a probabilistic, expected loss approach to determine a portfolio's credit risk. Expected loss is the average of all possible principal losses weighted by their probability. A portfolio's credit risk is quantified as the amount of loss protection needed to lower a portfolio's expected loss to the expected loss benchmark of the desired rating of the structured bonds.

For illustrative purposes, suppose that a transaction is backed by a single speculative-grade bond with a 30% default probability and the investment-grade rating sought is associated with a 5% default probability benchmark. Assume for now that defaulted bonds always lose 70% of par.

The expected loss of the speculative-grade bond with the 30% default probability and a 70% loss severity is 21%:

Probability of Default x Default Severity = Expected Loss

30% x 70% = 21%

The expected loss of the investment-grade bond with the 5% default probability and a 70% loss severity is 3.5%:

Probability of Default x Default Severity = Expected Loss

5% x 70% = 3.5%

We want to calculate the amount of credit protection necessary to lower the expected loss of the speculative-grade collateral to the expected loss of the investment-grade bond.

Probability of Default x (Default Severity – Credit Protection)
= Expected Loss

Solving the above equation, credit protection must equal 58.3%:

30% x (70% – X) = 3.5%

X = 70% – 3.5% / 30%

X = 58.3%

Note that the credit protection is not the difference between the two security's expected losses (21% – 3.5% = 17.5%). An intuitive explanation of this is that the credit enhancement is only used if there is a default on the speculative-grade debt and is therefore weighted by the default probability of the speculative-grade bond.

Probability of Default x Credit Protection = Change in Expected Loss

30% x 58.3% = 17.5%

With only one bond in the portfolio, there are only two possible outcomes: default or no default. As more bonds are added to the portfolio, the distribution of outcomes becomes more centered on the expected outcome. The more bonds added to the portfolio, the lower the necessary credit protection, as illustrated by adding one more speculative-grade bond in the example in Exhibit 14.

Solving the equation, credit protection equals 34.3%, substantially reduced from the 58.3% credit protection necessary for one speculative-grade bond to achieve the same expected loss as the investment-grade bond. That reduction in credit enhancement is a result of the decreased variance in the portfolio's expected loss.

Necessary credit protection also depends upon assumptions about the distribution of potential recovery rates on a defaulted bond. Suppose loss in the case of default can be 100%, 85%, 70%, 55%, and 40%, with equal probability. Exhibit 15 shows the relevant calculation.

Exhibit 14

Probability of 1 Default* x
(Default Severity if 1 bond defaults – Credit Protection)
+
Probability of 2 Defaults** x
(Default Severity if 2 bonds default – Credit Protection)
=
Expected Loss
or:
(2 x 30% x 70%) x
(35% – Credit Protection)
+
(30% x 30%) x
(70% – Credit Protection)
=
3.5%

*The probability of the first bond defaulting and the second bond not defaulting is the default probability of the first multiplied by one minus the default probability of the second. The probability of the first bond not defaulting and the second bond defaulting is one minus the default probability of the first multiplied by the default probability of the second. These two products are summed to obtain the probability of either one of the two bonds defaulting.

**The probability of both bonds defaulting is the probability of the first bond defaulting times the probability of the second bond defaulting.

Exhibit 15

Probability of Default x Probability of 100% Loss x (100% – Credit Protection) +
Probability of Default x Probability of 85% Loss x (85% – Credit Protection) +
Probability of Default x Probability of 70% Loss x (70% – Credit Protection) +
Probability of Default x Probability of 55% Loss x (55% – Credit Protection) +
Probability of Default x Probability of 40% Loss x (40% – Credit Protection)
= 3.5%

In solving the equation, portfolio credit protection equals 65.6%. Note that the credit protection is higher than that in either the one or the two bond case, where loss was assumed to be constant at 70%. That is because when losses are 40% or 55%, credit protection is capped at 40% or 55%, respectively, because an investor never receives more than 100% of par. To offset the reduced probability of using the full credit protection, the amount of credit protection must be increased.

The above examples introduce the four important quantitative factors that must be considered when assessing the credit risks of a corporate debt portfolio:

- Moody's ratings of the collateral, quantified as a default probability.

- Default loss severity and distribution.

- Diversifiable and undiversifiable default correlation, quantified as higher default probability and as an adjustment to the number of bonds assumed in the portfolio.

- Desired rating of the structured security, quantified as the target expected credit loss.

Default Probability and Loss Severity. Moody's study of default rates found 10-year average cumulative default rates as low as 1.0% for companies with **Aaa** senior unsecured ratings and as high as 31.6% for companies with **B** senior unsecured ratings. These default rates refer to the company rating at the beginning of the 10-year period and include the defaults of companies subsequently downgraded. An interpolation of these results to show default rates by numerical rating modifiers yielded the results shown in the left-hand column of Exhibit 16. Moody's stressed these interpolated default rates to allow for variations in future default rates caused by harsher economic conditions and undiversifiable default correlation. The resulting assumed default rates in any rating category are higher than those actually experienced over any 10-year period.

These default probabilities for single debt obligations are the basis for computing the probability of multiple defaults within a portfolio. A binomial distribution is assumed, where the probability of y defaults out of a portfolio of n debt obligations is as follows:

$$(n \text{ choose } y) \times (\text{Probability of Default})^y \times (1 - \text{Probability of Default})^{(n-y)}$$

Exhibit 16

Rating	Historic 10-Year Default Rates	Assumed 10-Year Default Rates
Aaa	1.0%	1.8%
Aa1	1.2	1.9
Aa2	1.4	2.0
Aa3	1.5	2.2
A1	1.7	2.5
A2	1.8	3.0
A3	2.3	3.6
Baa1	3.5	4.4
Baa2	4.4	5.4
Baa3	7.5	7.9
Ba1	11.9	17.4
Ba2	16.1	21.5
Ba3	20.6	26.0
B1	25.9	32.1
B2	31.6	37.9
B3	39.6	45.8

Several historical studies of bond defaults have shown that the average price of a bond shortly after default, without regard to lien position, is approximately 40% of par, although there is evidence that recovery rates have recently declined. Moody's uses a recovery distribution that varies from 0% to 60% and has a mean of 30%, which is lower than the historic average.

Moody's computes the portfolio's credit risk using the actual rating of the specific collateral in the portfolio (or if trading is allowed, the limit to which trades may be made) and the 0% to 60% recovery assumption. That method is possible because Moody's assessment of portfolio credit risk is stated in terms of expected loss, which is the product of default probability and default severity, and because the rating system is de-

Exhibit 17

Rating	Historic 10-Year Default Rates Without Special Events	Target Expected Loss
Aaa	0.0%	0.002%
Aa1 to Aa3	0.9%	0.06% to 0.23%
A1 to A3	1.1%	0.37% to 0.86%
Baa1 to Baa3	3.4%	1.25% to 3.33%

signed so that obligations of the same rating have the same expected loss. A senior-secured bank loan, for example, would have a lower loss severity but an offsetting higher default probability than a subordinated bond of the same credit rating. Since the expected loss of all obligations of the same rating category is roughly the same, and since the approach to calculating portfolio credit risk focuses on expected loss, an accurate assessment of the portfolio can be made by adjusting default probability while maintaining the same recovery assumption. That simplification makes it easier to compute the portfolio's credit risk and to monitor the trading activity of transactions with nonstatic portfolios.

Target Expected Returns. To determine expected losses commensurate with each investment-grade rating category, Moody's first computed historic default rates on investment-grade companies without counting defaults caused by special events. These default rates were then lowered to make investment-grade ratings harder to achieve, particularly for speculative-grade collateral. Finally, to arrive at expected loss, the reduced default rates were multiplied by a 60% loss severity assumption, which is a lower loss severity than that assumed for collateral. These assumptions, shown in Exhibit 17, lower the target-expected loss that a structure must achieve, and add another conservative bias to our approach to ensure that structured investors receive a structured security with the credit characteristics of the investment-grade rating.

PART IV
Distressed Debt

Chapter 11

Investing in Chapter 11 and Other Distressed Companies

JANE TRIPP HOWE, C.F.A.
VICE PRESIDENT
PACIFIC INVESTMENT MANAGEMENT COMPANY

Investors and analysts often shy away from distressed and Chapter 11 companies. On the surface, this hesitancy is understandable. Most investors would not willingly invest in bankrupt companies, which the Random House Dictionary defines as "as the end of one's resources" or in the state of "utter ruin, failure, depletion, or the like." Most analysts believe that analysis directed at healthy companies is more likely to be profitable. This avoidance of bankrupt and distressed companies is not wise for several reasons. First, investing in Chapter 11 companies can be highly profitable. Many companies use the bankruptcy process to reorganize. Often, the reorganization process gives companies a new start

I wish to thank George Putnam III, publisher of *Bankruptcy Datasource*, for his helpful comments and suggestions.

that can provide rewarding investment opportunities. The key to success is to differentiate between the companies that are truly depleted and those that will reorganize successfully. Secondly, a total avoidance of bankrupt companies may result in an investor selling a holding of a bankrupt company at its lowest price. The price of securities of companies that have filed for Chapter 11 often plummet when the filing is made. These prices often recover somewhat with time. Investors who immediately sell their securities upon news of a filing will often suffer a more significant loss than would occur if they had been patient.

Historically, most investors who owned companies in bankruptcy did so by default. Today, many investors actively invest in companies in reorganization. These investors intend to profit by taking advantage of the substantial inefficiencies in this market. This chapter gives the investor an understanding of the bankruptcy process and outlines a method for evaluating securities in bankruptcy.

The methodology outlined here can also apply to companies that are distressed but have not filed for bankruptcy. In the case of distressed companies, the analyst should value the company as an ongoing business as well as a business that has filed for bankruptcy. With these two valuations in hand, the analyst will be able to weigh the potential benefit/cost of investing in the security.

THE IMPORTANCE OF A BASIC UNDERSTANDING

Most investors believe that they will never have to deal with a company that has filed for protection under the Bankruptcy Code. Although this may be true for the majority of investors, as long as there are bankruptcies, there will be investors who own the securities of the bankrupt companies. The possibility of your owning the securities of one of these companies is increasing as the number of companies filing for protection under the Bankruptcy Code has been increasing in recent years. A basic understanding of bankruptcy analysis is also important in order to evaluate the potential rewards of this market.

OVERVIEW OF BANKRUPTCY

There are two types of investors who deal with the securities of companies in bankruptcies. The first type is the investor who owns the security by default. This investor purchases the security with the intention of profiting from a healthy company. The second type of investor buys the securities of bankrupt companies after the company has filed for protection. Regardless of how you came to own the security, the analysis of the holding is similar.

Investors who analyze their investment holdings carefully are unlikely to be surprised if one of their investments petitions for bankruptcy protection. The decline of a company into bankruptcy generally takes several years and is often the result of illiquidity and deteriorating operating performance. Although most bankruptcies can be predicted in advance with sound credit analysis, companies occasionally file for protection that are financially sound. For example, Johns Manville was profitable when it declared bankruptcy because of the contingent liabilities arising from claims of individuals suffering from asbestos-related diseases as well as claims from property owners who incurred costs for the removal of asbestos materials from their property. Although bankruptcy filings for nonfinancial reasons are less easy to predict, they should not be complete surprises. For example, sometime in the future, tobacco companies could be faced with a similar situation regarding their contingent liabilities for illnesses caused by smoking. The astute analyst should always be mindful of footnotes that outline contingent liabilities.

All companies that file for bankruptcy are governed by the Bankruptcy Reform Act of 1978, which then-President Carter signed into law on November 6, 1978. The Act became law on October 1, 1979. The purpose of the law is twofold: (1) to provide consistency to the companies filing for protection under the law and (2) to provide a framework under which a company can either reorganize or liquidate in an orderly fashion. Perhaps the most important facet of bankruptcy law is the protection it affords companies in distress. Filing for protection triggers the automatic stay provision of the Code. This provision precludes attempts of creditors to collect prepetition claims from the debtor or otherwise interfere with its property or business. This provision gives the debtor breathing room to formulate a plan of reorganization or to formulate a plan for orderly liquidation. Creditors are necessarily discouraged from racing to court to dismember the debtor.

The current Bankruptcy Code consists of 15 chapters. Each chapter deals with a different facet and/or type of bankruptcy. For most investors, an understanding of Chapters 7 and 11, which deal with corporate liquidation and corporate reorganization, respectively, are sufficient.

When a Company Files for Protection

When a company files for protection under the bankruptcy law, it can do so either voluntarily or involuntarily. A voluntary petition is filed by the company declaring bankruptcy. In an involuntary bankruptcy, the petition is filed by the creditors of the company.

When a company files for bankruptcy, the filing may include only the parent company and exclude one or more subsidiaries. For example, when Southmark filed for protection in July 1989, several of its subsidiaries were not initially included in the filing. These nonfiling subsidiaries included NACO Finance, Thousand Trails, Southmark California (Carlsberg Corp.), and Servico. In a similar manner, when Lomas Financial filed for Chapter 11 in September 1989, many of its operating subsidiaries were not included. In an effort to educate the investing public as to which of its subsidiaries filed and which did not file, Lomas placed a full page advertisement in the New York Times to outline the difference.

When a company files for bankruptcy, it files in the appropriate circuit and the appropriate district within that circuit. (There are 11 circuits and 93 districts.) The "appropriate" court cannot necessarily be predicted. Appropriate can mean the court with jurisdiction over the company's headquarters location or perhaps the court with jurisdiction over its principal place of business. Companies have some flexibility in their choice of geographic location for filing. Eastern Airlines, for instance, filed in New York even though its corporate headquarters is Miami. The airline stated it filed in New York because it has substantial operations in New York, and its financial efforts and lawyers are there. Many of Eastern's creditors are also in New York, which will facilitate meetings.

When a company petitions for protection, its petition is accompanied by several items, including basic administrative information and a listing of the 20 largest creditors. These creditors will be contacted by the court and called for a meeting. Other financial information is required within 15 days of filing. Sometimes, the financial information accompanies the filing. Other times, it is delayed. Included in this financial information is a listing of assets and liabilities as of the petition date. This listing represents the company's best estimate of its assets and liabilities. Often, this listing of assets and liabilities can cover several hundred pages.

Significant adjustments are often made to the assets and liabilities by the time a company completes its reorganization process. These adjustments are noticeable when assets are sold during the reorganization process and also when the asset values are compared with estimates of the liquidation value of the assets. This is principally because the values are based on the company as an ongoing business in its prepetition form. Revco's February 1989 sale of 113 sites exemplifies the discrepancy between listed asset values and realizable value. In its February 1989 sale, Revco was enabled (with bankruptcy court approval) to sell 14 sites. What is more significant, however, is the fact that no bids were made on several sites. the difference between listed market value of assets and the liquidation value of these assets can be even more dramatic. For example, in its September 5, 1989, Second Amended Plan of Reorganization, Cardis Corporation estimated that its inventory would be discounted by 52%. Cardis further estimated that its net plant, property, and equipment would be discounted by 23% in a liquidation. In fact, the only asset that will not suffer a discount will be cash.

Although the assets and liabilities filed with the Bankruptcy Court are not precise, they are useful in that they give an indication of the overall picture of the company. For example, when Manville filed for protection in 1982, it had more assets than liabilities and was a profitable company. On the other hand, when Worlds of Wonder filed on December 22, 1987, it listed $271.6 million in debts and $222.1 million in assets.

Once a company files for protection under the Bankruptcy Code, the company becomes a "debtor-in-possession." As such, the company continues to operate its business under the supervision of the court. Usually, the debtor-in-possession needs to obtain court approval only for major and unusual transactions (such as the sale of property). Generally, the United States Trustee for the particular district is assigned to the proceeding. The U.S. Trustee's duties are esentially administrative. The appointment of the U.S. Trustee has become fairly standard.

The increasing complexity of bankruptcies has resulted in the increased frequency of a second appointment to a bankruptcy case. This appointment is usually an examiner but can also be a trustee. The requirements for the appointment of an examiner are fairly broad. An examiner can be appointed if the appointment serves the interests of the creditors, equity holders, or other interests. For example, an examiner was appointed in the case of A. H. Robbins because management had shown an inability to follow the bankruptcy rules. An examiner was also appointed in the case of Eastern Airlines, whose slide into bankruptcy was at least partially caused by striking unions. Shortly after Eastern Airlines filed for protection, the unions petitioned the court to have an examiner appointed rather than a trustee so that it would have more flexibility in running its business. The federal bankruptcy judge in the Eastern case ordered the appointment of a "powerful" examiner, who was given a broad mandate to end the strike. Sometimes, if there are allegations of negligence or mismanagement, then an examiner will be appointed to investigate the allegations and report to the court. Occasionally, a trustee will be appointed by the court to take control of the business if there is gross negligence or mismanagement. This is relatively unusual. A recent case where a trustee was appointed was Sharon Steel, where there were allegations of fraud.

Proceeding Toward a Plan

The purpose in filing for protection under the Bankruptcy Code is to give the debtor time to decide whether it should reorganize or liquidate and time to formulate a plan for the chosen action. The intent generally is to successfully reorganize. The first step in formulating a plan of reorganization is the appointment of committees. Generally, only a committee of unsecured creditors is appointed by the U.S. Trustee. Frequently, this committee is comprised of an elected subcommittee of the 20 largest creditors. The committee represents a particular class of claimants. Its principal function is to help formulate a plan of reorganization that is equitable to all classes and that will be confirmed (approved) by the court and the claimants. The committee approach is necessary because plans are negotiated.

Although only one committee is usual, there has been a growing incidence of multiple committees, each representing a different class of creditors. For example, in the Revco D.S. bankruptcy, there are two committees—the Noteholders Committee and the Unsecured Creditors Committee. In the Allegheny bankruptcy, there were four committees: the Equity Holders Committee, the Secured Creditors Committee, the Unsecured Creditors Committee, and the Sunbeam Corporation Creditors Committee. Often, the existence of multiple committees slows the bankruptcy process as factions can develop that undermine the spirit of cooperation necessary to formulate a plan. Cooperation is necessary because plans of reorganization rarely work under the premise of absolute priority; that is, the most senior classes are paid in full before a less senior class receives anything. The negotiation process inherent in a reorganization generally grants all classes some token distribution in order to obtain their acceptance of the plan. This is the reason why shareholders often receive some percentage of the equity of the reorganized company.

(The percentage distributed to the equity holders varies considerably. In recent plans of reorganization, equity holders of Po Folks are proposed to receive zero percent, while equity holders of Allis Chalmers are proposed to receive 19%.)

After the committee of unsecured creditors has been appointed, the debtor generally makes specific decisions whether to assume or to reject its executory contracts (contractual commitments entered prior to bankruptcy for the provision of future goods or services). In many bankruptcies, the rejection of high-priced contracts has been beneficial to the debtor. For example, when LTV declared bankruptcy, it was able to reject several high-priced contracts for raw materials. Several debtors also rejected high-priced labor contracts. For example, in 1984, a bankruptcy judge upheld Continental Airline's decision to break its labor agreements with its pilots union. The laws have changed for the rejection of labor contracts. Currently, collective bargaining agreements cannot be rejected so easily. Although many executory contracts can be rejected, specific rules may apply to the rejection of certain contracts. For example, Chapter 11 companies may reject leases with the approval of the Bankruptcy Court, only after they have made efforts to sell the sites. This was the case with Revco. After Revco held an auction for 113 sites, the Bankruptcy Court was likely to grant Revco permission to reject the leases of sites for which no bids were received.

Formulation of a Plan

Once the committee(s) are in place, the formulation of a plan begins. The debtor has the exclusive right to file a plan of reorganization for 120 days. The length of the exclusive period is determined by the court and can be extended or shortened. (Generally, the period of exclusivity tends to be longer than 120 days.) No other plan from interested parties can be filed during this period. However, this exclusive period does not stop other parties from formulating plans. In the case of Allegheny International, the unsecured creditors formulated a plan during the period of exclusivity (which had been repeatedly extended) because of their frustration with what they perceived to be lack of progress in the Allegheny bankruptcy. Generally, the first plan of reorganization is not the final plan. It is common to see the first amended and second amended plans of reorganization. (During August 1989, Allegheny International filed its Sixth Amended Plan of Reorganization.) Sometimes, even the debtor knows that its first formulation of a plan is not its final formulation. For instance, Allegheny actually labeled its August 30, 1988, Disclosure Statement "Preliminary." It is important to remember that a plan is commonly amended at least once before it is confirmed. Amended plans often entail significant changes in the funding of the plan, terms of the reorganization securities, and distributions to classes. Investors must be certain that they are working with the most recent plan of reorganization.

Investors must also be aware of plans of reorganization filed by others. For example, in September 1989, four plans of reorganization were filed for Public Service Company of New Hampshire. These plans were filed by (1) Public Service Company of New Hampshire (the debtor), (2) New England Power Company on behalf of itself and New England Electric System, (3) The United Illuminating Company, and (4) Northeast Utilities Service Company. A potential investor in Public Service Company of New Hampshire's securities would have to be familiar with each of these plans.

There are several ways to ensure that the investor is working with the most recent plan. One way is to keep in contact with the debtor. A second way is to keep in contact with the court in which the petition was filed. A third way is to subscribe to a bankruptcy service such as *Bankruptcy Datasource* in Boston, which has the advantage of being timely and convenient.

In filing a plan of reorganization, a debtor with one or more subsidiaries must decide if the plan will incorporate substantive consolidation of the subsidiaries. Under substantive consolidation, all of the assets and liabilities of the entities in question are pooled and used collectively to pay debts. Substantive consolidation must be approved by the court. The approval is not granted lightly. In order for substantive consolidation to be granted, proponents must prove that the parent and the subsidiaries in question operated as a single unit. This can be proven by such means as intercompany guarantees and transfers of assets. The issue of substantive consolidation can have important ramifications for the investor. For example, in the case of LTV, the aerospace/defense subsidiary was profitable and had assets in excess of its liabilities. On the other hand, the steel subsidiary was unprofitable at the time of filing and had liabilities significantly in excess of its assets. If LTV is reorganized without substantive consolidation, investors owning the securities guaranteed by the aerospace/defense subsidiary will receive generous distribution. On the other hand, if substantive consolidation is granted, the distributions to these investors will be decreased as the assets of the aerospace/defense subsidiary will be pooled to pay the debts of the entire corporation.

Disclosure Statement

Once a plan of reorganization has been finalized (and generally has been informally approved by the major creditors), the debtor produces and files for approval a disclosure statement about the plan with the court. The disclosure statement provides enough information to allow reasonable investors to make informed judgments. The court does not approve a disclosure statement unless the judge is satisfied that the information presented is accurate and helpful to the impaired classes. A disclosure statement summarizes the plan. It also contains fairly detailed financial information about the debtor including the company's five-year pro forma statements, which are required by statute. It also presents a liquidation analysis of the company that supports the company's contention that creditors will receive a higher distribution under the plan than they would if the debtor were to liquidate. The disclosure statement also provides a brief history of the company, including reasons for filing and significant events since filing. The disclosure statement is generally more understandable and readable than the legal plan.

If the court approves the disclosure statement, the plan and the disclosure statement are mailed to the impaired classes for approval. Holders of claims that are not impaired (i.e., claims that are paid in full or whose interests are not adversely affected by the proceeding) are not entitled to vote because unimpaired classes are conclusively presumed to have accepted the plan. Classes that are entitled to vote are generally given 30 days to do so.

In order for a plan to be accepted, at least two-thirds of the amount and more than one-half of the number of claims allowed for voting purposes of each impaired class and at least two-thirds of the outstanding shares of each class of interest must accept the plan. If the plan is approved by the voting classes, it is sent to the court for confirmation. When the court confirms the plan, it approves the transactions specified in the plan and a date for the reorganization to take effect.

Cram-Down

It is interesting to note that a plan can be confirmed under the cram-down provisions even if the required number of creditors do not approve the plan. The confirmation of a plan under the cram-down provisions must meet several specific requirements. First, the plan must be shown not to discriminate unfairly against any impaired class. Such a determination includes the requirement that no class shall receive more than 100 percent of the amount of its claim. In addition, each dissenting class must receive as much as they would be entitled to receive under a liquidation. Often, plans state that the Bankruptcy Court will confirm the plan under the cram-down provisions if all the requirements are met except for the requirement that each class has accepted the plan. Second, a plan must be shown to be fair and equitable to a nonaccepting class. Under the Bankruptcy Code, a plan is fair and equitable to a nonaccepting class if, among other things, it provides that the nonaccepting class either (a) receives property of a present value equal to the allowed amount of such claims, or (b) if the class is to receive property of any lesser value, no class junior to the nonaccepting class receives or retains any property under the plan.

ANALYSIS OF COMPANIES IN REORGANIZATION

There are several different approaches that can be used to invest in the bankruptcy market. Large and aggressive investors buy a substantial block of the debtor's bonds and try to become a significant factor in the reorganization plan. Often these investors pool their resources in "vulture funds," which invest in the securities of bankrupt companies. Such funds often operate by acquiring large blocks of a particular class of securities and use their leverage in the reorganization process to formulate a plan favorable to their position. All such strategies are not profitable. In one case, a vulture fund acquired a large percentage of the subordinated debentures of a Chapter 11 company, hoping that it would receive a controlling equity interest in the reorganized company. Unfortunately for the vultures, more than 90% of the equity in the reorganized company was distributed to secured creditors.

Investing in Individual Securities

Another approach to investing in Chapter 11 companies, more suited to individual investors, is to buy specific securities in a bankrupt company. This approach has the advantage of not requiring a large investment, thereby allowing investors to diversify their investments. It does require, however, a significant commitment to analysis of the company but has the potential of being extremely profitable.

In buying the securities of a bankrupt company, the investor has the choice of investing for a general improvement in the overall condition of the company or of investing in situations (such as secured bonds) where the return is more quantifiable because of the assets.

Selecting the Universe

Selection of a universe of potential acquisition candidates is the initial step in investing in bankrupt securities. Thousands of corporations file Chapter 11 petitions yearly. However, many of these filings represent corporations whose securities are inappropriate for individual investment because the corporations are very small. In these cases, the individual investor could have difficulty obtaining sufficient financial information for analysis or purchasing the securities if analysis could be accomplished. Individual investors should confine their universe to companies that are publicly traded and have assets of at least $25 million. Potential candidates fitting this description can be collected from a variety of sources. An individual investor will probably find a sufficient universe from which to select simply by consulting the business section of newspapers. All listed bankruptcies are identified by a symbol. All bankruptcies listed on the New York, American, and the National Association of Securities Dealers Automated Quotation system's over-the-counter have "vj" preceding the name of the stock. For example, BASIX Corporation was listed on the New York Stock Exchange Composite Transactions as of September 26, 1989, as vjBasix. The NASDAQ National Market Issue listings include an additional indication of bankruptcy. These listings are identified by a four- or five-letter symbol. The fifth letter indicates the issues that are subject to restriction or special conditions. Securities that are in bankruptcy have a "Q" as the fifth letter of their symbol. For example, American Carriers was listed on the NASDAQ National Market Issues as of April 6, 1989, as vjAmCarriers ACIXQ. A reading of the business section of a major newspaper should keep investors current on recent bankruptcy listings.

Obtaining Financial Information

Perhaps the most difficult aspect of investing in Chapter 11 companies is obtaining financial information. Trading in the securities of small companies that have filed for bankruptcy can present problems if the companies are delisted. (If a company is delisted, its price can often be found on the National Daily Quotation Service "Pink Sheets," published by the National Quotation Bureau. The Pink Sheets also provide potential market makers for the issues listed on the sheets.) More importantly, financial information can be difficult to obtain after a filing. Although SEC filing requirements are not suspended for Chapter 11 companies, filing requirements are often neither strictly observed nor enforced. Therefore, a potential investor may want to limit his or her universe of investment candidates to those Chapter 11 companies whose filings are current. This is not always necessary, however, if the investor uses other sources of information and invests only in those securities that are clearly undervalued, employing alternative methods of evaluation.

Once a list of potential candidates has been selected, the collection of financial information should begin. For each company, the investor should obtain the most recent annual report, 10-K, and quarterly report. In addition, the investor should obtain the 8-K that reports on the bankruptcy because this document may have useful facts about the filing. These documents will give the investor some indication of how the company has performed historically and perhaps why it declared bankruptcy. (Old copies of *Value Line* are also useful for obtaining historical perspectives on companies.) The investor should also collect information on the company's publicity traded securities. For stock, such data would include current shares outstanding, par value, and current price.

The information that should be gathered for bonds is more substantial. Bond data should include a complete description of the bond, the amount of bonds outstanding including the amount of original-issue discount, price, and security (i.e., the specific assets supporting the bond). If the value of the security is known or can be estimated, this should also be listed. All bonds should be listed in order of seniority. Sometimes the securities data is found in the 10-K. More often, the investor needs to consult the appropriate *Moody's Manual* (industrial, public utility, etc). These are found in most libraries.

It is also important to stay current on the news items that affect each of the companies being considered. An easy way to accomplish this is to use a computer news retrieval service such as the Dow Jones News Retrieval, which lists all news stories from the past 90 days from the Dow Jones News Service (the Broad Tape), *The Wall Street Journal,* and *Barron's*. However, the Dow Jones News Retrieval is of little help if companies have been delisted. Finally, one should attempt to be placed on the mailing list of the companies being considered. This is sometimes difficult, particularly for those who do not own any securities.

Investing without a Plan of Reorganization

Perhaps the most important documents for the analysis of bankrupt securities are the most recent plan of reorganization and the accompanying disclosure statement. These documents specify what each class of claimants (including each class of security holders) will receive in a reorganization. If a plan of reorganization has not been filed, investors must speculate on the distributions to the classes. Because it does not lend itself to thorough analysis, investing without a plan of reorganization is not generally recommended for the individual investor. Although investors can make intelligent decisions regarding some of the more senior debt of the Chapter 11 company, the inability to analyze thoroughly causes trouble in the area of common stock. An analysis of distributions for numerous bankruptcies quickly reveals the variance of distributions made to holders of common equity interest who have received from zero percent to a major portion of the equity in the reorganized company.

Potential distributions to common stockholder can be further complicated if the "new value" principle is applied. This principle contends that the equity holders who contribute new money and management expertise to the reorganization should receive a substantial equity position in the reorganized company. Unfortunately for the holders of subordinated debt, the increased distribution to equity holders translates into a decreased equity distribution to them. Although this principle has been applied in some small bankruptcies, it is infrequently applied in the larger cases. This may change. Revco's preliminary proposal grants 55% of the new Revco stock to its stockholders in exchange for $150 million. Under the proposal, secured creditors would be paid in full, but subordinated debt holders would only receive stock and bonds valued at 25% of their claims.

The valuation of the securities of a debtor that has not filed a plan of reorganization is similar to a liquidation analysis with one important exception. The company is assumed to be an ongoing business, and therefore, no substantial discount is applied to the value of its assets. Under this approach, the assets of the company are totaled and the liabilities are systematically subcontracted from this total to give an approximation of how many assets are available to repay each class of claimants. Each class is subtracted in order of seniority. For example, the fully secured claims will be among the first to be subtracted. Although this approach is a quick valuation technique, it is imprecise. It can, however, be used even with somewhat dated financials. Further, this methodology can be usefully applied to both a full and a liquidation value of the company. This application would serve to bracket the value of the company with a worst case (liquidation value) as well as an optimistic case (full valuation). The application of this technique is outlined below.

Estimated Valuations of Securities

Total Assets			$xxx
Less:	Collateralized debt		
		Banks	−xxx
		Other	−xxx
Equals:	Amount remaining for distribution to other creditors		xxx
Less:	Amount due to other creditors (in order of seniority)		−xxx

This approach is generally not applicable to the valuation of the common stock simply because the assets are depleted before the common stock holders are eligible for a distribution. In order to estimate a value for common stock holders, one must make assumptions regarding a plan of reorganization and what percentage of the equity of the reorganized company the old shareholder will receive. If this approach is used, the valuation of the common stock should follow the methodology presented under "Investing With a Plan of Reorganization."

Secured Bonds

A major exception to the premise that investors should generally wait until a plan of reorganization is filed relates to secured bonds. When a company petitions for protection, it is subject to the automatic stay provisions of the Bankruptcy Code. These provisions generally disallow the accrual of interest during bankruptcy, except in the case of secured bonds. Secured claims are allowed to accrue post-petition interest during bankruptcy to the extent of the value of the collateral. (Although post-petition interest is accrued, the Code does not generally require that it be paid.) Given these provisions, an astute investor could conceivably purchase a secured bond whose collateral exceeds the principal amount of the bond at a substantial discount to par, knowing that the bond will eventually be either reinstated or be paid off at par plus post-petition interest. An example of how this provision of the Bankruptcy Code could have been beneficial to investors is provided by the LTV bankruptcy. When LTV filed for bankruptcy on July 1, 1986, all of its securities declined significantly. The overall decline overlooked the intrinsic value of the Youngstown Sheet & Tube First Mortgage bonds, whose collateral exceeded the value of the bonds. These bonds, therefore, were entitled to the continuation of their interest.

An additional exception relates to certain equipment trust financing. Much airline equipment debt and railroad equipment debt is exempt from the automatic stay provisions of the Code and the power of the court to repossess the equipment due to §§ 1110 and 1168 of the Bankruptcy Code, respectively. Instead, the court gives the debtor 60 days to reaffirm the lease on the equipment or return the equipment to the lessor. The debtor is unlikely to cancel the lease because the equipment represented by the lease is the operating asset of the company, without which the company cannot operate. Airlines cannot operate without airplanes! Generally, in cases of § 1110 equipment trusts, the debtor assumes the lease and resumes current interest payments, including interest payable during the 60-day period. Recent examples of § 1110 equipment trusts are Eastern Air Lines' 16.125 percent Secured Equipment Trust Certificates due 10/15/02 and Eastern's 17.5% Secured Equipment Certificates, Series A, due 1/1/98, and Series B, due 7/1/97. The fact that a particular equipment certificate is covered under § 1110 is not part of the general description of the certificate. The investor must refer to the "Events of Default, Notice and Waiver" section of the prospectus or indenture of a given issue to ensure that a particular trust certificate is covered. Although these Bankruptcy Code sections may provide some added protection to investors, the protection is not assured. The investor must also factor in the possibility that the carrier will liquidate. The investor must also consider the age of the aircraft and whether the debtor is likely to reaffirm a specific lease

Fraudulent Conveyance

Investors cannot rely blindly on the secured status of particular bonds. In some instances, the issue of fraudulent conveyance or transfer may become an issue. If fraudulent conveyance is proved, the seniority of debt may be reordered.

Fraudulent conveyance can become an issue when a company is restructured and security interests are granted in the stock or assets of a company. For example, assume that company A acquires company B in a leveraged buyout for $550 million. Prior to the buyout, company B's capital structure consisted of equity and $300 million in subordinated debt.

Assume further that the transaction was financed by $50 million in equity and $500 million in debt secured by the assets of company B. Company A subsequently files for bankruptcy within six months of the LBO. At first glance, one would assume that the secured bonds issued by company A would be paid in full with company B's bonds receiving a share in the remaining assets. In fact, company B's bonds could be deemed senior to company A's bonds if it can be proven that a fraudulent conveyance occurred. Fraudulent conveyance can be proven if fraud was involved. It can also be proved if, at the time of the transfer, company B received less than fair or less than reasonably equivalent value for the transfer and either (1) was insolvent or rendered insolvent by the transfer, (2) its remaining unencumbered property constituted unreasonably small capital, or (3) it is believed that it incurred debts beyond its ability to pay as such debt matured.

Investing with a Plan of Reorganization

The analysis of companies in bankruptcy that have filed plans of reorganization should be approached in the same systematic way that the analysis of any security is approached. However, there are two important differences. First, the analyst must place more emphasis on pro formas and place less emphasis on historical results. This emphasis is mandated because a reorganized company is generally significantly different from the company that filed for protection. Second, the analyst must be a combination equity/fixed income securities analyst. It is not always clear which of the securities of the reorganized debtor are the most attractive. Often, the relative rates of return among old securities are substantially reordered under the plan. The analyst must therefore be willing to value all securities of the debtor and purchase those that offer the highest potential returns.

Evaluation of the Plan

The first step in analyzing a company in bankruptcy that has filed a plan is to carefully read the plan and determine the distribution each class will receive upon reorganization. This effort should be conducted on a per share or per bond basis. Terms of new securities that are to be issued under the plan should be examined carefully so that they be valued properly. Often, securities issued in reorganization have unique characteristics. For example, the senior notes proposed under Texas International's April 28, 1989 Plan of Reorganization provided for an initial coupon payment 39 months after issuance. The notes proposed under Delta US's May 1989 plan provide that interest and principal repayments can be deferred for a specific period if cash flow and rig count, respectively, are below certain levels. Furthermore, an increasing number of issues proposed under plans of reorganization are bonds whose interest may be paid in kind at the option of the reorganized debtor.

The analysis of a plan should begin with a listing of each class of creditor, the amount of the claim, the proposed distribution per security—where applicable—and the value of the distribution. This part of the analysis could take the form for the hypothetical ABC, Incorporated, shown in Exhibit 1.

Frequently, there are only a total of 6 to 12 classes of creditors. These can be individually listed. Sometimes, as in the case of Allegheny International, there are over 50. In these instances, it is wise to itemize only the relevant classes or consolidate the classes to make them more manageable. The classes that should be listed are those classes that contain publicly traded securities or classes that receive securities to be publicly

Exhibit 1
Plan of Reorganization—ABC, Incorporated

Class	Amount of Claim	Total Distribution	Distribution per Security	Valuation per Security
1st mortgage bonds	$100 million	$100 million plus pre- and post-petition interest in cash	100%	100%
Debentures	$100 million	$100 million face value of debentures of reorganized debtor	100%	90%*

*The amount of discount attributable to the new debentures is a function of coupon, credit considerations, etc.

traded. By consolidating the proposed distribution in this manner, the investor can easily focus on the relevant securities.

It is also advisable at this point to chart the proposed equity ownership per class. This chart allows the investor to quickly convert changes in the valuation of the company into tangible values. A chart of equity ownership could take the form shown in Exhibit 2.

Western Company of North America's equity ownership is fairly straight-forward. The only dilution that has to be considered is that from the possible exercise of employee options. Frequently, the distribution of equity in plans of reorganization are more complex, with warrants and options affecting the fully diluted stock ownership of several classes. In such cases, it is helpful to include additional columns that outline the fully diluted common stock ownership. This chart could take the form of Exhibit 3, which outlines the equity ownership proposed under Heck's Second Amended Plan.

Exhibit 2
Distribution of New Common Stock of Western Company of North America: Second Amended Plan of Reorganization

Class	Number of Shares	% of Common
Senior unsecured claims	8,750,000	70.00
Senior subordinated claims	1,285,438	10.28
Junior subordinated claims	1,120,812	8.97
Old preferred stock	562,500	4.50
Old common stock	406,250	3.25
Management incentive compensation plan	375,000	3.00
Total	12,500,000	100.00
Reserved for employee option plans	956,250	7.1

Source: Western Company of North America's Second Amended Plan of Reorganization and Disclosure Statement dated January 19, 1989, *Bankruptcy Datasource*, Boston, MA.

Exhibit 3
Proposed Equity Ownership of Hecks

	Number of Shares		% of Common	Fully Diluted Number of Shares	% of Common
Unsecured claims					
and PNB	2,000,000		79%	2,000,000	68%
Shareholder actions	22,222		1	22,222	1
Old common	200,000		8	260,000	9
	60,000	warrants			
Key employees	225,000	warrants	0	225,000	7
Hallwood	294,967		12	442,451	15
	147,484	warrants			
Total	2,517,189	shares	100%	2,949,673	100%

Source: Heck's Second Amended Joint Plan of Reorganization and Disclosure Statement dated March 24, 1989, *Bankruptcy Datasource*, Boston, MA.

Determining a Price Per Share for the Debtor

Once the specifics of the plan of reorganization are known, including potential dilution, the valuation of the company can proceed. In this chapter, Cardis Corporation will be used for our analysis.

Cardis Corporation filed for bankruptcy on May 25, 1988. It has been engaged in the wholesale and retail distribution of automotive parts, supplies, tools, and accessories since 1917. Cardis also owns Tune-Up Masters, which operates 242 company-owned service centers principally in the western and southwestern United States.

Cardis's Second Amended Plan of Reorganization and Disclosure Statement were filed on August 11, 1989. The plan is premised on the sale of Tune-Up Masters (TUM) and the reorganization of the company around its remaining warehouse distribution centers and 29 retail stores. Importantly, however, the plan may be confirmed without the sale. Under the Second Amended Plan of Reorganization, Security Pacific National Bank (SPNB) will receive $15 million in cash, a $29 million seven-year note, a $20 million secured revolving credit note, and $8 million from the sale of stock or assets of TUM. The plan provides that if TUM is not sold within three months of the confirmation date, the debtor will issue 80,000 shares of new preferred stock to SPNB with a face amount of $8 million. The reorganized debtor will then convey its right and interests to the TUM stock to a trust for the benefit of SPNB and the reorganized debtor. The general unsecured creditors will receive 65% of the stock, old equity holders will receive 10% of the stock, and a final 10% of the stock will be reserved for management. This allocation of common stock is presented in Exhibit 4.

The analysis of Cardis should begin with the debtor's pro forma income statements, balance sheets, and cash-flow statements, which are provided in disclosure statement. Care should be taken to evaluate the debtor's assumptions in formulating these pro formas. Modifications should be made to the pro formas where the assumptions look doubtful. After the pro formas have been adjusted, an estimate of the company's value (in terms of price per share) should be calculated. One way of approaching this task is to apply valuation multiples. The analyst should

Exhibit 4
Proposed Equity Ownership of Cardis: Second Amended Plan of Reorganization

Class	Number of Shares	Percent of Common*
Unsecured creditors	7,540,000	65%
Subordinated debentures	1,740,000	15
Present equity security holders	1,160,000	10
Reserved for management	1,160,000	10
Total	11,600,000	100

*The percentages are subject to a potential dilution of 13% if the reorganized debtor exercises its right under certain circumstances to put 1,800,691 common shares in exchange for the new preferred stock.
Source: Cardis Corporation's Second Amended Plan of Reorganization and Disclosure Statement dated August 11, 1989, *Bankruptcy Datasource*, Boston, MA.

estimate what range of multiples the stock should command in terms of earnings, sales, book value, and cash. The analyst can use the traditional approach of averaging the appropriate multiples of comparable companies and then applying these multiples to the company being analyzed.

In the case of Cardis, the analyst must first determine the market multiples of the auto parts (replacement) industry. To estimate the auto parts industry multiples, one should first select an industry sample of companies. In this case, SPX Corp., Echlin, Federal Mogul, and Genuine Parts are used as the representative sample. These four companies were selected in part because they are all followed by *Value Line,* and therefore consistent projections of earnings, sales, book value and cash flow were readily available. Once the sample was selected, *Value Line's* estimates for 1992–1994 for each of the companies was listed. These estimates are listed in Exhibit 5.

Once the estimates of these values have been logged, the range of valuations relative to price/share can be calculated for each of the sample companies by dividing each estimate by the estimated prices. Because *Value Line* gives a range for estimated prices, it is necessary to divide the appropriate per share figure by both the high and the low price estimates. Once these calculations are made, the numbers should be aver-

Exhibit 5
Auto Parts (Replacement) Industry (1992–1994　*Value Line* Estimates)

	Price Range	Sales/ Shares	BV/ Share	EPS	Cash/ Share
Cardis*		10.43	.26	.16	.45
Echlin	20–31	32.75	13.50	1.80	2.75
Federal Mogul	40–48	73.90	18.95	3.70	6.30
Genuine Parts	56–72	60.00	18.80	3.85	4.25
SPX Corp.	46–64	69.65	25.95	4.65	6.90

*Company estimates from the disclosure statement.

aged to generate an average range of valuations for the industry, as shown below.

Price	
Sales/Share	.69 to .92
Price	
BV/Share	2.09 to 2.78
Price	
Earning/Shares	11.59 to 15.68
Price	
Cash/Share	8.37 to 11.28

To arrive at an estimated value for the common stock of Cardis, multiply the above multiples (or, more realistically, some discount of the multiples so as to reflect the problems associated with the debtor) times the appropriate variable for Cardis. When these valuations are multiplied times the pro forma estimates of Cardis' sales/share, book value/share, EPS, and cash/share, a value of $.54 to $9.56 per share is estimated for Cardis. If the multiples are discounted by 50% to reflect problems associated with Cardis, the valuation declines to $.27 to $4.78. This looked attractive versus a September 1989 price of $0.06. However, this price assumes that each old share of Cardis will own the same proportionate share of the new company. In fact, Cardis' August 1989 Plan of Reorganization provides that each old share will receive the equivalent of .20 new shares. Therefore, these prices must be discounted by a factor that reflects that a share purchased at current prices may only be worth .20 shares if the plan is confirmed. When the estimated valuation is discounted by 80% as required, the estimated value declines to $.05 to $.96. At these levels, the stock is valued at the low end of the projections. The projected prices must be discounted once more, however, to reflect the potential dilution of 13% should Reorganized Cardis exercise its put. If this potential dilution is considered, the projected range for Cardis becomes $.04 to $.83.

Once the valuation of the debtor's stock is complete, the analyst should proceed to investigate the other securities of the debtor, if any, to determine if another security is attractive. Frequently, this is where value is found.

As of 4/30/88, Cardis had outstanding $25.16 million 12.5% Senior Subordinated Debentures due 6/30/97. To determine if the bonds are undervalued or overvalued, the relationship between the current price of each bond and the valuation of its proposed distribution must be compared. In the case of Cardis, debenture holders are proposed to receive 69.6 shares per $1000 of face value of debenture. The analyst must value these distributions to see if the debentures represent an undervalued or an overvalued situation. If the valuation of cardis common stock outlined above is used, then the debentures should be worth between $2.78 and $57.77 per bond. This compares with a market estimate of $15 per bond. The bonds appear to be within the same relative range as the common (i.e., at the low end of the projections).

Both the common stock and the debentures of Cardis appear to have more upside potential than downside risk. The risk/reward trade-off will be a function of the price the investor actually pays for the securities. Frequently, securities of bankrupt companies are thinly traded and the offering price of a security may differ substantially from the most recent quotation.

CONCLUSION

The analysis of bankrupt securities involves several variables. The investor must analyze both the plan of reorganization as well as the pro forma projections of the reorganized company. The analysis should not stop once these two analyses are complete, however. Companies should be monitored in order to keep current on changes in the plan as well as on company prospects. Changes in this market can occur quickly and be significant. The likelihood of these changes must be factored into the analysis. They also signal the need for diversification in bankruptcy investing. The time element must also be factored into the analysis. Most bankrupt securities do not accrue interest during reorganization. Therefore, the investor must estimate when the company will emerge from bankruptcy to fully estimate (and discount) values. Because most bankrupt companies take at least a year to reorganize and some have taken over seven years (Manville), the time element can be significant.

Chapter 12

The Emerging Market for Distressed Senior Bank Loans

STEVEN C. MILLER
ANALYST
LOAN PRICING CORPORATION

Selling senior, secured, bank loans of distressed companies at a discount to par remains a fairly new and revolutionary idea for banks. Traditionally, mark-to-market concerns and tightly-knit bank groups helped discourage distressed sales. Over the past several years, the need to pare troubled loans has taken on a new urgency at many banks as a result of regulatory pressures and capital adequacy guidelines. At the same time, the large number of bank and thrift failures has left government agencies with a stockpile of bank loans to troubled companies. As a result, discounted sales of distressed credits have become more commonplace. In response, a large number of investors specializing in restructuring and

The author would like to thank Christopher L. Synder, Jr. and Floyd A. Loomis for their direction and feedback in conducting the research and analysis presented in this chapter.

bankruptcy (the so-called vulture funds) have begun to explore opportunities in senior loans.

During the second half of 1990 and into 1991, the market for distressed bank loans has picked up. Discount sales have been confirmed in Ames Department Stores (between 55% and 65% of face value), Morning-Star Foods (85%), West Point Pepperell (75%), Southland Corp. (80-86%), Hills Department Stores (41%), Interco (40%), Zapata Corp (52%), and Integrated Resources (24%). However, the market remains highly inefficient with the bid and offer side of some distressed situation as much as 15-20 percentage points apart. Further, the successful reorganization of some troubled debtors during the first quarter of 1991 has made some lenders less eager to sell troubled loans at a discount.

DETERMINING VALUE

The value of distressed bank loans remains an area of extreme mystery. Hence, the market for troubled loans is highly inefficient and presents banks, brokers, and institutional investors with extremely attractive arbitrage and valuation opportunities. Even the issue of how bank loans to distressed companies are valued is a major question. An investor needs to determine whether to view a potential purchase as an interest rate or asset play.

Interest Rate Play

In general, loans that are current are viewed as interest rate plays. The buyer determines what level of return justifies the risk associated with the credit, does a yield-to-maturity (YTM) analysis, and seeks to purchase the credit at a discount level which brings the desired return.

MorningStar, one of the nation's largest dairy operators, was spun off from Southland Corp., the troubled convenience store operator, in a leveraged buyout during the fourth quarter of 1988. The transaction involved $150 million of original issue, high yield bonds and a $155 million bank credit package. The company was hurt by rising dairy costs and generated insufficient cash flow to meet debt servicing costs.

Two members of the existing bank group, Long Term Credit Bank of Japan (LTCB) and NMB Postbank Groep N.V. (NMB), underwrote a new $140 million credit facility. NMB bought out three entities controlled by the Resolution Trust Company in August 1990 at 85 cents on the dollar.

This distressed purchase by the Dutch bank, which has dedicated a group to this type of investment, allowed the company to avoid bankruptcy by obtaining a more liberal repayment schedule from its bank group. Bankers Trust (Delaware) also stepped up with a $10 million credit facility which helped the company remain solvent. Since that restructuring, the company's financial condition continued to deteriorate.

MorningStar Foods completed an out-of-court debt restructuring in March 1991. Under the restructuring, senior creditors agreed to refinance the bulk of the company's long-term debt for higher spreads, lucrative fees, tighter collateral, and equity. Hicks Muse & Co. provided a $30 million cash infusion in exchange for nearly $3 million in fees, a 95% equity interest in the company, and warrants for a $30 million initial investment.

MorningStar used the proceeds of this cash infusion to pay off its senior bank debt and repurchase $110 million of its $150 million of subordinated debt at 52 cents on the dollar. The company also converted its outstanding equity stock to new, lower priority, securities. The ambitious package was arranged by Donaldson, Lufkin & Jenrette.

Exhibit 1 shows how creditors fared in the work-out process. The following is a review of the restructuring process from the standpoint of the bank creditors.

- The Original Bank Group. Under the reorganization plan, direct assignees to the existing bank credit agreement will be paid out at face value. The initial bank facility consisted of a $95 million term loan and a $30 million revolving credit. It was refinanced in 1990 to provide a more liberal repayment schedule due to tight cash flow. At the reorganization date, there was $59.9 million outstanding under the term loan facility and $22.2 million outstanding under the revolving credit. Interest on these facilities was set at 250 basis points over LIBOR. Also, Bankers Trust's $11 million term loan facility would be repaid in full. Bankers Trust Securities helped arrange the initial LBO transaction and was a major stock holder in MorningStar.

- The New Bank Group, NMB and LTCB will assume most of the new debt, with the residual $20 million of senior secured notes offered to members of the current bank group and other investors. The credit agreement consists of a $45 million working capital facility and a $95 million term loan. The revolving credit is

Exhibit 1
The MorningStar Restructuring

Existing Creditors Class	State Value ($ Mil.)	Outstanding 9/30/90 ($ Mil.)	Stated Coupon	Amount Outstanding After Restructuring ($ Mil.)	Offer
Bank Creditors					
Term Loan	$125	$59.9	L+250		Repaid in full.
Revolving Credit	30	30.1	L+250		Repaid in full.
Bankers Trust Loan Facility	10	11.2	L+250		Repaid in full.
Subordinated Creditors					
Debentures due 2001	$150	$149.3	13%	$39.3	Received $57.2 million in cash for $110 million of outstanding debt.
Equity Holders					
Preferred Stock	$17.2	$17.2	0		Received 200,000 share of common stock, or a 20% interest in the company
Common Stock	10.0	10.0	0		Will receive a 5% interest in the reorganized company, or 50,000 shares.

tied to a borrowing base. Borrowing under the facility may not exceed 40% of eligible inventory. The senior secured facilities are secured by principally all of the assets of MorningStar and its operating units. The new bank group will also receive some equity consideration in MorningStar.

The new facility will accrue interest at 325 basis points over the three-month LIBOR rate. This is 75 basis points (bps) higher than the spread of the current agreement. The senior secured lenders received $250,000 in due diligence fees and $250,000 in commitment fees. Also, the bank group received $4.5 million in commitment and facility fees, of which $2.5 million will be paid on the active date of the deal and the balance will be paid during the first year. In sum, the new bank group will receive $5 million in upfront and commitment fees, or 360 bps. Also, LTCB will receive $100,000 per year for administrative fees and the company will pay an annual fee of 50 bps on the unused portion of the revolving credit. Using the 360 bps fee as a discount, the implied purchase price for the banks is 96.4. This translates to an implied yield-to-maturity of 12.43% on the term loan facility, as of April 1, 1991.

In summary, the MorningStar case, NMB purchased in at 85 cents on the dollar in August 1990 and was taken out ostensibly at 100 cents on the dollar nine months later. This is a nominal gain of 17%, or 23% on an annualized basis (exclusive of the interest paid on the facility or origination fees associated with the refinancing package). This is an interesting case because NMB was, in part, taken out by itself. This shows the advantage a new, deep-pocket bank investor can bring to a distress situation.

Asset Play

Loans to companies which have filed for protection under Chapter 11 of the U.S. Bankruptcy Code are generally considered asset plays. The loans are often in default and, therefore, YTM analyses are, at best, implied. The major issue for buyers in the case of a defaulted loan is the value of the security underlying the loan in the event the company is liquidated under Chapter 7 of the bankruptcy code and the chances the company will be able to emerge from Chapter 11 with its prepetition claims intact.

Exhibit 2
The Post Restructured Company

Capital Structure	Status	Pricing	Initial Commit. ($ M)	Fees/Tpye ($000/bps)	Repayment Schedule	Other Kickers
Bank Lenders						
Term Loan	Sr Sec	L+325	$95	$250/due diligence, $4,750/commitment and facility	$7 million, 1992; $10 million, 1993; $15 million, 1994; $18 million, 1995; $45 million, 1996	An equity stake
Revolving Credit	Sr Sec	L+325	45	50 bps on unused		
Subordinated Debtholders						
Debentures	Sub	13%	74.95		Due in full in 2001	
Equity Holders						
New Equity Investors	Prefer		30	$250/due diligence $2,500/commitment		Warrants
Preexisting Equity Holders						
Preferred Stock	Common				Received a 20% ownership interest	
Common Stock	Common				Received a 5% ownership interest	

Under the Southland Corporation's prepackaged Chapter 11 reorganization program, banks have agreed to relax certain financial ratio and cash flow covenants, allowed the company to issue additional common stock, and freed some collateral in order to facilitate a debt-for-equity exchange at the subordinated level and a capital infusion from the borrower's Japanese affiliate. The troubled convenience store operator filed a prepackaged reorganization plan last November under Chapter 11 of the U.S. bankruptcy code. It made scheduled interest payment on its prepetition, senior secured bank debt during the four-month petition period.

Southland was one of the most interesting plays in the distressed loan market. The company is a "brand name" borrower with the clout to attract a $430 million equity investment from Ito-Yokado, a Japanese retail company which owns a controlling interest in Southland's Japanese affiliate. Ito-Yokado will also provide about $60 million in non-recourse loans to companies controlled by the Thompson family, which founded Southland in exchange for shares of newly issued Class 11 common stock equal to a 5% ownership interest. This stake may be diluted if other creditor classes exercise warrants issued as part of the restructuring.

The bid/offer range for Southland's bank loans generally has been 10–15 percentage points apart during the petition period. Early in the bankruptcy, a trade was reported at the 78–80% of par level. As the proceeding wound down, a trade was completed at 86% of par. After the plan was accepted and Southland emerged, the bid range for the bank debt moved up to about 95 cents on the dollar. Few banks were persuaded to sell at a discount because most felt comfortable in their position in the capital structure. The company's extensive due diligence shows that the banks could recover 100% of principal and interest over a two to three year period even in a liquidation. Under the restructuring, banks, continue to occupy the most senior position in the capital structure of a significantly enhanced borrower, with less subordinated debt and a better capital position (see Exhibit 3).

Other Issues

Another issue for lenders in determining value is the potential for fraudulent conveyance challenges to leveraged buyout and recapitalization transactions. This is because most of the actively sought or traded distressed loans are to companies taken private in LBOs or which underwent recapitalization programs that included large dividend payouts to

Exhibit 3
The Southland Restructuring Plan

Creditor Class	Initial Commit.	Current Claim	Offer/Concession
	($ million)		
Secured			
Bank Term Loan	$2,500	$1,299	Under the proposal, the bank agreed to: (1) allow the proceeds of stock sales not to be used to repay the term loans, (2) eliminate the limitations on the revolving credit and letter of credit facilities issued by the bank group, (3) reset cash flow and other financial covenants in line with current projections, (4) release capital stock pledged as collateral. Also, if Ito-Yokado reduces its share in Southland below 51%, the revolving credit line will be payable in full.
Bank Revolving Credit		215	
Unsecured			Received the following package for each $1,000 of principal amount tendered:
Senior Reset Nts	$593	$593	(1) $475 of 12% Sr Nts, due 12/15/96, (2) 86.5 shares of common stock, (3) $57 in cash, (4) a warrant to purchase one share of Class 11 common stock.
Sr. Sub Nts	395	395	(1) $650 of 5% first priority Sr Sub debt due 12/15/2003, (2) 40.5 common shares, and (3) warrants to purchase 7.5 Class 11 shares.
Sr Sub Disc Nts	392	392	(1) $555 of first priority debt, (2) 35 shares of common stock, (3) warrants to purchase 6.5 shares of Class 11 stock.
Sub Deb	592	592	(1) $500 of 4.5% second priority Sr Sub Deb due 6/15/2004, (2) 28 shares of common stock, (3) warrants to purchase 6.5 shares of Class 11 common stock.
Jr Sub Deb	50	50	(1) $257 of 4% second priority Sr Sub Deb due 6/15/2004, (2) 11 shares of Common Stock, (3) warrants to purchase 6 shares of class 11 common stock.
Equity			
Cumulative Preferred Stock			Received one share of common stock for each share tendered
			The Thompson family, who founded Southland and took the company private in the 1987 leveraged buyout, received an amount of stock equal to a 5% ownership interest in the company. This interest will be diluted if warrants are exercised.

shareholders. Recourse is another issue that has given pause to potential sellers of distressed bank loans, which will be discussed in a later section of this chapter.

WHICH LOANS ARE BEING SOLD?

The market for distressed loans is generally limited to troubled leveraged buyout and recapitalization credits for three principal reasons: (1) these credits have large, disjointed bank groups, (2) senior claimants are protected by the subordination of other creditor classes, and (3) potential investors have access to publicly available information and can therefore make more informed decisions.

Bank Groups

Bank groups that funded leveraged buyouts are typically large and disjointed, as a result of primary and secondary syndication. Foreign and regional banks bought into a large number of nationally syndicated, LBO credits in the 1980s. With the volume of nonperforming loans mounting, many banks are under pressure from regulators and management to reduce their nonperforming loan portfolios. As a result, many regional, and even superregional, banks have been willing to sell loans of distressed companies at a discount. Many foreign and regional banks have built large loan loss reserves, which are not disclosed on a loan-by-loan basis, against their large, nationally syndicated, HLT portfolios. If one of these banks, for instance, has reserved 35% against a given credit and is offered 75% of par value by a fund, it is not only able to remove "bad" credit from its balance sheet, but also enjoys a recovery contribution to its income statement.

A good precedent for this type of activity was established in the less developed countries (LDC) debt market. Regional banks acted quickly to cut their losses by writing off LDC loans and declining to extend new credit to these nations. This is because regional banks typically have limited LDC exposure and thus are able to exit the market without taking severe earning hits. Interestingly, some regional banks are seeking to use their experience in trading LDC paper to start up trading operations for troubled C&I loans. NMB Postbank Groep (NMB), for instance, has set up a unit to invest in troubled loans and another to trade these instruments. NMB is a major player in the international LDC debt market.

Subordination

Most investors consider LBO credits to be safer than most nonperforming and distressed credits, particularly middle market loans (factoring out the fraudulent conveyance risks which are discussed later in this chapter). In general, troubled middle market companies gradually fall into financial distress, during which the assets of these companies deteriorate in value and the company's cash flow and retained earnings have been exhausted. Therefore, the banks are often forced to take a "haircut" in the event of a middle market failure and liquidation both in terms of interest and principal.

Companies taken private in leveraged buyouts, by contrast, usually fall into financial distress in short order. Though these companies have typically exhausted their equity, the assets of some companies still retain a good deal of value. This was the case with Southland Corp., Revco D.S., Doskocil Industries, and a number of other distressed companies. Also, the comfort level of senior, secured creditors is boosted by the subordination of other classes of creditors. This subordination may not be present in the middle market, where companies have limited access to the public capital markets. Therefore, in theory, banks should be in a better position to come out whole in an LBO transaction, even in a liquidation scenario.

Subordination varies widely among transactions. In the case of Allegheny International, which has filed for Chapter 11, pre-petition senior, secured bank debt totals $175 million. Other classes of pre-petition debtors hold $346 million of unsecured debt. This is nearly a 2:1 ratio, providing bankers with a substantial "comfort" level in terms of lower class subordination. In the case of MorningStar Foods, senior bank creditors held about $130 million of the company's debt, while bondholders hold $155 million of face value securities. In this example, the ratio is closer to 1:1. The Revco D.S. transaction was also structured with a similar percent of bank debt to subordinated debt. This 50/50 ratio has become the accepted standard on large corporate deals structured over the past year. The $1.5 billion Saks Fifth Avenue transaction, closed in May of 1990, was financed with $775 million of bank debt, with the balance financed through subordinated debt and equity.

Comfort Level

The comfort level for banks on some large transactions has declined over the past year due to the collapse of the high-yield bond market. This is because bridge loans and other bank facilities which were supposed to be refinanced through the public bond market have been converted into permanent facilities. In addition, some debtors have been forced to refinance bond issues with new bank lending. This has been the case with the $2.25 billion recapitalization package completed by RJR Nabisco in 1990. The borrower decided to retire public bonds which were issued as reset notes in order to avoid converting these instruments to higher paying facilities.

Bondholder Activism

Another issue for banks is the increasing activism of public bondholders and the growing number of "bond raiders" who buy subordinated debt of troubled companies. These investors buy notes at a discount and seek to coerce the company into taking them out at a substantial premium to their purchase price. These investors will purchase subordinated securities at a given discount to par, say 50%, and threaten to block reorganization plans, introduce fraudulent conveyance litigation, or throw a company into Chapter 11, unless they receive a payout of 65-75% of par. Though this practice is still rare, some bondholders have been able to force an early payout. These payouts reduce the available assets of the company and effectively lower the comfort level of senior, secured bank creditors.

Information

Distressed debt investors can tap the large body of publicly available information concerning LBO credits, either through secondary sources and publication or through SEC disclosures. This is an important consideration in a market driven, in large part, by information.

WHO IS BUYING DISTRESSED LOANS?

As previously mentioned, small syndicate banks and institutions that have purchased credits through secondary syndication represent the most likely sellers of distressed bank loans. The Resolution Trust Company (RTC) and survivor institutions created by the Federal Deposit Insurance Corporation (FDIC) to hold the "bad" assets of failed banks also represent likely sellers. Two major buying constituencies are emerging in the distressed market: the vulture funds and other banks in the syndicated group.

Vulture Funds

The Loan Investor Services database lists over 60 vulture funds which are currently buying, or are considering the purchase of, bank loans. These funds are often involved with the company as subordinated creditors. In addition, many securities firms have actively sought to purchase or broker distressed bank loans. Salomon Brothers, Goldman Sachs, Bear Stearns, and Merril Lynch & Co., are among the major investment banks which have attempted to apply their knowledge of the market for publicly-traded, speculative grade "junk" bonds and distressed debt to the bank loan market. In addition, such high-yield investors and traders as MJ Whitman, Oppenhiemer & Co., and Jeffries & Co. have entered the distressed bank loan market. Some vulture funds which concentrate on equity or subordinated debt, such as the Zell/Chilmark fund, Equity Strategies Fund, and Goldman Sach's Water Street Fund, have also purchased bank loans. In these cases, the funds may take out syndicate members who are "holding up" the restructuring or workout process.

As a rule, vulture funds seek 30-40% returns on their investments. If they can purchase a credit in the 60% range and cash out at 80% within a year, they are able to meet this goal. Unlike most banks, vulture funds tend to view the distressed credits they purchase in the context of their portfolio. In other words, if they overpay in one situation and underpay for another credit, they can still meet their portfolio goals. For example, if one vulture fund holds a large stake in the subordinated debt of Interco, Southland, and Integrated Resources and Interco and Integrated Resources generate large returns but Southland is unprofitable, the investor can still meet its return goals. Also vulture funds are owned by investors who expect a high risk/reward profile. Therefore, these funds have more latitude to invest in troubled debt than do banks, which are federally insured institutions.

Agent banks

Agent banks are also likely to purchase distressed loans from smaller syndicated members in an effort to keep vulture funds out of the bank group. These banks are not likely to be receptive to new, nonbank investors which often bring a new agenda to the workout process. Vulture funds investors typically buy in at a discount and may seek to make a quick "killing." In other words, they may be willing to settle for less than 100% of interest and principal in exchange for a quick resolution which allows them to "cash out" at a profit.

In addition to seeking full repayment on a given credit, agent banks which are involved in a large number of distressed situations clearly would be averse to setting a precedent by accepting less than full payment in a given workout or liquidation. Also, highly leveraged transaction constraints aside, agent banks for leverage buyout transactions are deep pocket players which have the resources necessary to keep new players out of the bank group.

Competitive Advantage—The Information Factor

Agent banks work closely with the borrower. They need to attend all workout meetings and typically have the largest staffs of analysts, lawyers, and other bankruptcy experts. Therefore, the agent banks typically are in the best position to value a distressed credit and present potential sellers in the syndicate group with the most knowledgeable bid.

LEGAL ISSUES

Fraudulent Conveyance

The senior status of bank loans is being challenged under the Uniform Fraudulent Conveyance Act (UFCA) in a number of distressed situations. Under the UFCA, senior loans used to finance an LBO or recapitalization program can be subordinated to the liens of preexisting creditors if it is determined that the transaction rendered the company insolvent. In other words, the company was left with an unreasonably small capital base to meet expenses and service existing debts as a result of the LBO. In such a case, the company and its pre-existing creditors may not have received fair consideration. Fraudulent conveyance suits have been brought by pre-existing bondholders against a large number of LBOs including Revco D.S., Circle K Corp., Allied Department Stores, and RJR Nabisco.

An examiner in the Revco case issued a report in August 1990 which cleared the way for fraudulent conveyance laws to be applied to LBOs. the rationale in applying the UFCA to LBO transactions is that funds borrowed in the transactions are often routed directly to shareholders. Therefore, the company and its pre-existing creditors do not receive fair consideration and the company often is left with an insufficient capital base to survive its post-transaction debt burden. The Revco report, issued by Barry Zaretsky, a Professor at Brooklyn Law School, is likely to prompt a large number of UFCA suits as bondholders become more organized and the number of LBO insolvencies grow. For instance, pre-existing pre-merger noteholders in Interco Inc. are considering bringing fraudulent conveyance litigation. In the case of Darling Delaware, the company paid out a substantial dividend to its owners. The company soon became financially distressed as a result of higher debt servicing costs and slower revenue growth. Though equity holders have agreed to disgorge some of the dividend, the bondholders have still suffered lower credit quality as a result of the transaction.

The specter of fraudulent conveyance has slowed the growth of the distressed loan market because many potential investors are demanding the inclusion of fair representation clauses in the representations and warranty ("reps and warranty") sections of loan sales agreements. A fair representation clause functions like a put option. In the event that a transaction is proved to be fraudulent under the UFCA, the buyer has the right to sell back the loan to the original holder at the purchase price. Sellers are often unwilling to include a fair representation clause for this very reason. The value of the fair representation clause is elusive and varies widely between transactions, given the potential for a successful UFCA challenge. As a result, the fair representation clause has become a major point of contention in trading distressed loans and has helped to slow the market.

Recourse

Outside of the fair representation clause related to fraudulent transfer, a number of other potential sources of recourse exist for a buyer of distressed bank loans. This has discouraged the sale of loans at a discount, because if the situation turns out positive the buyer has little need to search for an implied "put" option in the documentation. However, if a meltdown occurs, buyers may search the sales agreement for a loophole.

In the February 1991 *Extra Credit Publication*, Martin Fridson, Manager of High-Yield Research at Merrill Lynch & Co, lists a number of other potential triggers for recourse. These include: covenant violation, or a change in the repayment schedule or pricing. Other material changes in the credit or in the borrowers' operating strategy may expose the seller to recourse.

SUMMARY

The distressed bank loan market can be viewed as a speculators' market, with new players bringing fresh money and a new agenda to the game as some of the original investors are seeking a way out. It is clear that the valuation process in these situations is extremely tentative and that the ultimate payout depends not only on such fundamental factors as asset values and revenue, but on external factors such as legal issues, economic trends, and documentation. Regardless, with a large number of regional and foreign banks under pressure to reduce distressed loan holding and HLTs, and many vulture funds and high-yield investors exploring opportunities in senior loans, it appears that the market is likely to expand rapidly.

A key question is whether trading prices truly reflect either the value of a credit or its market price. In other words, does a single trade in a distressed name constitute: (1) the market, (2) a firesale by a regional bank which was not in touch with enough potential buyers to get a true sense of the demand, or (3) a purchase by a relationship lender at a price which is overly optimistic.

Another question is whether banks will be willing to sell enough troubled debt to make troubled bank loans a viable market. The favorable experience of banks in several large reorganizations completed during the second half of 1990 and the first quarter of 1991, including MorningStar Foods, Southland Corp., Harcourt Brace Jovanovich, and JPS Textiles has helped to raise the perceived value of distressed bank loans. This could potentially drive an even larger wedge between the offer- and the bid-side of the distressed bank loan market. In other words, banks would keep the price of these instruments at levels which would not allow vulture funds and other investors to meet their hurdle rates. This, in turn, could stymie the growth of the market.

APPENDIX A

FEDERATED RECOVERY LEVELS AND TRADING RANGES

Initial trading ranges for securities issued as part of Federated Department Stores' reorganization plan provide an interesting case study of how banks fare in a large, disjointed workout. Federated emerged from Chapter 11 protection in early February. The securities issued to bank lenders had a combined trading value of about 81 cents for each dollar of the prepetition principal claim. In sum, banks received about 91 cents on the dollar for accrued interest, 81 cents on the dollar for principal, and 83 cents on the dollar for the total petition claim plus accrued interest. Holders of Federated's original issue high-yield bonds received 0.6 shares for each $100 claimed plus 0.3 warrants. This implies a recovery level of less than 20 cents on the dollar.

Background

Federated was merged into CRTF Corporation, a Campeau Corp. subsidiary, on May 3, 1988 in a $6.4 billion leveraged acquisition. The transaction was financed with $3.15 billion of bank loans, $2.1 billion of subordinated notes from CRTF and $1.4 billion of equity. The bank loan consisted of a $800 million mortgage bridge tranche, an $1.65 billion asset bridge tranche, a $750 million working capital facility, and a $1 billion receivables tranche. The credit was secured by capital stock in Federated's principal subsidiary units and receivables. The transaction was also financed with a $500 million bank equity loan from Bank of Montreal and Banque Paribas.

The company issued unsecured bonds and made asset sales in order to repay bridge loans from CRTF. In September 1989, the company amended its prepetition credit agreement to increase the cash draw amount of its revolving credit by $50 million to $650 million, extend scheduled repayments of the mortgage bridge and asset bridge loan by three months to April 30, 1990, relax fixed charge and other financial ratios, and waive the annual clean-up period for the working capital facility.

The amendment cost the company 37.5 basis points. Federated also paid Citibank $2 million for work completed in connection with the amendment. The company also deposited $250 million from asset sales into a cash collateral account to secure debt under the asset bridge facility. The asset bridge was repaid on January 3, 1990.

Federated received $500 million from Allied Department Stores, another Campeau unit, for a 36.2% interest in the company. The funds were used to repay the bank equity from Bank of Montreal and Bank Paribas. This transaction was later challenged under fraudulent conveyance laws. As a result, Bank of Montreal and Paribas received an equity stake in Ralph's Grocery in exchange for the claims against Allied.

Repayments Prior to Default

The company filed for Chapter 11 protection in February 1990. The bank loans had been paid down $1.7 billion, or 53%, at the time of the filing. The repayments were made primarily through asset sales.

Treatment During the Petition Period

During the petition period, banks received $197.7 million of interest as part of the agreement with DIP lenders. Federated's $400 million DIP credit was provided by a group of lenders led by Citibank, which served as agent on the prepetition agreement. The facility allowed for the payment of interest on the prepetition bank credit with 50% of excess cash flow. Federated made payments of interest on the prepetition agreement until May 3, 1991.

Settlement

Federated emerged from bankruptcy protection on February 15, 1992. Bank creditors received a package of senior secured notes, convertible debentures, and equity (Exhibit A-1). Banks' claims totaled $1.853 billion

Exhibit A-1

	($ Mils.)
Original Commitment	3,215.00
Repayments Prior to Default	1,711.00
Repayments/Initial Commitment	53.22%
Petition Amount	1,504.00
Petition Interest	349.10
Interest Paid During the Petition Period	197.90
Net Interest Accured	151.20
Total Claim	1,655.20
Current Value	1,345.25
Recovery From Original Commitment	81.27%
Interest Claim	349.10
Repaid During Petition Period	197.90
Net Interest Accrued	151.20
Net Present Value of Accrued Interest	122.89
Total Interest Recovery	91.89%
Recovery on Total Claim of Principal and Interest	
Total Claim	1,853.10
Recovery	1,345.25
Interest Received	197.90
Total	83.27%
Recovery From Initial Principal Amount	95.06%

at the effective date, including principal and interest. The banks received $197 million interest payments during the petition period, which lowered the claim to $1,504 million of principal and $152 million of interest.

Bank creditors were offered a package of fixed- or floating-rate secured notes, convertible bonds with an initial accrete value of $260 million and an ultimate face value of $311 million, and 19.02 million shares of common stock. About 30% of the stock is not restricted from sale, with the balance restricted from trading. After eighteen months, the level of unrestricted shares will increase to 70%. Unrestricted shares are bid about $2.50 higher than restricted shares.

The banks chose a package of either series B and D fixed-rate or series A and C floating-rate secured notes. Many of the banks opted for the floating-rate notes, which are tied to a spread of LIBOR plus 250 basis points. The series B and D fixed-rate notes carry a rate of 10% and 9%, respectively. The B notes have a progressive repayment schedule with a final maturity of February 2000. The D notes have a bullet maturity of August 15, 1997. Holders of the D notes also receive a 3.25% fee at the active date and annual fees paid on the amount outstanding of 1% in years one through three and 2% in the final two years. Given a bid of 93.5 for the series B notes and a bid of 96 for the series D notes, both would offer a yield-to-maturity of about 11.2%.

Traders say that the fixed-rate notes are trading five to six percentage points higher than the floating-rate notes. This is because institutional buyers generally prefer fixed-rate instruments and it is not feasible to swap the Federated floating-rate notes for a fixed-rate income stream due to the potential for prepayment. Also, three-month LIBOR is about 4.25% (as of February 15, 1992), meaning that the floating-rate notes have a current yield of 7.75%.

Bids for the convertible securities range from 50–55% of face value. Bids for unrestricted stock are $17.25 per share, with restricted stock shares bid at $14.50 per share.

Recovery Values

Initial trading values for the securities distributed as part of Federated's restructuring plan imply a recovery of 81 cents for every dollar of principal, 92 cents for every dollar of interest (because banks had received over half of the interest during the petition period in full), and 83 cents on every total dollar claimed.

Banks total repayments from initial commitment, including repayments prior to default and recoveries following default, totaled 95 cents for every dollar lent.

Trading Perspective

In the calculation of returns for potential investors, a post-reorganization recovery value of 80 cents on the dollar will be assumed. Based on bid prices collected by LPC, investors could have potentially garnered annualized returns on 20% to over 50% and nominal returns of 7–20% by investing in Federated bank debt (see Exhibit A-2) over the past three quarters (exclusive of the cost of closing the transaction). Last April, the bank debt was bid about 65 cents on the dollar. Assuming a LIBOR-based rate of 7% during the petition period and a current sale price of 75

Exhibit A-2
Indicated Bid vs. Potential Return: Federated Bank Debt

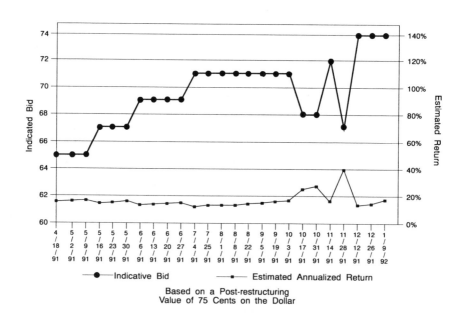

Based on a Post-restructuring
Value of 75 Cents on the Dollar

cents on the dollar, an investor would have realized a 25% annualized return.

During the third quarter, several large trades in Federated were reported at about 71 cents on the dollar. The trades occurred as large regional banks came under pressure to reduce highly leveraged transaction holdings, in general, and nonperforming assets, in particular. If an investor had purchased Federated bank debt in the third quarter and sold the debt at the current when-issued prices, it would have realized an annualized return of 20–30% and a nominal return of 11–13% (depending on the timing of the purchase). Clearly, the later the purchase, the better the return.

After the reorganization plan was filed in October 1991, bids for the bank debt increased to about 72 cents on the dollar. It retreated for several weeks in November due to uncertainty over acceptance. This was the most lucrative buying opportunity. If an investor was able to find a lender with available paper at 67 cents on the dollar, it would have enjoyed an annualized return of 66% and a nominal return of 14%. Since December, Federated bank debt has moved steadily higher as confidence in the current reorganization plan grew.

Summary

Federated provides clear evidence that distressed loan investing can meet the hurdle rates of vulture fund investors, which generally range from 30–40%, despite the relatively high purchase price of the loans during the petition period. Other distressed loans that have produced similar returns for distressed loan investors over the past year include Southland Corp., JPS Textiles, Lomas Financial Corp., and Doskocil Industries.

Federated also shows that equity is an increasingly important component of the package of securities received by banks in distressed reorganizations. In order to facilitate the restructuring process, and ensure the economic viability of companies' post-restructurings, banks often need to accept partial reduction in principal recovery, in this case about 19% of the petition principal claim and 10% of interest accrued during the petition period.

However, it is important to note that secured bank loans stand up far better in the reorganization process than unsecured debt. Also, when repayments prior to default are factored in banks' total nominal losses (excluding workout costs) can be far less than that of bondholders. In the case of Federated, holders of unsecured bonds that financed Federated's leveraged acquisition took a haircut of over 80% of their initial commitment. By comparison, bank creditors' total principal losses totaled about 5%.

Chapter 13

Investing in Distressed Bank Loans and Securities

MERIDEE A. MOORE
FARALLON CAPITAL PARTNERS

The late 1980s and early 1990s have seen a market develop for investors looking for capital appreciation through investment in deeply discounted bank loans and other debt securities. One of the reasons opportunities exist in this market is that many distressed investments are "fallen angels"; they found their way into securities and loan portfolios before they became distressed. In addition, consolidation in the banking industry has increased many banks' exposure to some distressed credits. Regulatory constraints, capital requirements, highly leveraged transaction disclosure requirements and the prospect of write downs or a money default all encourage selling of distressed loans for other than purely financial reasons. On the demand side, the analytical process involved in assessing distressed investments, and the risks and time necessary to realize a re-

Special thanks to Martin J. Whitman and Peter M. Lupoff of M.J. Whitman & Co., Inc.

turn, make the field less populated than more mainstream investment strategies. These factors combine to create a market that many believe to be inefficient and undervalued. Whether the market in general is undervalued is unclear, but the sheer quantity of distressed loans compared to the funds dedicated to invest in them indicates an opportunity.

Although interest in distressed investing has increased, the field remains essentially underresearched. Some brokerage firms have encouraged their high-yield fixed income research analysts to undertake the analysis of distressed companies, but the equity-like nature of distressed debt makes the transition for fixed income analysts difficult. In addition, Wall Street's inherent growth bias and short attention span makes distressed investment analysis less glamorous than other disciplines. Finally, very few firms or private funds employ inhouse bankruptcy counsel, and legal analysis is crucial to the evaluation of loans and securities of distressed companies.

Profitable distressed investing requires three key capabilities: first, the ability to perform fundamental financial analysis, both of the company's enterprise value and of the various layers in its capital structure; second, a comprehensive understanding of the validity, priority, and transferability of claims; and third, access to the market makers of these distressed loans and securities.

DISTRESSED INVESTMENT ALTERNATIVES

A distressed security is most often defined as any security that has suffered a money default, or, if performing, yields more than ten percentage points above the comparable maturity Treasury security. This definition works for fixed-rate, term obligations, but due to the quantity of distressed floating-rate securities that now trade in the secondary market, especially bank loans, the definition has come to encompass any security or loan which is offered at a substantial discount to its originally issued value due to financial or operating distress.

The public market for distressed debt is an outshoot of the $200 billion of high yield bonds issued between 1979 and 1990. It has been supplemented by the public debt of fallen angels, those companies whose debt ratings have fallen below investment grade due to operating problems or financial distress subsequent to the debt's original issuance. Although some public distressed bonds are senior securities, much of the public market is made up of junior, subordinated debt and preferred stock.

The private market for distressed debt is comprised of bank debt, mezzanine financing, private placements, trade claims, and other liabilities and contractual claims. Although investment opportunities exist in many private securities, this chapter will focus specifically on bank debt, and will attempt to assess its investment attributes and risks in the broader context of investing in distressed companies.

WHY IS THE COMPANY DISTRESSED?

A company can be distressed due to fundamental operating problems or an unworkable capital structure, or both. Like any value investment, a business that can be shown to be viable long term, one with competitive products or services and competent, experienced management, makes the best investment. This leads most financial buyers to focus on businesses whose distress has resulted from an over-leveraged capital structure or a one-time, debilitating litigation—there are simply less contingencies in an investment in a company with competitive core operating businesses and a reliable management team.

Investing in businesses that are financially instead of operationally constrained often means current management will continue to run the business, which can help existing employee morale and relationships with customers and suppliers. Often, however, the management that led the company into financial demise has lost its rapport with these important constituencies. When new management must be introduced, the most successful teams tend to have superior leadership ability, in-depth knowledge of the business, history of success in turnarounds, and the ability to make tough decisions.

A company with a sound operating business, but with an over-leveraged capital structure or cash poor balance sheet, often can be rehabilitated through an equity infusion, while operations are maintained with a debtor-in-possession working capital line. If the structure of the reorganization is not bitterly contested or if the company does not need the relief provided by the "automatic stay" provisions of the Bankruptcy Code, the reorganization may be accomplished through a pre-packaged plan or out-of-court exchange offer. If the claimants and parties in interest agree on a plan, the company is less likely to have to weather a protracted,

combative bankruptcy during which the investor's claim could lose significant value.

DISTRESSED INVESTMENT APPROACHES—ACTIVE AND PASSIVE

Active

Investment in distressed loans and securities takes two forms, active and
passive, either of which may be appropriate for an investment portfolio.
An active investor takes an active role in the negotiation of the reorganization, and may attempt to control or influence day to day management
decisions, by buying and holding a substantial portion of the most senior
impaired claim in the distressed company's capital structure. If the investor becomes privy to inside information, he is restricted from trading
in the securities without appropriate disclosure. In addition, should he
choose to sit on a creditors' committee, his ensuing fiduciary duty may
prohibit selling his position at all until the information conveyed to the
creditors becomes public.

An active investor's objective is to acquire enough of the troubled
issue to require either payment of his claim in full or a veto over any
proposed reorganization plan. The active approach, due to its control nature, can lead to hostility between the investor and the management of
the company. It is important to note, however, that unlike the original
creditors whose goal may be to extract value for their claim in cash or
near cash securities at all costs, the secondary market participant's objective should be to rejuvenate the company and realize a return from improved performance through reorganization.

Often the active investor in bank debt will want to receive some equity in the reorganized entity in exchange for his claim, which may enable him to participate in the control of the company, frequently at a
hefty discount from par. Although the original bank lenders and participants are in the best position to take advantage of this inexpensive way
to acquire equity in a reorganizing company, most banks, as lenders, are
restricted by regulators from holding equity under certain circumstances,
and may prefer to forgo potential capital appreciation in favor of a near
cash debt obligation or a cash payment, even if it is at a discount to the
bank's original claim.

Any active investment, but especially one in which the investor becomes a significant equity holder, requires a working knowledge of the company's operating businesses as well as a variety of other factors. For example, what are the objectives of the company's management and its board? Who are the other constituencies involved with the company and what are their attitudes and objectives? If the company is regulated, are there issues concerning approvals, licenses or constituencies the regulators are legislated to protect? Are other secondary market participants interested in the same stake? Can the purchase be structured so as not to trigger adverse tax consequences for either the company or the investor, and to preserve tax attributes, such as net operating loss carry forwards (NOLs)?

Working out the company's problems will probably be more complicated than anyone can imagine at the outset and it is important to manage the process and seek outside advice when any assessment—legal, industry, economic, value or tax—is outside of the investor's realm of experience. A small expenditure made on an industry consultant or appraiser, for example, may be worth many times its cost if the expert points out a legal or operational black hole.

An active investment is a long-term investment and the investor must be prepared to ride with the company through the sometimes arduous turnaround process. Time is a key factor in measuring return: as part of the analysis it is important to estimate the time the actualization of the best and worst case scenarios will take, in addition to measuring economic and business risk, and weighing all against potential reward. Finally, the active investor must have in mind an exit strategy. A greatly enhanced investment is worth only as much as a targeted public market or strategic buyer will pay for it.

Passive

A passive investor, as opposed to an active investor, sees an undervalued or overvalued situation and buys or sells a portfolio position. The investor has no access to material nonpublic information and thus can trade freely. When evaluating a passive portfolio position, it is best, to the extent possible, to complete the same financial and legal analysis and due diligence review as is undertaken in evaluating an active investment. Since the passive investor has no control over the reorganization process, however, the price of the position must reflect his confidence in the operating prowess of existing management or active financial investors.

Philosophies differ about the parameters of the best portfolio investments. Some investors restrict their portfolio positions to junior unsecured debt that sells at a significant discount, anticipating a greater return once the market recognizes a turnaround in the company's prospects. A more conservative strategy is to restrict passive investments to senior, usually secured securities or bank debt, and target a better than 20% annualized rate of return over a one to two year period, based on fundamental and legal valuation, for each investment.

FINANCIAL ANALYSIS

Evaluating potential risk and return of a distressed security requires fundamental financial analysis of both the company's prospects as an enterprise and of the value inherent in the specific security the investor is reviewing for investment.

Enterprise Value

In order to value both active and passive investments, the first step is to establish an estimated value of the entire company as a reorganized going concern. The factors in assessing enterprise value include: projected free cash flow; anticipated access to the capital markets, if any; value of disposable non-core assets; capital expenditures, including any additional expense necessary to recuperate capital expenditures that may have been neglected by the company once it began experiencing financial distress; and hidden liabilities, including environmental, pension or health care liabilities, and any off balance sheet assets, such as NOLs.

These factors are much easier to list than to value. Often the reliability of a distressed company's published reports is in question and outside research reports, if available, do not emphasize a company's potential problems. If a company has filed for protection under Chapter 11, there may be a delay before a reorganization plan or a disclosure statement is made available to outside investors, although monthly cash flow schedules are supposed to be filed with the Bankruptcy Court on a timely basis and are publicly available. Prior to a filing, a company may be under such pressure to meet financial ratios under its credit agreements that it may misrepresent the actual state of its business, by accelerating booked sales or accounts receivable, for example, or by failing to write down assets or write off excessive inventory. Even if properly stated, historical numbers may be of little help in analyzing a distressed or reorganizing company; projected operating cash flow becomes the basis for the determination of enterprise value. For this reason, in addition to reviewing the available financial statements, credit agreements and contracts, it may be helpful to supplement the company's disclosure by doing on-sight due diligence or obtaining the view of an industry consultant.

Going concern enterprise value. The three key elements of reorganization value are cash flow, earnings, and separable non-core assets. The investor's first step should be to identify separable, salable assets and adjust operating profit assuming the assets were sold. For companies taken private in leveraged transactions in the late 1980s, most salable assets will have already been divested and cost cuts implemented. On the other hand, for special situation bankruptcies, such as those caused by a major litigation, there may be substantial non-core asset value and cost cutting potential.

The investor's next step is to project cash flow and apply a conservative multiple to the restructured operating cash flow stream. Since there are substantial risks to any reorganization, the appropriate multiple should be at the low end of the range of comparable companies with similar, de-leveraged capital structures. The company's enterprise value must also be adjusted (or the multiple lowered) to take into account non-operating assets of the healthy comparable companies, such as cash and other liquid investments, real estate or NOLs.

Although a multiple of projected cash flow provides the best proxy for going concern enterprise value of a distressed company, it is also important to review earnings, or the amount of wealth the company can create while consuming cash. However, valuation based on earnings is hampered by the fact that cash consuming businesses need access to the capital markets, which is often unavailable to a reorganizing company.

The enterprise valuation analysis used here is similar to that used to value a leveraged buyout, but the risks involved in a reorganizing troubled company are much greater: the analysis of a distressed company's prospects can be much more difficult, financing is much harder to obtain for a troubled company, and timing and other contingencies of reorganization can swamp even a conservatively projected return.

Liquidation value. In addition to going concern enterprise value, the prudent investor will estimate liquidation value to establish a floor on

the value of the company. The company or other party in interest pro-
posing a reorganization plan must also determine liquidation value,
since the plan will not be approved unless the court believes that the
creditors' claims on the company will be more valuable in reorganization
than in liquidation. Asset liquidation values are difficult to pinpoint,
since, except for cash, assets may be carried on the books for much more
or, occasionally, much less than the values achievable in liquidation. The
investor must determine the discount or premium to book value of each
specific asset with reference to economic, geographic and competitive
factors, as well as the uniqueness or obsolescence of the asset, the availability of a buyer, and the time frame of the expected sale. The difficulty
of assessing liquidation value argues in favor of investing in the senior,
secured layers of a company's capital structure which have first claim on
whatever the liquidation value of the assets turns out to be.

Valuation of Individual Securities

Senior secured debt. After estimating an enterprise value, the investor
can systematically assign a value to each layer in the company's capital
structure, both in liquidation and as a going concern. The first step is to
value the senior, secured debt of the company, which will include the
bank debt. When evaluating the asset coverage of debt secured by all the
assets of a going concern, the market value of the collateral (or reorganization value, if the company's reorganization plan is available) can be
assigned to the debt to determine whether it is adequately secured. If the
collateral value is less than the face amount of the claim, the remaining
asset value of the enterprise should be allocated to the unsecured portion
of the claim according to the rule of absolute priority. The rule of absolute priority states that in liquidation, each class of securities must be
repaid in full in order of priority before the next lower class receives any
of its claim. Thus, partly secured bank debt is only worth 100% of face
value if there are adequate assets to cover the secured as well as all of
the unsecured creditor's class. Although in practice, allocations according
to the rule of absolute priority are rarely exact for the middle and lower
layers of a company's capital structure, the rule does allow the investor
to project a ball-park value, especially in the case of bank debt, which is
usually secured and occupies a senior position in the company's capital
structure.

   If adequately secured, a bank debt holder will receive post-petition
interest in a bankruptcy, either accrued or in cash, which, depending on

his rate of return requirements, allows the investor to be more flexible about the time frame of any reorganization. Since most bankruptcies last several years, receipt or accrual of interest has real value which can be added to the expected capital appreciation. More importantly, secured debt is assigned to a separate class in bankruptcy, which is senior to the claims held by the unsecured creditors. This is especially advantageous if the size of the unsecured creditor class is difficult to estimate due to significant contingent or off balance sheet claims. For these reasons, fully secured debt is the most conservative investment, but if collateral value is greater than cost, an under-secured obligation may be perfectly acceptable. As long as the collateral value does not deteriorate during the proceeding, it should essentially provide a floor on the value of the investment, one that may be significantly higher than the investor's cost.

A reorganized going concern value will, in most cases, exceed the value of an enterprise in liquidation. The same holds true for the value of the collateral that underlies the secured debt holder's claim. The appropriate discount or premium must be applied to book value to assess the liquidation value of the collateral and again the rule of absolute priority is used to estimate the allocation of asset value to each security.

Unsecured senior and subordinated debt and preferred stock. After the senior, secured debt is assessed, any remaining enterprise value is assigned to the senior unsecured debt (which includes the unsecured portion of the bank debt), subordinated debt, preferred stock, and finally the common equity. If cash flow is adquate, holders of long term, relatively low coupon obligations are likely to be reinstated in reorganization, in which case the holder's yield should be calculated to the original maturity or to the estimated date of an improved credit rating. Although reinstatement may provide less total return than equity or other reorganization securities received in exchange for the original debt, the reinstated debt will usually be more senior than the reorganization securities and should pay interest in arrears, as well as cash interest from the reinstatement date.

Investing in the junior layers of a distressed company's capital structure can provide the greatest returns, but bears the most risk. In addition, the unsecured claimholder does not necessarily know the size of his class at the outset of any reorganization, since perfected off-balance sheet liabilities and contingencies (such as underfunded pension plans, environmental and other legal claims), and claims relating to rejected executory contracts are assigned to the unsecured class as they are quantified.

Most leveraged companies that are experiencing financial distress will need an infusion of equity to de-leverage the company's capital structure and allow operating income to cover capital expenditures and interest and dividend expense. The new capital structure will either be part of the company's proposed reorganization plan or it may be a plan put forth in a filing by a creditor or shareholder group. Often the plan will include a distribution of equity to impaired debt holders with the largest percentage of claim value being distributed to the junior most layers in the pre-reorganization capital structure. Of course, any significant equity infusion will affect post-reorganization equity value, but the negative effect of dilution may be offset to a large degree by the better prospects of the reorganized entity, and the benefit of any retained earnings generated while interest and dividend expense is stayed.

LEGAL CONSIDERATIONS AFFECTING THE PURCHASER OF BANK DEBT

The legal issues that the secondary market purchaser of bank debt must consider are those affecting transferability, validity, and value of the purchased claim. When evaluating the transferability of a bank creditor's claim, the investor must determine the structure of the loan as well as the restrictions on transfer of ownership, both under the loan agreement and under the bankruptcy rules.

Transferability

When banks committed funding for leveraged transactions during the late 1980s, often a primary underwriter would enhance return on committed capital through syndication or participation of its commitment. In a syndicated transaction, each bank in the syndicate has a direct commitment to the borrower: it must share in any additional funding undertaken in the original agreement and may modify some terms of its obligation independently. In a loan participation, the original underwriting bank retains the ultimate control over all terms of the loan, except that core covenants cannot be waived without the consent of the participating bank. Core covenants are those that specify principal payments and any pre-payment premium, interest rate, and loan term.

The structure of the loan is important to the non-bank investor since the structure may limit assignment. A syndicated loan may require borrower or agent bank approval, which may be reasonably or unreasonably withheld, depending on the language in the original agreement. These same agreements may allow participations without the consent of the agent bank or the company. Some loan agreements specify that all transfers must be to a bank or financial institution or carry a minimum capital requirement for transferees. A minimum dollar amount for each sale is sometimes stipulated. These provisions are meant to protect borrowers from secondary market investors who might be unable to meet future funding requirements. The company may also withhold consent for less concrete reasons; for example, if it fears the investor may attempt to control the reorganization process or embolden the other creditors, causing them to step up their scrutiny of management.

Other Legal Considerations That May Affect Value

In addition to restrictions found in the specific loan documentation, the following considerations may affect the validity, value, and transferability of a claim:

- The sequence of documentation may have a bearing on the value and rights of claimants; most distressed companies have had a series of capital infusions, and have repaid loans or agreed to prioritize repayments to different creditors in different loan agreements over time.

- Rule 3001 of the Bankruptcy Code restricts transfer of some claims, including bank debt, without proper filing and seller approval.

- There may be unpredicted third-party claims, such as claims for taxes, environmental claims, claims for mismanagement of the business, and tainted claims which, if shown to be valid, will either be classified as priority claims or will be assigned to the unsecured creditors' class. In either case, these claims may affect the value of any unsecured portion of the bank debt holder's claim.

- There may be a risk of equitable subordination, or the subordination of a senior claim to that of a junior claim (or all junior claims) due to an act of inequitable conduct by the original claim holder. Some courts have found that an assignee of the claim (the in-

vestor) is not protected against a valid claim of equitable subordination against the original lender.

- The investor's claim may be compromised to the extent that preferential payments were made or property was transferred to the
creditor within 90 days (or one year if an insider) of a Chapter 11
filing, out of the ordinary course of business.

- The investor may be forced to accept a plan of reorganization that
another creditor or shareholder class or management proposes,
which the bankruptcy judge deems to be "fair and equitable," but
which may undercompensate the investor. So long as the investor
receives at least as much as an absolute priority distribution
would provide him if the company were liquidated, he has no
negotiating position to refute such a "cram down." An investor
can also be outvoted by other members of his class and forced to
accept the distribution that is approved by the required percentages of class number and claim amount.

- Although infrequent, if the company is structured as a holding
company with various operating subsidiaries, debt issued by different entities may be treated as a whole, or substantively consolidated. If the claim the investor is reviewing for purchase was
originally a loan to an unleveraged operating subsidiary, for example, it may pay to review the value of the claim assuming the
debt is consolidated with the leveraged parent, especially if it
could be argued that the company operated as a single business
unit.

- Depending on the jurisdiction, a bankruptcy court may allow a
pre-leveraged buyout creditor to claim that the debt incurred in
the buyout was a fraudulent transfer of assets to his detriment. If
this situation were to occur, the creditor who benefitted from the
conveyance, the lender of LBO bank debt, might be subordinated
to the pre-LBO creditor. Although actual subordination rarely
happens in practice, a valid claim of fraudulent conveyance may
bolster the pre-LBO creditor's negotiating position.

- Finally, corporate governance issues arise in a bankruptcy. Although the pre-petition management team may retain control
after bankruptcy is filed (unless ousted by the board or by a court

ordered change), management's fiduciary responsibility changes. In addition to its duty to the shareholders, management must undertake fiduciary responsibility for its creditors. Corporate governance issues can affect the value of the creditor's claim, since management accustomed to operating the business for the benefit of the shareholders, the LBO mentality, may have trouble recognizing its duties to creditors. Also, creditor scrutiny may interrupt or delay the reorganization process.

Risk Shifting

The bundle of rights and obligations embodied in the loan can be purchased by the investor either in whole or in part. In most cases the bank and the assignee or participant will allocate rights and risks during the documentation negotiation process. A participant will often want representations from the bank that the loan or the claim is not subject to compromise for preference or equitable subordination, or subject to any undisclosed set-offs or counterclaims. The investor will usually attempt to leave any lender liability risk with the bank, and future funding commitments, especially under unfunded letters of credit or other third party commitments, are contingencies that must be understood and either purchased or left with the seller, depending on the investor's assessment of the likelihood of future drawdown and the discount he receives for assuming the risk.

INVESTING IN THE DISTRESSED LOAN MARKET

Once the investor completes his financial and legal analysis, he must locate the debt and execute the trade. The private market for bank loans is a less developed, emerging market. Recently, an increased supply of distressed bank debt has surfaced from domestic and international commercial banks, most of which have been pressured by regulators to improve capital through monetization of troubled loans. Less often the bank will have written down an obligation to a lower value than the market will pay, which provides an inducement to sell. A bank may have timing or diversification portfolio considerations that make divesting of particular obligations attractive. Finally, a lending institution may be unwilling or unable to accept equity of a reorganized company offered in exchange for its claim, and will prefer to sell the claim outright.

The buyers of distressed loans are other banks, brokerage firms (either for customers or for their own account), independent investors, and dedicated funds. Unlike the merchant banking funds established in the 1980s to make equity investments in and bridge loans to leveraged buyouts, some of the new funds dedicated to distressed investment have more conservative investment profiles and more modest return expectations, which are well suited for investing in distressed bank debt.

Similar to the initial trades in LDC bank loans in the mid-1980s, no standard procedure or documentation currently exists for the purchase and sale of distressed bank debt. After an agreement is made on price, documentation, settlement and closing may take up to two months, especially if the debt of the particular credit has not yet traded in the secondary market. The loan sale is usually structured as a direct assignment or participation, but may also be structured as an interest in a trust. The trust format allows the investor to buy a certificate in a pool of claims accumulated and packaged by another investor or a broker. The trust structure streamlines the closing process since documentation and most terms are predetermined by the seller, but trust certificates are not necessarily offered in the investor's chosen credit or on his terms.

Each distressed bank loan trade will specify its own terms with respect to indemnification and assumption of additional liabilities. When an educated investor bids for a piece of bank debt, he will ordinarily bid a price that reflects his understanding of the loan sales language in the original loan agreement, the credit worthiness of the lender of record, which may have additional funding commitments under this or another loan commitment to the same borrower, and whether he requires any indemnification for claims arising after settlement of the trade. Bank loan traders will often attempt to spell out each of these understandings, requirements and contingencies in an initial commitment letter. If, after a commitment is made, an agreement cannot be reached on the terms required by both parties, the transaction never settles. Although some investment firms boast that they close up to 90% of commitments, the market average is closer to 50%.

Notwithstanding the potential variations in contingencies and hidden liabilities among the terms of bank debt offered for sale, pricing is relatively tight. The 25 to 30 active buyers of bank debt, four or five of which may bid on any particular offering, often price their bids within a percentage point of one another. The bid-ask spread between buyer and seller is much larger, of course, since often banks have failed to write down loans to reflect the market clearing price, and are unwilling to accept the discount secondary market participants require for assuming the risks inherent in holding the loan through a reorganization or liquidation.

PORTFOLIO MANAGEMENT CONSIDERATIONS

Unlike investing in more liquid markets, investment in distressed loans and securities poses particular portfolio management problems. A completely diversified portfolio across industries and maturities may not be feasible, especially if the investments are chosen company by company. On the other hand, the contingencies involved in distressed investing make being too concentrated riskier than over-concentration in a more traditional value portfolio. It may be necessary and advisable to take larger portfolio positions in companies in which the investor plans to have an active involvement, given the investors access to management, better information and influence on operating and financial decisions.

The most important portfolio management consideration in distressed investing is the long-term nature of the investments. Although some managers may be able to do well actively trading in these markets, the inefficiencies in the market, and thus the opportunities, exist because the primary sellers of distressed bank debt, the banks, do not want to hold their stake for other than purely financial reasons. Timing of an individual investment is always important, but it is difficult, and may be counterproductive, to try to time major market trends. Most successful investors select a few loans and securities that meet an aggressive hurdle rate and do not sell unless their perception of value has been accepted by the market in general, the financial or legal analysis originally accepted is proven wrong, or some irresistible opportunity comes along in which the portfolio manager deems the fund's capital put to better use.

CASE STUDY: INVESTMENT IN HILLS DEPARTMENT STORES BANK DEBT

Hills Department Stores Inc. is a discount retailer that was taken private in 1985 in a leveraged buyout lead by management, Drexel Burnham Lambert, and Thomas H. Lee, an outside investor who happened to be the grandson of the founder of Hills' predecessor company, Shoe Company of America. Since 1985, Hills' business strategy has been to attract a primarily female discount customer base with everyday low prices, especially of apparel, footwear, and other family-oriented dry goods. Hills clusters its stores in various markets in the northeastern and midwestern United States for efficiency in marketing and economies of scale in management and distribution.

From 1980 through 1989, Hills expanded its operations through new store openings of from two to ten stores per year. In addition to adding eight new Hills stores in 1989, the company purchased 33 Gold Circle Stores from Federated Department Stores with a view toward converting the more elegant locations to Hills' discount format, while retaining and building on the existing customer base. Hills' history of expansion was arrested in late 1990, when, thanks to the recession in the northeast, Hills' historically profitable operating business did not generate enough earnings to meet interest, dividend and principal commitments. Hills proposed a restructuring plan which included an infusion of capital and the closing of 28 unprofitable stores (including 15 of the ill-conceived Gold Circle stores), but the plan failed to satisfy all interested parties. On February 4, 1991, after trade creditors refused to deliver merchandise, the company filed for protection under Chapter 11 (see Exhibit 1).

Enterprise Value

Immediately after the filing, M. J. Whitman & Co. explored the possibility of investing in Hills' bank debt. The first step in reviewing a potential investment was to estimate Hills' enterprise value, both as a going concern and in liquidation.

Hills was deemed to have a valuable franchise that managed to maintain moderately strong sales notwithstanding the recession in many of its key territories. Still, the discount retailing business had grown more competitive over the late 1980s, with Wal-Mart, the well-capitalized discount powerhouse, threatening to move into Hills' key markets. On a pure store count basis, even after store closings, Hills had a greater presence in New York, Ohio, Pennsylvania and West Virginia; but the number of Wal-Mart stores exceeded Hills stores in the other four states in which Hills did business. Given the continuation of the recession, pressure from the better capitalized competitor was considered the key risk to Hills' viability as an operating enterprise. Other threats included:

- Inability of all the parties to reach agreement on the restructuring plan put forth by management prior to filing, which might foretell a protracted negotiation period in bankruptcy.

Exhibit 1

Hills Department Stores Inc.   Timeline and Summary of Events January 1, 1990–August 18, 1991

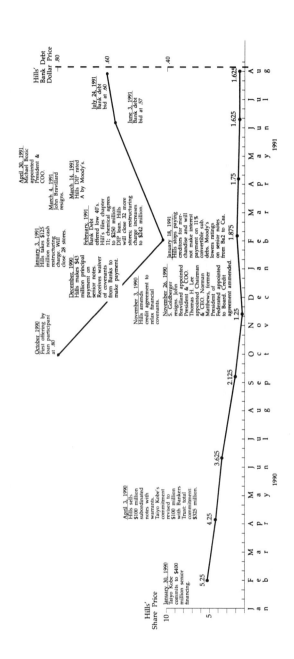

- The difficulty of obtaining the necessary equity financing from outside investors or convincing senior creditors, especially the banks, to accept equity in exchange for their claims.

- Employee and middle management disillusionment caused by continuous senior management changes and resentment that the company's burdensome debt load was the only thing hampering profitability.

On the positive side, the company had no major labor issues or environmental or pension liabilities and no other major litigation was pending or anticipated. As of February 3, 1991, the company had a $21.1 million NOL, although there was no guaranty that either the NOL or the tax benefits resulting from other recorded expenses would be preserved in the bankruptcy.

Although risks to the enterprise existed, the principle cause of Hills' financial distress was considered to be the inability to meet increasing competition in an economic downturn due to an inflexible capital structure. Once unprofitable stores were closed and capital expended to refurbish existing stores, Hills was believed to be capable of achieving its historical level of operating profitability.

To extrapolate post-reorganization earnings before interest and taxes (EBIT), sales were projected assuming 154 stores at a slightly enhanced historical sales per store number of $10.5 million per year. M.J. Whitman assumed cost of sales would remain at the historical average of 73%, with selling, general and administrative expenses also constant at 22%. Year end 1992 earnings before interest and taxes (EBIT) were projected at approximately $80 million, and earnings before interest, taxes, depreciation and amortization (EBITDA) were projected to reach $130 million.

To determine enterprise value, the appropriate multiple of operating cash flow was determined with reference to a group of regional and national department stores and discount retailers. Although there were size and strategy differences within the group, all were well capitalized going concerns (see Exhibit 2). The operating risks inherent in the Hills investment argued in favor of applying a conservative multiple of five times EBIT and three times EBITDA bringing Hills going concern enterprise value to approximately $400 million. Hills pre- and post-reorganization income statements are set forth in Exhibit 3.

Hills' enterprise value in liquidation was less rosy. The majority of the approximately $275 million enterprise value was made up of inventories, assumed sold at a substantial discount (40–50%) to going concern

Exhibit 2
Hills Department Stores Inc.—Income Statement and Balance Sheet Ratio Comparisons (a)

	Number of Stores	Avg. Store Size (sq. ft.)	Same Store Sales Growth	Cost of Sales/ Sales	Selling, G&A/ Sales	EBIT/ Sales	EBIT/ Interest	EBITDA/ Interest	LT Debt/ Total Capital- ization	EBIT Multiple (c)	EBITDA Multiple (c)
Hills											
Pre-reorg	214	80,000	1.3%	73%	24%	3.2%	.6x	1.01x	neg.	NM	NM
Post-reorg	154(b)	80,000	NA	73	22	5.0	3.2	5.3	43%	5.0	3.0
Jamesway	134	30–107,000	4.8	73	27	1.4	.87	2.0	45	12.4	5.3
Venture Stores	79	100,000	4.8	74	22	4.8	4.9	6.3	41	5.0	3.9
Ross Stores	185	23,000	(3.0)	71	23	5.7	5.7	7.4	29	4.7	3.7
Price Company	51	116,000	7.9	89	7	3.7	19.3	22.0	24	11.9	9.9
Wal-Mart	1,721	100,000	10.0	78	16	5.9	13.1	13.6	26	15.6	13.2
KMart	4,180	40–120,000	8.6	74	22	3.6	2.8	4.1	42	10.4	7.3
Dayton Hudson	708	80–220,000	7.4	72	17	10.9	5.0	6.1	63	5.8	4.7
J. C. Penney	1,799	22–212,000	1.6	67	29	6.9	3.8	4.8	32	9.6	7.6
									High:	15.6	13.2
									Low:	4.7	3.7
									Median:	9.6	7.6

Hills Post-reorganization Valuation as % of Median: 52%   39%

(a) All numbers as of fiscal year end 1990, except Price Company EBIT and EBITDA based on LTM ending March 1991. Hills post-reorganization are 1992 estimates.
(b) As of February 2, 1991.
(c) Market value of net capital/EBIT and EBIT and EBITDA, respectively. Market value of equity at or around April 1, 1991. Total debt, preferred stock, cash and investments in unconsolidated companies taken at book.

Exhibit 3
Hills Department Stores Inc.
Pre- and Post-reorganization Income Statements ($ in millions)

	February 3, 1991	*February 3, 1993 (E)*
Sales	$2,141	$1,617
Cost of Sales	1,560	1,180
Selling G&A	513	356
EBIT	68	81
EBITDA	116	131
Interest Income	2	1
Interest Expense on DIP Loan (a)	NA	(9)
Interest Expense on Capital Leases (b)	(26)	(10)
Interest Expense on Long-term Debt (b)	(88)	(10)
Other Expense	(3)	(1)
Provision for Store Closings	(242)	NA
Taxes (benefit) (c)	(15)	18
Preferred Dividend	(2)	NA
Net Income	(276)	34

(a) Assumes $90 million average outstandings at 10% average rate over the 1992 fiscal year.
(b) Long-term debt and capital leases reduced to $325 million. Assumes rejection of certain capital lease obligations and adjusts expense for store closings.
(c) Assumes NOL not available to offset income in 1992.

retail value. The balance was made up of existing cash, receivables, and property and equipment calculated at estimated realizable value.

Valuing Hills Bank Debt

Hills' capital structure in order of seniority as of February 3, 1991 is set forth in Exhibit 4. All liabilities are of Hills Stores, the company's principal operating subsidiary, except the 11% Convertible Subordinated Debentures. Hills Department Stores Inc.'s principal asset is its investment in Hills' Stores.

Hills' bank debt, although it was the most senior claim on the company's assets at the time of the filing, was not secured by inventory or leases that by their terms could not be pledged. Its only collateral was the pledge of receivables, various contracts, equipment, and general intangibles such as trademarks and computer programs, and the pledge of stock in the operating company by the parent in support of the parent's obligation under the guarantee of the loan in favor of the banks. The value of the assets pledged was estimated to be a little more than half of the banks' claim in liquidation. This under-collateralization held two consequences for the purchaser of bank debt. First, upon filing Chapter 11 the company determined that the banks' collateral was insufficient to require payment or accrual of post-petition interest. Second, the part of the banks' claim deemed to be unsecured would be assigned to the unsecured creditor class.

In calculating the price M. J. Whitman & Co. would be willing to pay for the debt, three factors were held to be paramount: first, return must be calculated based on capital appreciation alone, without the benefit of cash interest payments or accruals; second, the market price should be less than the assessed value of the security in liquidation and thus provide a floor value for the investment; and third, the time it takes the company to liquidate or to emerge from bankruptcy must not be so long that the rate of return is unduly compromised.

The going concern value of Hills' bank debt was derived by applying Hills' enterprise value of $400 million first to the secured portion of the claim. The majority of remaining enterprise value was then distributed to the senior unsecured claimholders, including that portion of the banks' claim that was deemed to be unsecured. Since the claims of the unsecured creditors' class exceeded the remaining enterprise value, seniority became important (see Legal Analysis below). After determining that the banks' claim was covered by Hills' going concern value, Whitman deter-

Exhibit 4
Hills Department Stores Inc. Capital Structure ($ in millions)

	2/3/91	2/3/93 E
Bank Debt (a): Working Capital Credit Line Reducing Revolving Loan (b)	$110	90 (c)
13.5% Senior Notes due 1992	87	—
Capital Leases	138	125
Trade and Misc.	339	130
Other (pension and uncompromised)	17	20
14.125% Senior Subordinated Debentures due 1997	92	—
14.625% Subordinated Debentures due 1997	51	—
15% Junior Subordinated Notes due 1998 (w/warrants)	100	—
11% Convertible Junior Subordinated Debentures due 2002	40	
New Long-Term Debt		110(d)
Total Long-Term Debt and Capital Leases	524	235
Preferred Shareholders' Equity	27	—
Common Shareholders' Equity (Deficit)	(259)	275
Total Liabilities and Shareholders' Equity		$750

(a) Expires December 1992 and provides for an additional $25 million in standby letters of credit.
(b) Paid down.
(c) New bank financing line.
(d) Reorganization long-term debt.

mined that the liability would be money good if Hills could successfully reorganize. If the debt could be purchased at less than 50 cents on the dollar, the annualized rate of return over a conservatively estimated two year reorganization period would be over 40%.

The banks' claim in liquidation was only slightly impaired. Although the banks' interest was not secured by inventories, it was determined that the value of the collateral securing the debt still exceeded the market price. When the remaining enterprise liquidation value was allocated to the unsecured portion of the banks' claim according to the rule of absolute priority, the total asset value available to the banks was estimated to exceed 95% of the banks' dollar claim at filing.

Legal Analysis

Hills provides a ready example of the integration of legal and financial analysis in distressed investing. In order to assess value, it was important to become familiar with the various agreements that pledged and secured assets in favor of Hills' creditors. Unbundling the flow of loans, security, and guarantees was made more complicated in the Hills case due to the complex structure of the original LBO and the multiple infusions of capital that were repaid or refinanced, in whole or in part, by subordinated or pari passu instruments. In addition to the Credit Agreement documenting the company's obligations to the banks and the indentures in favor of the various note holders, the relationship between Hills' creditors and the pledge of stock of Hills' stores were documented by an Intercreditor Agreement and Senior and Subordinated Pledge Agreements, respectively.

It was the Subordinated Pledge Agreement that provided the final affirmation of the value of Hills' bank debt. Although the company's financial statements ranked Hills 13.5% Senior Notes pari passu with the company's obligation to the banks, under the Subordinated Pledge Agreement, the holders of the $130 million Senior Notes agreed to subordinate their interest in the stock of the operating company to the banks claim on the same collateral. Thus, the value of the Senior Notes in the event of default was less than that of the banks for two reasons: the Notes were not secured by receivables and equipment, and their right to the capital stock in Hills owned by Hills' parent and supporting the guarantee was subordinated to the banks' claim.

Legal considerations affecting Hills' bank debt. Bankers Trust Company and Taiyo Kobe Bank, Ltd. were the lead lenders under Hills' Credit Agreement. Along with the co-agents, ten other banks had direct obligations to the company under the syndicated loan, including commitments to fund under the standby letters of credit. A bank party to the agreement could only assign its interest to an outside bank or financial institution with the consent of the company. Although additional funding requirements are stayed once a company files for bankruptcy, Hills still had the authority to reject a potential secondary market investor if the company deemed the investor unable to meet future funding requirements or for other technical reasons. The Credit Agreement did allow the syndicated loan to be sold in the form of a participation, however, in which the syndicate bank would dispose of its claim but still retain all funding responsibilities. This structure was the transaction format eventually chosen by M.J. Whitman & Co. in its purchase of Hills bank debt.

Obligations to third parties are not stayed when a company files for Chapter 11 and thus the selling bank's commitment to fund under the stand-by letters of credit remained a real liability for the purchaser. The Credit Agreement capped each syndicate member's liability, however, so the potential funding requirement was agreed to be purchased as part of the loan.

One of the attractive features of the Hills purchase was that the debt was relatively free of the other issues that could cloud a purchaser's claim: equitable subordination, substantive consolidation and potential cram down. As for fraudulent conveyance, there remained an outside chance that the debt issued in the 1985 LBO and supplemented in 1990 could be construed by the court as a fraudulent conveyance to the detriment of the unsecured creditors. The remaining risk was the threat of impairment that stemmed from a principal payment that the company made on the Reducing Revolving Credit Facility. The payment was made within 90 days of the bankruptcy filing, and if found preferential, could require disgorgement of the amount paid to the selling bank, or, more likely, could result in a compromise to the banks' claim during negotiations. Although section 547 of the Bankruptcy Code provides an exception in the case of payments in the ordinary course of business, it is possible that the "reduction" of the "reducing" loan would be deemed out of the normal course, and therefore preferential. Given these risks, M.J. Whitman requested indemnification from the selling bank for any impairment to the investor's claim that would occur if the court were to find either fraudulent conveyance or preference.

Execution and Portfolio Considerations

Although M.J. Whitman & Co. had been in contact with Hills' various lenders since late 1990, it was only after the filing that some of the banks assessed the liability at a low enough price to meet the investor's aggressive hurdle rate. Due to the size of the commitments for sale, the investment was never an active investment, although the financial and legal analysis would have supported such a commitment at the right price.

The purchase was structured as a participation, as mentioned above, and commitment to price was accompanied by a commitment letter, drafted by the investor, which outlined M. J. Whitman's required representations concerning indemnification for any loss incurred by the investor due to a finding of preference or fraudulent conveyance. The commitment letter also spelled out how M.J. Whitman proposed to fund the banks' outstanding letter of credit commitment. Negotiation of the commitment letter and internal approvals took less than one month and the trade closed two weeks thereafter.

After holding the position for only three months, the investor was approached by another investment house that proposed to buy the commitment at a substantially higher price than M.J. Whitman's cost. The deal fell through, however, when the prospective purchaser was unsatisfied with the representation in the participation agreement against preference risk. Six weeks later, another secondary market investor offered a slightly higher price than the failed bid and was willing to accept the participation on its terms. Given the substantial appreciation of the debt over such a short period of time, it was decided to sell the position and invest the appreciated funds elsewhere, rather than wait through the reorganization process for any further increase in value.

CONCLUSION

Investing in distressed bank loans and securities is value investing with a wrinkle; each investment must be evaluated from both a financial and legal standpoint and the operating and financing risks of distressed businesses are much larger than those of healthy going concerns. In the spectrum of distressed investment vehicles, bank debt may be the most attractive alternative for the patient investor. It is usually secured, and covenant protections limit borrowers' flexibility without lender approval. Secured bank debt ordinarily has the highest priority of any class of creditors in a bankruptcy, except for administrative claims and debtor-in-possession financing. Bank debt is becoming more available at discount prices as the original lenders continue to monetize their holdings of distressed loans, often for other than purely financial reasons. There are no formal 13D-type filing requirements for acquisitions of bank debt and bank loans are less affected by general market trends in the debt or equity markets. The purchase of bank debt at a discount may be the most cost-effective way to invest equity in a reorganizing, "pre-leveraged" company in the age of overextended or reluctant new lenders. Finally, due to the risks, research hours and the indefinite time it may take to realize a return, the investment strategy is not for everyone, which allows those patient investors willing to commit to avail themselves of substantial opportunities.

Chapter 14

Opportunities in Bankruptcy: Retail Insolvencies and Debtor-in-Possession Lending

STEVEN C. MILLER
ANALYST
LOAN PRICING CORPORATION

This chapter concentrates on the opportunities and challenges for banks in one of the fastest growing areas of commercial lending: Debtor-in-possession financing to retail companies.

Beginning in 1990, many retail companies taken private in the leveraged buyout binge of the 1980s have become distressed or insolvent, including such prominent names as Allied Department Stores, Federated

The author would like to thank Christopher L. Synder, Jr. and Floyd A. Loomis for their direction and feedback in conducting the research and analysis presented in this chapter.

Department Stores, Ames Department Stores, and Amdura Corp. This has created a rapidly growing and lucrative lending opportunity for banks to provide third-party debtor-in-possession (DIP) financing.

WHAT IS A "DEBTOR-IN-POSSESSION?"

Under the U.S. Bankruptcy Code, a company that files for Chapter 11 protection is a "debtor-in-possession" of its assets. It is essentially a new entity which is able to operate unencumbered by its pre-existing, or pre-petition, debt burdens until the company and its creditors agree on a viable reorganization plan. The bankruptcy court may give DIP, or post-petition, creditors a "superpriority" claim on an insolvent company's cash flow as well as unencumbered assets which are not pledged to senior, secured prepetition creditors.

Retail companies are a particularly attractive market for debtor-in-possession financing because: (1) retailers' inventories are often unencumbered assets which can be used to secure post-petition claims, and (2) retail companies, when their prepetition liabilities are stayed, effectively become cash-flow machines which typically build a large cash reserve and therefore may be in a position to pay off post-petition claims and emerge from Chapter 11. DIP loans are due in full once a company adopts a reorganization plan and emerges from Chapter 11. Therefore, in order for a debtor to leave Chapter 11 as a solvent entity it must first pay off DIP creditors under the superpriority clause. This entitles DIP lenders to the war chest of cash generally built by retail companies under Chapter 11 protection.

PRICING AND STRUCTURING

DIP transactions for large retailers are generally structured as revolving credits which are priced at LIBOR plus 300 basis points and carry steep fees between 200-250 basis points. According to Loan Pricing Corp.'s Public Deals database, $741 million of retail industry DIP loans were registered with the Securities and Exchange Commission during 1990. This represents 57% of the $1.3 billion of DIP loan filed during the year. During just the first five months of 1991, $1.36 billion of retail industry DIP loans were registered. This represented 67% of total DIP financing during the year.

Bankers generally agree that DIP loans are a viable form of financing for retail companies with over $10 million in revenues. Smaller retailers generally do not have the cash flow coverage, receivables, or inventory levels necessary for banks to rationalize the risks associated with DIP financing.

SIZE

In the past, most banks in the DIP market were able to arrange and hold an entire DIP credit. With many DIP credits for insolvent retailers reaching the $300-800 million level, even money center banks have syndicated these loans in an effort to reduce exposure. Chemical Bank syndicated a $250 million facility for Ames Department Store, which was closed May 1, 1990, to a group of eight bank and nonbank participants. Chemical Bank also syndicated the $300 million Allied Stores inventory DIP facility and the $721 million Allied Stores receivable securitization.

SECONDARY SALES

Most DIP loans continue to be structured like club transactions, though the majority of large credits allow primary banks to make participations and assignments. The $400 million DIP loan to Federated Department Stores allows assignments and participation to be sold in minimum amounts of $5 million at a fee of $2,500 payable to the agent (Citibank). Similarly, the $300 million Allied Department Stores, underwritten by Chemical Bank, included loan sales language allowing secondary sales in minimums of $10 million, with a $3,000 fee. These assignment fees are typical of most large corporate credits.

To date, banks have not actively sold DIP credits to secondary investors. These loans may become more attractive to secondary investors because regulators have determined that DIP loans will not be classified as highly leveraged transactions for reporting purposes. Many secondary investors have expressed interest in DIP loans, according to Loan Pricing Corp.'s Investor Database, because of the rich margins and over-collateralization associated with these credits. However, DIP lending remains a highly specialized area of finance which is complicated by legal and transactional risks. Therefore, it may not lend itself to secondary sales.

Finance companies, leasing companies, and foreign and regional banks represent the most likely investor base for DIP loans. Bank loan mutual funds and other institutional investors generally do not purchase revolving credits. With DIP loans to retailers typically structured in this way, most institutional investors are not likely to be active buyers.

QUICK TURNAROUNDS AND SYNDICATION RISKS

In the DIP market, turnaround times are very tight, with banks often originating loans in less than a week. This makes syndication and under-writing risk a very real concern. Before a troubled retail company files for Chapter 11, trade creditors often lose confidence in its ability to pay trade payables. As a result, these creditors may require payment on de-livery or refuse to ship merchandise altogether. This was the case with Allied, Federated and other Campeau Corp. units after the giant Cana-dian retailer began to experience financial difficulties.

In order to assure trade creditors that they will receive payment for goods, a distressed retailer needs to obtain DIP credit lines in short order or it may lose confidence among its trade creditors. For this reason, DIP financings need to be approved in as little as two to five days. This ex-tremely tight timeframe increase the underwriting and syndication risk associated with DIP loans.

COLLATERAL AND VERIFICATION RISKS

The collateral underlying DIP loans to retailers generally takes the form of inventories and receivables. Though prepetition creditors and trade creditors may protest the superpriority status of a DIP lender, bank-ruptcy courts have generally been willing to grant such guarantees. This is because Chapter 363 of the U.S. bankruptcy code allows the courts a good deal of latitude in granting security to post-petition creditors in order to keep a company in operation and preserve jobs. Courts can even subordinate the claims of unsecured, prepetition creditors. However, this type of "priming" meets with heated objections from prepetition credi-tors and is therefore very difficult to accomplish.

BORROWING BASE CALCULATION IN DIP LENDING

Lenders typically use a borrowing-base formula in originating DIP loans, which are similar in nature to asset-backed loans. In general, banks are willing to lend 40 cents for every dollar of inventory underlying a DIP loan, though overcollateralization can reach 400-500%. Despite this wide cushion, DIP lending remains a high-risk form of financing because third-party lenders may not have sufficient time to verify inventories or properly research prepetition claims. Most banks actually send personnel to check the inventory rooms of retailers and warehouse locations to verify that the debtor is, in fact, in possession of the inventories it has pledged.

MELTDOWN RISKS

The major concern for lenders in any DIP financing is the prospect of a "meltdown," or liquidation. The value of the assets which underlie DIP credits are secure as long as a company is able to generate cash flow and can successfully emerge from Chapter 11. DIP loans are considered to be administrative expenses and therefore take priority over all free cash and unsecured assets. If the company is unable to emerge from Chapter 11 and a liquidation ensues, the DIP lenders' superpriority status may apply only to unsecured creditors (see Exhibit 1). In most cases, the post-petition lender has no claim on the assets pledged to prepetition, senior, secured lenders if a company converts from Chapter 11 to Chapter 7 and is liquidated under the bankruptcy code. Another complication in a meltdown situation is that the inventory claims of post-petition creditors are likely to be challenged by prepetition lenders and trade creditors.

The risk of meltdown is mitigated in the case of a retail company because retailers generally produce strong cash flow when interest payments on their prepetition debts, including bank loans, trade debt, bonds, and tax withholding, are stayed. Therefore, most retail companies have been able to emerge from Chapter 11 under a reorganization plan. However, with consumers curtailing retail purchase, the risk of meltdowns for retail consumers may increase.

Exhibit 1
The Repayment Chain in the Ames Department Store Case

- Administrative expenses (DIP loans are generally categorized as administrative expenses)

- Wages and salaries

- Contributions to employee benefit plans

- Certain customer deposits

- Certain tax claims

Source: Ames Department Store 10Q Filing, Second Quarter, 1990

THE RETAIL MARKET

About one-third of the 2,300 leveraged buyouts completed during the 1980s involved retail companies, according to merger and acquisition experts. While most of the retailers taken private in a leveraged buyout over the past decade continue to be economically viable, sluggish consumer spending suggests that a growing number of retailers are likely to experience financial distress over the next six to twelve months. In fact, Dunn & Bradstreet reported that 10,803 retail trade companies failed last year, the second highest industry failure rate behind the service industry. This follows 11,487 retail failures the previous year. While the vast majority of these failures involve small retail shops, the volume indicates that demand for DIP loans from retail operators should be strong over the next several years.

In fact, our analysis shows that retail companies have the highest default rate among highly leveraged transactions (see Chapter 7). Most of these retail transactions were based on high cash flow expectations. This is because many of the transactions took place during the consumer spending binge of the 1980s and most retail companies are asset-poor and cash-flow rich. Further, the primary assets of most retailers—outside of their name franchise—are inventories, which are pledged to trade creditors; leases, which have declined in value as vacancy rates have in-

creased; and real estate. As consumer spending slows, many highly leveraged retailers lose their key value, cash generation. While this is true
for non-retailers, most of these companies have salable assets which can
be seized and liquidated in a default.

MAJOR COMPETITORS

Third-party underwriters and arrangers have increased their share of the
DIP market in recent years. In the past, DIP financing was almost always
provided to a Chapter 11 entity by its prepetition bank group. The size of
most bank groups has grown makedly over the past five years as a result
of syndication and secondary sales. In many cases, the original bank
group is unable to agree on a single proposal for post-petition financing
in a timeframe necessary to assure a retailer's trade creditors and suppliers. Therefore, the market has opened up to third-party players who
have become expert in providing DIP financing to troubled companies
(and are willing to do so in short order). In the retail DIP lending market,
some of the major banks include Chemical Bank, which continues to be
the acknowledged market leader, Continental Bank (Chicago), Bankers
Trust, General Electric Capital Corp., Mellon Bank, Societe Generale, Ca-
nadian Imperial Bank of Commerce, and Citibank. Institutional investors
which have pursued the market include Heller Financial and General
Electric Credit Corp. DIP credits are sometimes syndicated back to the
original bank group by the third-party arranger.

CONCLUSION

Third-party DIP financing, pioneered by Chemical Bank near the outset
of the LBO boom in 1984, has become one of the most profitable and
fastest growing areas of bank financing. DIP lending is sometimes characterized as this decades answer to the merger and acquisition binge of
the 1980s. Many retail companies taken private through LBOs in the
1980s are currently suffering under the weight of slow economic growth,
high debt burdens, and sluggish consumer demand. Therefore, banks
which are able to develop expertise in DIP financing to retail companies
are likely to find lucrative lending opportunities and strong loan demand
over the next three to five years.

ACRONYMS/ABBREVIATIONS

ABA: American Bankers Association

BHCA: Bank Holding Company Act of 1956
BEY: Bond Equivalent Yield

CAPEX: Capital Expenditures
CapMAC: Capital Markets Assurance Corporation
CBO: Collateralized Bond Obligation
CD: Certificate of Deposit
CF: Cash flow
C+I Loan: Commercial and Industrial Loan
CLO: Collateralized Loan Obligation
CMO: Collateralized Mortgage Obligation
COGS: Cost of goods sold

DIP: Debtor-in-possession
DM: Discount margin

EBIT: Earnings before interest and taxes
EBITDA: EBIT depreciation and amortization
ESOP: Employee Stock Option Plan

FASB: Financial Accounting Standards Board
FDIC: Federal Deposit Insurance Corporation
FGIC: Financial Guaranty Insurance Corporation
FRENDS: Floating-Rate Enhanced Debt Securities
FSA: Financial Security Assurance

GAAP: Generally Accepted Accounting Principles

HLT: Highly Leveraged Transaction

I/C: Interest Coverage
IRR: Internal Rate of Return

LBO: Leveraged buyout
LDC: Less Developed Countries; lesser-developed country
LIBOR: London Interbank Offered Rate
LOCOM: Lower of cost or market

M&A: Mergers and acquisitions

NASDAQ: National Association of Securities Dealers Automated
          Quotation
NIF: Note Issuance Facility
NOL: Net operating loss carry forward
NYSE: New York Stock Exchange

O/C: Overcollateraliztion

PIK: Payment-in-kind
PRIME: Prescribed Right to Income and Maximum Equity

RAP: Regulatory Accounting Principles
RM: Relationship Manager
RUF: Revolving Underwriting Facility

SG&A: Selling, General and Administrative expenses
SEC: Securities and Exchange Commission
SIA: Securities Industry Association
S&P: Standard & Poor's
SPV: Special Purpose Vehicle

UCC: Uniform Commercial Code

YTM: Yield to maturity

INDEX